VERGINA

THE ROYAL
TOMBS

Publishers: George A. Christopoulos, John C. Bastias
Managing Editor: E. Karpodini-Dimitriadi
Translation: Louise Turner
Lay-out: Angela Simou
Special Photography: Spiros Tsavdaroglou, Makis Skiadaressis
Colour separation: Ekdotike Hellados S.A., K. Adam
Printed and bound in Greece by Ekdotike Hellados S.A.,
8, Philadelphias Street, Athens

VERGINA

THE ROYAL TOMBS
AND THE ANCIENT CITY

MANOLIS ANDRONICOS

EKDOTIKE ATHENON S.A.
Athens 1994

ISBN 960-213-128-4
Copyright © 1984
by
EKDOTIKE ATHENON S.A. AND MANOLIS ANDRONICOS
1, Vissarionos St., Athens 106 72
Printed in Greece

To my wife, Oly

CONTENTS

PROLOGUE

I know that it is unorthodox for a book such as this to be written before the detailed systematic study and publication of all the finds from the excavation has been completed. Nevertheless, after much thought, I have decided to undertake the task for two reasons, albeit with hesitations. The unexpected finds of recent years made the whole world familiar with this region; requests for information about Vergina and its antiquities flood in from many places. But everything that has been written up to now is either confined to strictly archaeological reports which are inaccessible, and often incomprehensible, to the non-specialist, or it is concerned with the rich finds in "Philip's tomb". In view of the very real and very warm interest expressed in many quarters I considered that I no longer have any right to remain on one side. The second reason carries more weight with me. I know that the scholarly treatment of the material, its study and final publication will require many years yet. In the meantime, only brief archaeological reports can be published from which everyone will extract the information he requires. But, knowing from personal experience how trying it is to be obliged to further research without the aid of what one knows exists, I thought it my duty to other scholars to offer a preliminary, brief but authoritative presentation of the finds, hoping that my good will be not turned to ill account.

These two reasons do not contradict each other, but neither have they the same goals. It has, however, been necessary to link the two differing aims and to try to produce a text which will serve the needs of the specialist without ignoring those of the general reader. Such attempts are far from easy in execution and not infrequently succeed only in sacrificing academic integrity without providing adequate information for the non-specialist. It is not for me to say if I have achieved what I set out to do. Nevertheless, in addition to the text, there are the illustrations to the book which I believe contribute to the success of its purpose as I have defined it. A picture is always the best means – after the objects themselves – for every reader, specialist or not, to gain a closer idea of archaeological finds.

Once I had decided to write the book I considered it essential not to limit myself to the recent impressive finds from the royal tombs, but to set before the reader a synoptic but solid account of all the archaeological finds in the area. In this way its considerable interest becomes comprehensible – an area which has yielded graves containing hand-made prehistoric pottery and bronze jewellery, a magnificent architectural complex dating to the last years of the fourth century, the theatre of a city, a small temple and a series of monumental Macedonian tombs with unique painted compositions of the classical period, masterpieces of jewellery made by Greek goldsmiths, of miniature sculpture and the most magnificent products of Greek metalworking. The brilliance of the latter sheds new light on the older finds so that these acquire their proper perspective.

In addition to all this, the finds from Vergina provide new information about Macedonian Hellenism, our knowledge of which so far is based almost exclusively on literary sources emanating from Athens. It is natural that that city, the only serious political rival to Macedonia, should frequently distort its enemy's true face and denigrate its historical contribution to the development of Hellenism, at least before the meteoric rise of Alexander the Great.

I trust that all these reasons will justify my decision to proceed with this preliminary and at the moment provisional presentation of the results of many years efforts which are not yet at an end.

MANOLIS ANDRONICOS

PREFATORY NOTE

Before the Second World War archaeological excavations at Vergina were financed by the University of Thessalonike. From 1952, when the excavation of the Cemetery of the Tumuli was begun, the expenses were met by the Archaeological Society of Athens. From 1959 onwards the University of Thessalonike again met the cost of excavation. For all these years until 1976 the money I had at my disposal was very limited. In 1977, thanks to the initiative of the retiring Rector, John Anastasiades, the Rector John Deligiannis and the Rector elect, Theophanes Christodoulou, we received support sufficient to enable us to proceed to the uncovering of the royal tombs.

From that time onwards the excavations at Vergina have continued with abundant financial aid secured thanks to the personal interest of Constantine Karamanlis, President of the Republic (then Prime Minister). It is my happy duty to express in public my warmest thanks both for the practical assistance, which was decisive in the successful continuance of the work, and for the moral support which was extremely valuable and helped surmount many difficulties.

Through all the years of my archaeological commitments at Vergina my wife has stood by me with love, devotion and a calm judgement which has served me well. With me she shared the difficulties of the earliest years as well as the joys and agonies of the later years. I know that without her presence I might well have lacked the courage to follow my path so unswervingly. It is to her that I dedicate this book with love and gratitude.

When I began excavating at Vergina in 1952 as Epimelete of Antiquities I had to work alone; in addition to the archaeological tasks, I was also draughtsman, photographer, accountant and foreman. From my appointment to the University, first as reader and later as Professor (1957-1983) I had both the pleasure and the opportunity of help from many university assistants and from my students who came on the excavation and thus acquired useful archaeological experience. It is not possible to name all my fellow workers individually, but I should like to thank them warmly and to say that I always remember them with much affection, especially those who later became members of the Archaeological Service or university teachers. I do, however, feel the obligation to mention by name those of my colleagues who from 1976 until today have worked in every possible way to carry out the difficult work undertaken at Vergina.

My immediate archaeological colleagues in these years have been university lecturers and assistants, Styliani Drougou, Chrysoula Saatsaglou-Paliadeli, and Panayiotis Faklaris who, imbued with a deep sense of responsibility, worked unflaggingly and methodically. In addition to archaeological duties, in which they demonstrated their earnestness and reliability, I entrusted them with the thankless and complicated task of handling the financial affairs and other practical matters. Next to these, first as students, were Angeliki Kottaridou and Bettina Tsigarida and, for a shorter time, Grigoris Vasdekis; each made an important contribution.

For architectural drawing I had the assistance of John Kiagias and George Athanasiades who drew up all the plans of the excavation. The topographical plotting of the site was undertaken by colleagues of the Professor of Topography, Demetrios Blachos, in particular by Constantine Tokmakides. For the drawing of all the finds and the wall paintings I had the collaboration of my former pupil with a degree in Archaeology, George Miltsakakis whose remarkable sensitivity enabled him to bring the unique shape of the objects to life in his drawings.

From the very beginning of the excavation I entrusted the photography to my unforgettable friend, Spiros Tsavdaroglou. His memory remains vivid to all who participated in the work at Vergina. His monument, not only to his skill, but even more to his love of the objects, remains in his achievement. The reader too may appreciate his work which renders my tribute superfluous. When of necessity we had to do without his help, I was fortunate enough to have the services of Makis Skiadaressis, the quality of whose work needs no words from me. The photographs, the product of his artistic sensibilities, speak for themselves.

The advice of my colleagues responsible for the conservation and restoration of the finds was of particular importance. Sheer good luck willed it that two outstanding members of the Conservation Service should be my old and dear friends; Photis Zachariou and Tasos Margaritov. The first was responsible for the conservation of the wall paintings. He, together with his gifted colleagues John Thomas, George Portalios, Sotiris Koutaboulis, Petros Sgouros, Dionysis Kapizionis, Lefteris Kotsenos and George Constantinides, succeeded in saving the unique wall paintings after five years toil. Wisely directed by Photis Zachariou, whose many years spent preserving wall paintings has given him unique and valuable experience, they showed what can be achieved by the ability, the conscientious labour and especially the love which moves the Greek craftsman. On many occasions Tasos Margaritov was an invaluable counsellor on the conservation of the finds. I should perhaps mention in particular his achievement in preserving the unique gold and purple fabric from "Philip's tomb". With his colleagues Jacob Michaelides and Stavros Angelidis he flung himself into a great adventure and succeeded in restoring the magnificent piece of ancient material almost to its original beauty.

I should especially like to thank another colleague who is now also a friend, George Petkousis. With unparalleled devotion, verging on self-sacrifice, he dedicated himself to the conservation of the organic material which we had the good fortune to find in unbelievable abundance in the royal tombs. Exercising both dexterity and patience he removed all this material from the tomb, transported it to the laboratory, cleaned it and treated it. With near-missionary zeal he established himself permanently at Vergina and has worked there for all these years. His greatest achievement has been the restoration of the chryselephantine shield which he put together from thousands of fragments – a unique and exemplary effort. The same single-mindedness was shown by those who worked with him for long periods, Fouli Skamagouli and Nike Kalfopoulou-Kapizioni and, for shorter spells, Vasi Sakellari, Helen Moraïti, Andreas and Marina Stratsiani and Michael Larentzakis.

Almost the entire conservation and restoration of the metal finds has been undertaken from the very first by the technician of the Archaeological Museum of Thessalonike, Demetrios Mathios. His experience, his talent and his exemplary zeal have combined to restore all these finds to their original appearance. Part of the metal finds had to be taken to the laboratories of the National Archaeological Museum in Athens. Here the cuirass, the helmet and the sword were treated. This was difficult and delicate work and we owe the miraculous results to Chr. Chatziliou and his colleagues, G. Damigos, St. Kassandris and A. Magnisalis. Finally, the willing assistance of the sculptor Stelios Triantis in the conservation of the marble stelai was most effective.

We had scientific advice from the chemist at the National Archaeological Museum, Constantine Assimenos in all this work. His examinations on the spot, his chemical analyses in the laboratory and the cooperation of his entire team made a decisive contribution to the important work of restoring the finds. Limited in duration but very effective was the contribution of St. Baltoyiannis.

Throughout the excavation the help of craftsmen in under-pinning the monuments discovered was essential; it was carried out under the supervision of a civil engineer. And in this sphere too we were fortunate to have the services of the engineer of the Ministry of Culture and Science Nicholas Kaboulakos who on repeated visits inspected the buildings and gave the necessary orders to the craftsmen, in particular to Spiros Kardamis and his sons Themis and Stephanos to progress in their complicated work. Master Spiro's many years experience and the ingenuity of his sons in overcoming many difficulties has ensured the safety of the monuments which had indeed suffered severely from the passage of time and the weight of earth. In one important and urgent instance the help of the technician Sideris Karalis from the Archaeological Museum of Thessalonike solved a very acute problem.

Though the advice of all these collaborators has proved invaluable and decisive, it is impossible to over-estimate the help offered by the craftsman George Stephanides. Because he lives in Vergina and was therefore always available, he dealt with every technical problem arising from the progress of the excavation with unparalleled dexterity and marvellous ingenuity. The immediate roofing over of all the tombs in record time protected the monuments from adverse weather conditions; but, more than this, his continuous presence has ensured their safety.

It is clear that throughout this period the cooperation and assistance of the archaeologists in the XVIIth Ephoria of Classical Antiquities, to which Vergina belongs, was essential. The Ephor, Mairi Siganidou, good, long-standing friend and colleague, once again showed both her concern and her willingness to make our path as smooth as possible. In this she had, and thus we have had, the support of all her colleagues. The necessity of transporting all the finds to the Museum of Thessalonike, their conservation and eventual exhibition within its walls required the consent of colleagues who worked there, in particular of its director, Aikaterina Rhomiopoulou. However great the satisfaction of enriching the Museum and whatever the success of the exhibits, each its own reward, it would be a serious omission on my part if I did not mention the care and devotion she showed, in particular in the early days, when the problems created by the earthquakes in Thessalonike were exceptionally exacting.

I have also the pleasant duty to thank my old colleague and friend Nicholas Yialouris who, as Inspector General of Antiquities in the Ministry of Culture and Science rendered every possible assistance in the fastest and most appropriate way to solve the problems which were inevitably created by such an excavation. His support was the more fruitful in that the Ministers of Culture also displayed an especially enthusiastic interest. I should particularly like to thank Constantine Trypanis who immediately visited the site, Dimitris Nianias whose practical help was of inestimable value at one point in the excavations and Melina Mercouri whose genuine enthusiasm has supported me in recent years.

However, all the invaluable cooperation and assistance of those I have mentioned up to now cannot compare with the toil, the devotion and the dedication of the workmen themselves, the men who, with pick and shovel, often with their bare hands, patiently uncovered the magnificent monuments which luck desired us to find. Old colleagues, some of them friends of more than twenty years, shared with me the joy and the pains of archaeological investigation, the countless burning summers when we searched for the remains of our forebears' history. Some were local people, born and bred on Macedonian soil, others were refugees from "the other shore", far off Pontus, who believed that effort expended to bring the ancient myths to life was worthwhile. It is not possible to express my gratitude to each one of them by name; nevertheless, each has my profoundest thanks. I shall mention only the three no longer with us; Theophilos Amprikides, Elias Papailias and Nikos Xanthopoulos. I must also mention Costas Pavlides, now the custodian of the antiquities, and for the last six years patient foreman of the excavations; his unstinting dedication, his love for our work and his genuinely inquiring spirit did much to contribute to our success.

It remains only to thank those without whose understanding and practical help we might never have achieved our magnificent results. I mean the then Rectors, John Anastasiades, John Deligiannis and Theophanes Christodoulou. When, on their initiative, the University gave financial backing to the excavation, they became the instigators of success; they have continued to follow the progress of the work with affection and warm enthusiasm, my much loved friend, John Anastasiades in particular.

I am quite certain that without the help of all these people it would have been impossible for us to make progress in our difficult task. I know that there are many more who I do not forget, but who I cannot single out for mention; all gave us their loving support. To each and every one of them both I and my immediate colleagues proffer our sincere and heartfelt thanks.

THE ANTIQUITIES
OF VERGINA

THE SITE OF VERGINA
THE HISTORY OF ITS ARCHAEOLOGICAL INVESTIGATION

The western and southwestern edges of the plain of Thessalonike are bounded by the mountain ranges of Vermion and Pieria, separated by the river Haliakmon as it flows down from western Macedonia to water the level lands before running into the Thermaic Gulf. A short distance northwest of the river, on the northeastern foothills of Mt. Vermion, where the flat land ends and the hills began to rise, lies Veroia. East of the river, on the northern slopes of the Pierian hills we come first to Vergina and immediately after to Palatitsia, two adjacent villages which mark an area rich in archaeological material. In recent years the landscape has changed radically in appearance, for the uncultivated waste and poor fields have been turned into orchards and high yielding land thanks to irrigation works. The mountain however which rises directly to the south of the two villages still keeps its rugged beauty; peaks extend from northwest to southeast, rising one above the other, each overtopped by the next, their size decreasing only towards the Pierian plain. Its southern boundary provides safe natural protection for the area, for whoever controls these passes commands the huge plain which spreads far out of sight, the life-giving heart of the Macedonian kingdom.

Of the two villages, Palatitsia and Vergina, the former is the older, mentioned in a document of the fourteenth century.[1] Until 1922 two small hamlets occupied the site of Vergina – Koutles and Barbes; they were amalgamated and raised to the status of a village with the advent of the refuges from the Pontos. It was then that this new settlement acquired the name it has today, a name derived from the popular legend of Queen Vergina who, as the older inhabitants recounted, had at some time lived in the palace nearby. The name of the first village of course came from the ruins of the palace (*Τα παλά-τια*) which survived in good condition and were visible before the first archaeological investigation. Without knowing anything about their history or their purpose the locals perceived that they had to be ruins from antiquity which, throughout Macedonia, are associated with the name of the great king, Alexander. During the Turkish Occupation this area south of the Haliakmon was called Roumlouki which means the area inhabited by the *Romioi* (= Greeks), those who carried on the traditions of Greek culture, Hellenism.

Though these ruins were known to the enslaved Greeks, until 1855 they were entirely unknown to the travellers and archaeologists who travelled through the better charted and much celebrated lands of ancient Greece. In that year a young French archaeologist, Léon Heuzey, made a tour of Macedonia in search of archaeological remains off the track beaten by his predecessors in the quest for ancient Greece. But even then the ruins of this area would have remained unknown if Heuzey had not been lucky enough to encounter an "educated priest" – to use his own words. Heuzey wrote;[2] "The story of the first discovery of the ruins of Palatitsia are a good example of how those who travel to explore the Orient for ruins should never tire in the perpetual interrogation to which they subject the inhabitants. I had passed within a few leagues of this village several times without learning so much as its name and without learning anything from the peasants about its antiquities. It was not until I had left Olympos, on the occasion that I was travelling with M. Delacoulonche in the region

1. → General view of the site of Vergina from the air. On the right are the ruins of the palace; in the background the village of Palatitsia; to the left the area of the lower town of Aigai where a theatre and the temple of Eukleia were found. Part of the Cemetery of the Tumuli is visible on the left edge.

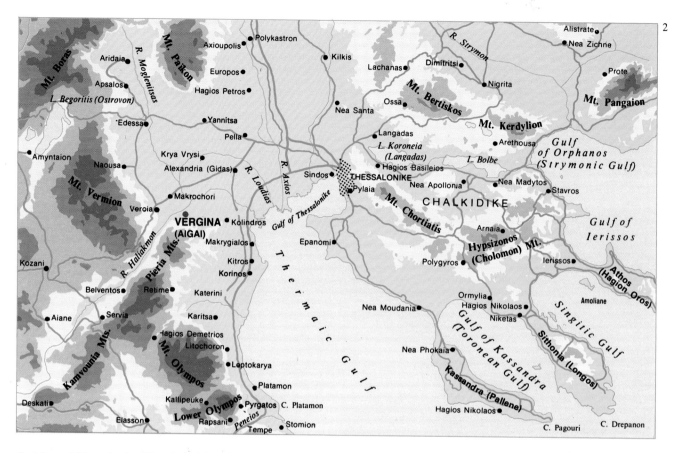

2. Map of Macedonia. The site of Vergina has been identified with the first capital of the Macedonians, Aigai, the centre of their power.

of the lower Axios, that converse with an educated priest revealed their existence to me. Taking a guide, I left my companion for a few days and, crossing the Haliakmon again, I recognized, not without surprise, that the discovery I was on the verge of missing was to be by far the most interesting."

When Heuzey returned to France he set down his observations from his travels and published his book, *Le Mont Olympe et L'Acarnanie*, (Paris 1860). Six years later, in 1861, Heuzey returned to Macedonia, this time as the head of a specialist research expedition under the august protection of the French emperor Napoleon III. The French archaeologist was now accompanied by his invaluable assistant, the architect Henri Daumet. They arrived at the hamlet of Koutles together with fifteen sailors from the frigate which the emperor had placed at their disposal and established themselves there since it was the nearest inhabited place to the ruins they intended to explore. With the sailors

from the boat and forty local workmen they began their excavation which lasted for only forty days because the malaria which was then the scourge of the area forced them to stop and to return to their boat. This excavation was confined to the eastern part of the palace but it was nevertheless fruitful and revealing. At the same time Heuzey excavated a subterranean vaulted tomb near Palatitsia, one of the two first "Macedonian" tombs to be discovered at almost the same time (the other was at Pydna, which Heuzey also excavated with M. Delacoulonche – see below, p. 31). The results of the excavation, with the magnificent drawings and reconstructions by Daumet, were published in their monumental book, *Mission Archéologique de Macédoine*, (Paris 1876), a work which is still valuable today for all who are interested in the history, topography and archaeology of ancient Macedonia. In the book Heuzey also commented on the Cemetery of the Tumuli (see below, p. 25) and on the Great Tumulus. At the end of his report on the palace he wrote, "Will those who rake over the same ground after us and bring our work to completion wish to be tied to turning over the confusing debris to look for the lines of constructions buried below the ground? We earnestly hope so, without being able to be sure that it will indeed be so. If indeed there is a chance to solve the mystery which envelops the history, the institutions and even the topography of Macedonia, if there is still some hope of rescuing from deep oblivion the antiquities of a people who played a significant role in the world, we are convinced that the answer to these difficulties is concealed in the hills of Palatitsa. Whatever the name of this unknown city, the importance of its ruins for Macedonia will be comparable to those of Pompeii. For us there will be a certain distinction in having been the first to have persisted in drawing the attention of travellers and scholars to the spot."

These prophetic words began to come true a hundred years after the publication of their book (1876-1976). And certainly the successors of Léon Heuzey render him all the respect and honour which are his due.

Even though it was only slowly realized, the desire of this pioneering explorer was fulfilled after many decades. The misfortune is that during all that time the locals used the ruins of the palace as an inexhaustible supply of building material and thus what the passing of time had failed to destroy the efforts of man removed in the interval which elapsed between the first excavation and 1938. In that year the Professor of Archaeology at the newly founded University of Thessalonike, Constantine Rhomaios, one of the great Greek archaeologists, took the initiative in renewing excavations. They were continued in the subsequent years until the declaration of the Greek-Italian war. The expenses were met by the University of Thessalonike assisted by substantial contributions from the Archaeological Service, then an arm of the Ministry of Education, and by the Chamber of Commerce of Thessalonike. Under Rhomaios' wise direction technicians, students and labourers worked enthusiastically for three years to uncover several more apartments of the huge palace. Thus there came to light a part of the central court, a number of rooms in the southern wing and two rooms on the west side. Work started to establish the basic plan of the outlines of the building.

In the first year's excavation, 1938, Rhomaios discovered a second Macedonian tomb in the area, close to Vergina. It is one of the most elegant and most impressive with a marble throne still in the main chamber.

After the war the Singer-Polignac Institution made substantial funds available for the excavation to continue under Professor Rhomaios in collaboration with Charalambos Makaronas, Curator of Antiquities (1954-1956). In these two years another room in the south wing of the palace was uncovered, together with the peristyle all round the central court and the full length of the foundations of the north wall.

Excavation was interrupted for two years. In 1959 the Singer-Polignac Institution again offered its support; this was supplemented by the financial backing of the University of Thessalonike which thus once again resumed its former obligations to this systematic undertaking. From this date the excavation of the palace was undertaken by the Professors of Archaeology, Manolis Andronicos and George Bakalakis who remained in charge during the succeeding years until the completion of the work in 1974. From 1970 the collaboration of John Travlos was of the utmost value. Throughout this period assistant lecturers and students in the Archaeology Department, many of whom are now employed by the Archaeological Service, participated.

The author of this text has had the good fortune to follow the excavations at Vergina from the very first efforts of K. A. Rhomaios who was his much-loved and respected teacher. From 1937, when, as a first year student he first visited the ruins in the company of his teacher, until 1940 when general mobilization stopped further progress, he worked on the excavation of the palace, becoming well acquainted with the area and acquiring a deep love for it. Perhaps Fate had some hand in linking him with this place, for when in 1949 he was appointed Epimelete of Antiquities he was assigned to Veroia which meant that he was responsible for the antiquities at Vergina. This fact took him there immediately and it provided him with the opportunity to embark on the exploration of another area, the Cemetery of the Tumuli, as well as of the Great Tumulus. The first efforts began on the Great Tumulus in 1952 and in the same year excavation of the first five mounds in the cemetery took place. Excavation continued in the cemetery the following year and, after an interval of three years, it was resumed between 1957 and 1961. The results of these excavations were finally published in 1969. In 1962 and 1963 excavation of the Great Tumulus was recommenced, with the opening of a deep trench on the eastern side. The excavation of the palace and the lack of funds forced his efforts to a halt until 1976 since when they have continued, bringing results so important that even his most optimistic hopes could never have led him to expect. From 1976 to 1980 excavation effort was concentrated on the Great Tumulus where the royal tombs and their unique finds were discovered; the story of the excavation of the royal tombs is the subject of a separate section. Although work in the area of the royal tombs has continued since 1980, archaeological investigation was no longer confined to that area.

The next aim of the excavation was to lay bare the walls of the town which had collapsed and been covered by the thick undergrowth of the forest on the hill above the palace to the south. In 1980, starting from the site of the *Palaioporta* (Old Gate) where there is still a good gate in the defences, we started clearing the ground to the east and west, at the same time freeing the ruins of the walls from the stones and earth which covered them. The continuous line of the wall which headed towards the acropolis on the southwest edge of the hill can be seen on the southern crest.

Lastly, one other goal was to discover the area occupied by the town at its lowest points, where the defences have not survived. Trial trenches, about 500 m. east of the palace, revealed the walls of houses of the Hellenistic period.

In the excavation season of 1981 we continued to uncover the whole extent of the fortifications and we excavated at two points on the western arm on which a small tower was found; on the southwest there was a room, probably for the shelter of the guards. Important buildings on the acropolis seem to have been destroyed in recent years so that their limestone blocks could be used for the construction of the new village of Vergina. The excavation of the residence east of the palace was resumed; only its foundations remain and it had been much damaged by the cultivation of the soil above. The attempts we made to locate other public buildings such as a temple, a theatre and others were fruitless.

The tomb which Heuzey had excavated in 1861 had been destroyed long since and only the trench, covered by thick bushes, remained. I thought it would be useful to check the extent of the damage in the hope that something might have been preserved. It was soon clear that my hunch was not ill-founded. Beneath the bushes and the earth which had slipped down into it, the walls of a building appeared. Of course, the entire vault was missing and we could not judge to what height the

side walls had stood. This had to wait until the following year.

Not far from Heuzey's tomb was a mound, marked on the French archaeologist's plan. Ploughing in recent years had considerably modified its shape and its swell could only just be distinguished from the surrounding cultivated area. My long-cherished desire to investigate it was about to become reality. Set apart from the large Cemetery of the Tumuli it seemed probable that it covered some large Macedonian tomb. Its excavation not only justified our expectations, but far surpassed them. Within a few days we encountered the vault of a large Macedonian tomb which had certainly been robbed. The interior had filled up with a deep layer of earth which had penetrated through the opening made by the tomb robbers; it concealed the marble and poros items which the tomb robbers had broken and hurled hither and thither in the chamber. Nevertheless, the doric facade and the interior of the chamber and antechamber compensated us for our pains.

Careful examination of the soil made us suspect the existence of a second tomb northeast of the first. The exploratory trenches we cut proved rewarding. A second Macedonian tomb – admittedly only its main chamber – but with a very well preserved wall painting on the facade appeared from the earth. The well-drawn figures were not in the same spirit as the paintings on the royal tombs. These of course were unlikely to be repeated, and it would have been unduly optimistic to hope for such a find again. However, this new wall painting could be added to the few we already knew and was indeed a reward for our labours.

The discovery of this second tomb made us more vigilant, and thus it was that within a few days we had discovered a third. This was much smaller and had a much plainer facade. It too had been robbed, but nevertheless the simplicity of its shape fittingly complemented the group. It is no mean achievement to uncover three complete buildings, still standing to their original height, from the earth!

To cap our excitement, a small square tomb, wedged one might say between the three others, poked up from the earth. It seemed not to have

3. The palace of Vergina and in the background to the left the modern village of Vergina. The road on the left follows the outer limits of the western wall of the town of Aigai. In the area to the right of the road foundations of houses and of public buildings were discovered.

been robbed; nor was it. But the charred bones and above them a small gold wreath were all it contained. Excavation had to be interrupted at the higher levels of the facade. One joyous task awaited us the next year.

So it was that in 1982 we started first on the clearing of the facades of these tombs, and then of the interiors. The chamber of the first contained a beautiful stone couch sarcophagus, the second a marble throne and the third a massive sarcophagus. This task occupied the two first months of the excavation season.

Later on we returned to the area of the town; one team continued the uncovering of the building which we had found the year before, while the rest of us explored the area between the palace and Rhomaios' tomb. Wherever we dug we came across the foundations of walls. However, we quickly concentrated our attention on the foundations of a building which indicated that it was possessed of particular interest. At the same time we noted an impressive wall very close to the palace. Two huge surprises awaited us at both these points; we were fortunate enough to find exactly what we were looking for, though our chances of finding it were almost nil. I, at any rate, had begun to believe that the gratification of finding the theatre – the place that is, where Philip was murdered – would not be mine. But, in our trench close to the palace, it took only two days to be certain that we had indeed located the theatre. The curve of the orchestra began to be quite clearly traceable; then came the gutter for the rainwater and the first row of seats, all of them intact and stable, all again seeing the light of day after so many centuries. When we had completed the excavation we had uncovered the entire first row of seats, the two side corridors, a large part of the foundations of the *skene* and the thymele (altar to Dionysos). It was a discovery so unbelievable that it might almost deliberately have been put in our way.

My younger colleagues voiced outright what I myself was thinking but feared to express; all that remained was for us to find the temple! Its fluted columns must surely rise somewhere close to the palace and the theatre. But where? Certain architectural members which appeared in the thick fill of the theatre strengthened our hopes. But we had to guard against being drawn into aimless and unmethodical effort. Besides, we had so much work to complete the excavation of the theatre, while our other area, a few metres lower down the hill, produced something interesting every day. We did not take long to realize that we were not dealing with a private house. Chrysoula Paliadeli, the supervisor of this area, had already called it the "oikos" in her excavation notebook, a term which denotes a building with a religious function. And she was not mistaken, rather the reverse. When sufficient earth had been removed and the tiles which covered the inner areas had been disposed of, we saw that we had uncovered a small temple, with *pronaos* and *sekos*, and the bases for two cult statues in the corners; between them was the offering table. Even if we had not discovered the temple of Aigai, we had at least discovered a small temple!

At the time we did not of course know which deity was worshipped there, but that did not diminish our satisfaction. I never expected that very soon even this would be revealed. Outside the west wall of the temple appeared a magnificent statue base; next to it a second and beyond that the foundations of a third. On the vertical surface of the first the incisions of an inscription began to be visible – beautiful letters executed with rare care and certainly dateable to the fourth century BC. We read ΕΥΡΥΔΙΚΑ ΣΙΡΡΑ ΕΥΚΛΕΙΑΙ.

The divinity therefore was Eukleia, a goddess familiar in many regions of southern Greece and in Athens. The statue had been dedicated by Eurydice daughter of Sirra. I assumed that she must have been one of the wealthy women amongst the Macedonian nobility. The name rang no bell in my memory at that moment for Eurydice is a common name in Macedonian history. But only one of these Eurydices had the unusual patronym Sirra – where even philologists had difficulty with the spelling (some preferring "Sirra" others "Irra"); she was the wife of Amyntas III, father of Philip II. So the woman who had erected this statue was Philip's mother. Willy-nilly, I was once more caught up in the royal family of the king against whom Demosthenes, the orator whom I had admired as a young man, had fulminated.

With this unexpected bonus the excavation season of 1982 drew to a close, as I too am determined to bring this section to an end so this book may indeed reach the reader.

THE CEMETERY OF THE TUMULI

The Cemetery of the Tumuli, between the villages of Palatitsia and Vergina, extends over an area of more than 1,000 *stremmata* (one sq. km.). In it are more than three hundred small mounds or tumuli, denser towards the south. The diameter and the height of the mounds both vary; most are 15-20 m. in diameter and from 0.50 to 1.00 m. high, though others are both larger and higher. Archaeological investigation has shown that the oldest of the mounds belong to the early Iron Age (1000-700 BC) and the most recent to the Hellenistic period (up to the second century BC). This means that we are in a region where some kind of settlement had been established at least as early as 1000 BC and that it continued to exist without interruption to the end of the ancient Greek world. The finds from the excavations also suggest that in its first phase this was a settlement of some importance whose inhabitants enjoyed a high standard of living. A second prosperous phase was observed in the fourth and third centuries BC. However, only the exhaustive archaeological investigation of the cemetery will allow us to trace its complete history and to draw more certain conclusions, especially for the period 650-400 BC for which our evidence is very meagre.

It seems that the oldest mounds were constructed in the northern part of the cemetery, that is, a long way from the probable site of the settlement. With the passing of time the cemetery extended southwards, that is it came closer to the town. However, the town and the necropolis were always divided by an important natural barrier, the winter torrent (*Το «ρέμα της Παλιοπαναγιάς»*) which gushes down from the western edges of the settlement and curves east immediately beyond its northern boundary, thus defining the southern and eastern limits of the cemetery. The oldest mounds were part of dense groups of three to eight mounds, which means that they belonged to some tightly-knit unit, perhaps a clan. The same may be true of the later mounds, but they are so close together that we cannot differentiate the groups since almost all the mounds touch each other.

Many burials had been laid within each tumulus. Mounds with four to five inhumations have been found and mounds containing as many as fifteen. It is clear from the finds that within the same mound there were both male and female burials, which means that each mound was a family burial ground in use over a long period of time, often for more than one generation. Some of the mounds were surrounded by a low circular stone wall which testifies to more careful construction or to an even more exact delimitation of the burial area. These observations lead to the conclusion that the cemetery belonged to a community well organized into families and family units which we may perhaps even call clans. We shall learn more about this society from the finds brought to light by the excavation of the burials.

First of all we should say that the custom of inhumation prevailed; to date, traces of cremation are few. Nevertheless, the instances where the skeletons of the dead have survived are very rare, and this must be due to the composition of the earth of the tumuli which everywhere is of exceptionally pure red earth (the only remains of the deceased being the teeth). A second observation is that the dead were buried in simple shaft graves whether this was in the fill of the mound or deeper down below the original ground level. In a few instances we encounter a simple stone construction and in considerably more cases the deceased were placed in large pithoi. All of this is useful information, but its general character does not greatly augment our knowledge of the people who lived in the area from 1000 BC and later, until at least 700 BC. By contrast, the contents of the tombs offer not only valuable

4 . Part of the large Cemetery of the Tumuli which spreads east of the village of Vergina. Most of the mounds form groups which perhaps belonged to clans.

evidence for study, but also an impressive picture of their civilization.

As we noted above, each mound covers both male and female burials; this is shown by the objects found in them. There were almost twice as many female burials as male; this should be regarded as natural if we consider that in older times the mortality rate amongst women was very high. It is, however, worth noting that in one case we found eight male burials and only two or three female – a very rare exception. Once again human behaviour offers the archaeologist rich material for study because the female inhumations are much more opulent than the male, for the simple reason that the

women were buried with all their jewellery, which has survived, while the men took only their armour, which consisted of far fewer objects, to the grave. Over and above this two pots were usually placed in both male and female interments; in a few cases we find three, more rarely still four. One of these was a jug for some kind of liquid (? wine) placed next to the head of the deceased and the other an open vessel for food.

Male burials tells us only about weapons. All the weapons were iron (in only one tomb excavated so far, which must be one of the oldest in the cemetery, was there a bronze sword). The most common weapon was a relatively small knife, but the most important was of course the sword. The swords from Vergina, whose number is not inconsiderable, are large in size. They form a very important group for the study of the sword in the Geometric period.

26

5. General view of the Cemetery of the Tumuli from the west. The area of the Great Tumulus with the royal tombs (below the roofs) appears in the lower part of the picture. These tombs were found on the west edge of the Cemetery.

Sometimes the dead man had both a sword and a small knife, while occasionally arrowheads lay beside the sword. Cases where the dead was given a spear are fewer still; of course only its iron tip has survived. Instances where the deceased had only a relatively large knife are infrequent. The only other fact contributed by the finds is that swords were placed in a wooden scabbard which sometimes had a very simple decoration of bronze bands.

Compared with the finds in the male burials those in the women's were both much richer and much more enlightening, so much so that they allow us to reconstruct, at least in imagination, the woman's attire. Almost all the objects are bronze; the jewellery found where the head would have been was unusually opulent and individual in style; the most common was a kind of circular tube (the ancient Greek term must have been σύριγγες)

which hung from the temples and down the back of the head; very often these were a pair, but sometimes many more were found (as many as four to the left and right and six at the back). On most occasions a kind of large button with a neck on the inside was found with these. We should probably imagine that this covered the point from which the little tubes hung. I imagine also that this heavy jewellery was fastened onto some kind of head covering, possibly of leather, possibly of cloth. Rings too were found by the head; these may well have decorated ringlets of hair, while others,

6

7

8

"*σφηκωτήρες*" (a ring-like jewel with more than one circle) sometimes gold, probably embellished the ends of plaits. There are frequent instances where the neck was decorated by a necklace made of flakes of sardis, sometimes very rich, while in poorer burials the flakes are few and of bone. A neck decoration of bronze is not unknown, but it is quite rare.

The most commonly found decoration, which also had a functional use, were the spectacle brooches (the bow fibulae and the simple clasps are rarer), all of which are found where the shoulder would have lain. Most of them are fairly large (from 0.10 - 0.18 m.) and from them we may deduce that the material which was secured on the shoulders was thick and heavy. The fastening of material on the shoulders implies that the garment so held was the peplos, well known in ancient Greece and wide-spread amongst all Indo-European peoples. This kind of peplos did not have long sleeves, hence the existence of very heavy bracelets on both arms of the woman; these were sometimes made up of more than ten coils. Other finds suggest that at least in some cases this garment has a belt, either of the same material or of leather. Though the belt has completely disintegrated two or three bronze shield-like bosses which were fastened to the belt have survived at the waist. Such belt buckles are not dissimilar to those on more modern local cos-

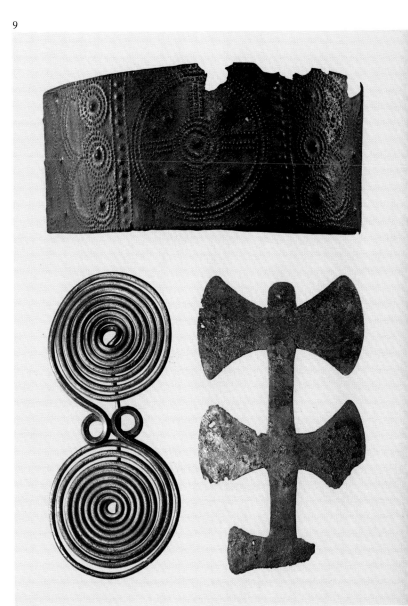

6. Male burial dating to the early Iron Age; the skeleton has disintegrated completely. Close to the head lay the jug (shown below) and at the feet was an open vase (shown above). There was an iron sword by the dead man's side.

7-8. Rich female burial. Close to the head were two vases (shown below) while a third (shown above) was placed at the feet. Opulent bronze jewellery decorated the head, the waist and the hands of the woman, and held her peplos on her shoulders. The clasps placed at her shoulders, the bracelet whose position shows that her arms were folded and the three shield-like bosses which buckled the belt can be seen.

9. Three typical pieces of bronze jewellery from female burials in the Cemetery of the Tumuli. Above, the "diadem" decorated with circles, the central one inscribing a cross which represents the sun symbol. Left; a large spectacle-fibula: right, the triple double-axe. This must have been a symbol of priestly authority.

10. A beautiful Protogeometric vase, a skyphos, bearing the characteristic decoration of concentric circles. This vase must have been imported from southern Greece and dates to around 900 BC.

tume. The whole length of the belt was studded with decorative bronze buttons (tutuli).

In addition to this functional jewellery there were some relatively few instances where small buckles at other points of the body and finger rings were found.

Some unexpected bronze objects found in a few inhumations are of particular significance. These were triple double-axes made from a thin bronze sheet; the three double-axes, of the shape familiar from Minoan Crete, spring to right and left of a central stem. All of them were found at the level of the shoulders as though they had been attached to some wooden rod which the deceased woman had held in her hand. We may be almost certain that these axes were some kind of distinguishing token, either priestly or temporal, the more so since they are associated with some of the most splendid burials.

One other unique and notable find was discovered in a woman's burial. This is a diadem made from a thin bronze sheet (0.075 m.) decorated with concentric circles themselves patterned with dots made by hammering on the inner face. The largest circle, at the centre, contains an inscribed cross, usually interpreted as a sun symbol. With the discovery of the sun-burst on the cover of the two gold larnaces found in the Great Tumulus the symbol on the diadem assumes greater importance, and may lead to interesting speculation. Unfortunately the burial to which it belonged had been disturbed and almost all the other jewellery which would have helped us arrive at its correct appraisal and interpretation has been lost. We may say with reasonable certainty that the diadem was kept on the head by a strap which passed under the chin, itself decorated with small bronze studs.

All these finds paint an impressive picture of female dress; they allow us to discern the northern inheritance of this civilization which is related to the Bronze Age cultures of central Europe. Furthermore, together with the jewellery and the weapons, we have also, as we said, the pottery.

Most of the pottery is handmade and it testifies to the continuance of a local tradition in pottery which we know in Macedonia from the second millenium BC. Very few of the shapes can be related to those of more northern European lands while a number of others follow the styles of southern Greece, known as Protogeometric. The Protogeometric pottery of Vergina is all wheel-made and bears the typical decoration of concentric circles or semi-circles; one at least of these vessels could have been imported from a region further south, but most of them would seem to have been fashioned in Macedonia, most probably close to Vergina. Certainly the existence of Geometric pots reveals that the inhabitants of the area had some contact with Greece further south, perhaps with Thessaly or with the Aegean islands.

Even though excavation of the Cemetery of the Tumuli has not taken place over its whole extent we may nevertheless venture to say that the most important and the greatest number of burials date to the ninth and eighth centuries BC. It is possible that the burials of the subsequent centuries – down to the fourth – lie in another area of the cemetery which has not yet been excavated. That this is indeed very likely is suggested by the fact that we have chance finds from the Vergina area which date to the sixth and fifth centuries, while an excellent relief stele of the fifth century was found in the overburden of the Great Tumulus.

There are many mounds covering burials of the fourth century BC and of the Hellenistic period. The finds from undisturbed graves are the usual clay pots, iron weapons and a few small objects, for all these were the burial places of men of relatively humble social standing. Wealthier members of the community constructed stone-built tombs in which they laid the very valuable offerings of gold, silver and bronze jewellery, and vases. All these tombs were found robbed. This, linked to the innumerable grave stelai which were found in fragments in the overburden of the Great Tumulus means that the Cemetery of the Tumuli was systematically pillaged in antiquity. Nevertheless, only the methodical and exhaustive excavation of all the mounds will permit us to draw a correct picture of its history, as well as of the history of the settlement to which it belonged, if indeed its investigation is supplemented by the archaeological exploration of the settlement too.

THE MONUMENTAL MACEDONIAN TOMBS

In 1855, when Léon Heuzey visited the area for the first time, the inhabitants showed him a subterranean vaulted building a short distance west of Palatitsia. It was then impossible to investigate it, for the autumn rains had flooded it with water. However, in 1861 he returned with the architect Henri Daumet to excavate the palace and, following on his investigation of the tomb at Pydna, the first Macedonian tomb to be known, he proceeded to excavate the "Tomb of Palatitsia". Despite the fact that he knew of no comparable monuments Daumet carefully observed and drew the unusual features of the facade. "The upper part of the facade," he wrote "ends not in a pediment but in a simple horizontal crowning member in the ionic style; the arrangement and the style of the whole possess great originality." It is indeed true that crowning the integrated surface of the facade was a third century ionic entablature which was supported to left and right on two capitals which were no more than simple decorative elements, since there were no pillars between them. At the centre of the facade was the opening for the door, flanked by marble jambs and topped by a lintel. On the outside the door was sealed by a strong wall of poros blocks to protect it from the pressure of earth. The door had had double marble leaves which were found flat in the antechamber where the tomb robbers had pushed them, probably in antiquity. The interior of the tomb consisted of an antechamber, 1.45 m. deep and 3.85 m. wide and a main chamber 3.10 m. deep which was reached through a marble double-leafed door. The plastering of the lower part of the walls had been painted red while the upper part (the vault) was white.

The most interesting fact about the chamber was the two stone couches resting on a slightly raised base next to the side walls. The couches were made of limestone slabs coated with plaster. Their shape shows that the framework imitated that of a wooden couch and rendered the shape of a mattress on the upper surface. Daumet noted the absence of painted decoration on the legs, but it is likely that it had faded with time. Red could be seen only above and below the cross-piece which joined the two legs.

All this made a great impression on the excavators, especially the marble doors, the first example to come to light. Consequently they were removed to the Louvre where they and the funeral couch from the Pydna tomb can still be seen. It is not easy to date the tomb from the evidence supplied by Heuzey and Daumet, but it is probably to be regarded as one of the earliest Macedonian tombs for which an acceptable construction date would be the end of the fourth century BC.

In the summer of 1981 we re-excavated the site of the tomb which had silted up after so many years. We ascertained that only the lower courses of the vertical walls had survived. The excavation of the facade showed that Heuzey had confined himself to uncovering the door; by extending the trench over the whole length of the facade we obtained one find of importance for the dating; an amphora from Thasos whose shape and, even more, whose seal, dates it to the last third of the fourth century BC, thus confirming the date which we have put forward up to now.

The second Macedonian tomb in the area was discovered by K.A.Rhomaios in 1938. It is sited at the northern end of the terrace which forms to the northwest of the palace, towards the plain, and is bounded to the south and west by the stream, known as "*Το ϱέμα της Παλιοπαναγιάς*". Remains of houses have been noted on this terrace, so that it is an odd site for a tomb. Its proximity to the last houses in Vergina, from which it is only separated by the stream, caused the excavator to christen it the "tomb of Vergina" and by this name it is known in archaeological literature. Nevertheless in the unofficial language of archaeologists, as indeed also in the everyday speech of the local residents, it is known as " Rhomaios' tomb" to distinguish it from the preceding tomb which is called "Heuzey's tomb".[3]

Like Heuzey's tomb – and like almost all the Macedonian tombs which had been discovered before 1977 – this too had been robbed; it was found almost half-filled with earth which had fallen through the opening in the vault made by the tomb robbers. The absence of every movable object from the interior was therefore to be expected. Nevertheless its well preserved condition and its carefully balanced architectural form was satisfactory compensation for the activities of the plunderers.

This tomb is the longest of the Macedonian tombs (± 8.50 m.) except for " Philip's tomb", and the most elegant in its architectural design. K.A. Rhomaios showed that all its dimensions, both of the internal areas and of the architectural members are governed by carefully determined proportions based on a specific modulus, that is a unit which serves as the base and when multiplied determines all the measurements. But there is more than this; for the first time the architect succeeds in linking the temple-like facade of the building to its vaulted sections in the most expeditious fashion. The facade springs from a low base which acts as its stylobate. On this stand the simple bases of the four ionic half-columns which support the two-part ionic entablature. Above the entablature is a narrow frieze with painted decoration of twigs and flowers which are repeated with a flexible mobility but also with geometric discipline against a deep blue surface which sets off their white, yellow, red and green colouring. There follows the ionic cornice and finally the pediment. The entire facade (like the rest of the building) is constructed in limestone blocks; the roughness of the stone has vanished under the exceptionally fine coating of stucco which permitted the application of richly painted decoration to the architectural members. The only exception to this treatment were the doors, where threshold, jambs, lintel and leaves were of marble. The leaves of the outer door, which were 3.14 m.

high and 0.85 m wide, were found as they had collapsed into the inside. But, as the reader may understand from the reconstruction drawing, the entire doorway made up one of the most impressive elements of the facade.[4]

The building consists of two rooms, the antechamber and the chamber. The antechamber is 4.56 m. wide, 2.50 m. deep and 4.34 m. high. At the top of the vertical walls, 2.22 m. above the ground, namely at the spring of the vault, there is a narrow band or frieze decorated with painted flowers; the flowers are arranged in rhythmic succession against a deep blue background, red, blue, white, blue, yellow, blue, white, blue, red and so on, while the white stalks and green leaves add their own colourful touch to the design.

A second marble door divides the antechamber from the main chamber which was square (4.56 × 4.56 m.) and 4.44 m. high – that is ten ancient feet. Thus the curve of the vault, projected in the imagination, forms a circle whose bottom edge touches the floor of the chamber; this too shows that the structure was carefully studied to confirm to a perfect geometric design.[5] A band corresponding to the one in the antechamber decorates the top of the walls, but differs in that it has no other embellishment than its dark blue colour. At intervals above this band there are nails on which wreaths and other objects for the deceased might have hung. At the back of the tomb were two interesting pieces of "furniture". In the northeast corner was an impressive marble throne and a little further west a rectangular stone construction which Rhomaios, not without hesitation, labelled a "bed".

The throne remains unique, both because of its size and because of its state of preservation. "Although it was found smashed into four large pieces and many smaller ones, its reconstruction is correct in every detail," wrote Rhomaios. It stands on a marble base measuring 1.40 × 1.12 × 0.15 m. with a total height of 1.98 m. while a graceful separate footstool at the front completes the beautiful and impressive picture. It is obvious that this marble object transferred the features of the older, wooden throne to the novel magnificent material. The two front legs, with their delicate shape and coloured decoration which today is largely lost, the two sphinxes above which were the terminals of the two arm-rests and the back-rest divided into nine squares, also with painted decora-

11

tion, must have excited the admiration of the viewer who stood before this unusual seat. It is possible that there was a painted scene of some kind on the band created on the front part of the throne between the legs and immediately below the level of the seat. This too has disappeared with time. In contrast, on the corresponding band on the side the scene has been preserved reasonably well; it depicts two griffins attacking a deer one from the right, the other from the left.

The robbing of the tomb and the fact that it had remained accessible to the curious for centuries explains the absence of even the slightest traces of its contents. I would suggest that the very few sherds of Corinthian and other vases noted by Rhomaios fell into it after it had been plundered, along with the earth which covered it. Thus the only evidence for its date are the architectural details

11. The facade of the tomb discovered during K. A. Rhomaios' excavations at Vergina in 1938 (drawn by Chr. Lefakis). This tomb with its slender ionic half-columns, its light superstructure dominated by the narrow ionic frieze with its lively floral decoration is undoubtedly the most elegant of the Macedonian tombs which has been found up to now.

and its plant decoration. Rhomaios believed that the tomb was almost contemporary with the palace. Now that we know more about the palace and about other monuments in Macedonia we are in a better position to observe the time difference which separates the two buildings. I think that if the palace dates to the last years of the fourth century BC, it is possible to date the tomb to the first half of the third century.

It is important to note that this splendid tomb

33

12. The largest of the three Macedonian tombs found in the "Bella Tumulus". The walls of the paved *dromos*, 7.80 m. wide, can be seen; (the marble door which had collapsed into the inside has been placed temporarily against the right wall). The doric facade with its four half-columns acquires unusual height through the addition of a singular cornice above the pediment.

13-14. The two outer edges of the long side of the couch-sarcophagus. Two feet bear relief decoration emphasized by paint. The nine rectangular divisions of the upper part, decorated with chariots, are characteristic; their yellow colour is in imitation of gold sheets which existed at this height on sumptuous wooden couches like those which were found in the royal tombs. Between the two legs is a frieze decorated with griffins.

13

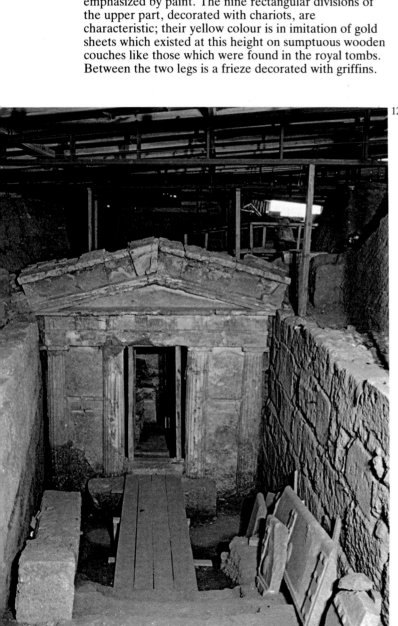

12

14

was not covered by a tumulus; Rhomaios' theory that the mound had either been washed away by rain or destroyed by ploughing does not seem very likely to us because the earth of all the mounds at Vergina has proved to be very resistant to the effects of rain, while ploughing with the means to hand until the time of the excavation in 1938 could not have levelled the mound. It is equally significant that this tomb stands at a distance from the cemetery where up to now only remains of houses had been noted.

Not far from the tomb excavated by Heuzey a low mound stands on the property of the brothers Bella. Ploughing in recent years has reduced its height and spread its perimeter. When we started excavation it was no higher than one metre above the level of the surrounding earth while the diameter was rather greater than 45 m. Within the circumference of the mound and below the original ground level we found three Macedonian tombs which had been plundered and a smaller, fourth tomb, unrobbed. The largest of them was entered from the south while the other two were oriented from east to west and had the entrance on the west side. The first had a built *dromos*, 7.80 m. long, which was narrower at its starting point (2.60 m.) and widened out at the facade of the tomb which it touched at either end. The facade (4 m. wide and 4.80 m. high) incorporated features of the doric architectural style; four half-columns, an architrave, triglyphs and metopes and a pediment above which was a singular tall cornice which added height to the building. The opening in the facade was closed on the outside by a poros wall; the customary marble door had never existed. The interior consisted of an antechamber and chamber, between which was a marble two-leafed door which the tomb robbers had smashed. It had fallen backwards into the chamber. The antechamber (1.23 × 3.02 m.) had a flat ceiling over which ran false "beams" made from special poros blocks parallel to the axis of the building. 1.75 m. above the floor on all four walls was a kind of decorative frieze (a projecting band) painted to imitate a polychrome marble surface. Above the band the surface of the walls was Pompeian red in colour. Below it the plaster was white and imitated large square stone coursing separated by sunken bonding joints. The plaster work is not well preserved.

The chamber (3.06 × 3.04 m.) is covered by a vault. At the same height as in the antechamber

there is an identical frieze; above it the surface is white, while beneath it is yellow. In the northwest part of the chamber there is a stone couch-sarcophagus, made up of many fragments; its eastern part had been completely destroyed by the tomb robbers who threw the pieces into the chamber, but almost all survived in good condition so that it can be reconstructed. The lid of the sarcophagus represents a mattress; because of this the stones at the sides are curved and are painted red. The stones which occupied the place for the pillow were similarly shaped and coloured. The two outside legs of the bed were shaped and decorated with relief work (spirals, palmettes, rosettes etc.). Furthermore, the moulded details were painted to make them stand out. Between the couch's two legs was a narrow strip-frieze painted with yellow griffins against a red ground. The top narrow band of the frame of the frieze has miniature scenes; only one, a semi-recumbent male figure towards which slinks an animal like a wild cat (? a panther) can be distinguished from amongst these.

The architectural elements and the sherds of pottery vessels which were found on a pyre, probably for sacrifices, next to the *dromos*, suggest that we may date the tomb to the second half of the third century BC (250-200 BC).

The second tomb had only one chamber (3.50 × 3.00 m.) and its facade, apart from the marble which framed the door (the jambs and the lintel) lacked architectural embellishments; it consisted only of a plain wall ending in a cornice. The emphasis on height is remarkable; since the facade was 3.87 m. long the height reaches 4.95 m. On the surface above the door there is a wall painting which shows three figures. In the middle, immediately above the door, a young warrior is shown full face; in his raised right arm he holds a spear and though his body is slightly turned to the right his head turns slightly in the opposite direction. He wears a cuirass and his red tunic is girded about the waist and bunched up in his left hand. His weight falls on his right leg while the toes of the left foot are only just on the ground, as if he were moving gently to his left. His high footwear covers the whole calf. The entire figure, which must represent the dead man, has a monumental character, and we may describe it as "heroized".

Some distance to the left of the soldier (to the viewer's right) is a very tall female figure, in profile. She wears a chiton and himation. In her right hand, extended towards the hoplite, she holds a gold wreath. It is clear that her gesture denotes the crowning of the brave fighter for his military prowess. I do not think that the female figure depicts a mortal, for she is of unusual height, and taller than the warrior, but I believe that she represents a personification either of Macedonia or more probably of Virtue and is thus associated with the deeds which brought the young warrior to his death.

On the other side, and again at a meaningful distance from the upright warrior, is the seated figure of a young man presented in profile. His cloak falls behind him and to his left, so that the right side of the youthful body is left uncovered while his himation folds over his leg. Below the body a circular shield bearing the device of an eagle is to be seen. The young man's right hand rests on his sword hilt, while his left is extended in a graceful gesture. The shield conceals a large part of his "seat" and it is difficult to see what this is. However, it is certainly not a throne nor a backed chair and it seems not to have any legs. What is visible behind the "seat" can only be interpreted as three shields placed on top of a base. This means that this youthful figure should be regarded – like the female figure – as a personification, probably of war. Whether we may interpret him as Ares, or even as Alexander, still requires more thought and systematic investigation.

The standard of the painting, without equalling that of the royal tombs, is very high. Its marvellous condition gives us the chance to augment our knowledge of Hellenistic painting. It is worth noting that before the tomb was covered with earth the painting had been treated with a thin coat of white plaster, probably made of powdered stones, which was a decisive factor in its preservation. We may also add that the earth was not heaped over the tomb immediately after the execution of the painting; quite some time elapsed before it was covered, which allowed both the plaster and the paint to dry thoroughly.

The simple, and architecturally unpretentious, frieze does not denote any sloppiness in the construction of the tomb. Rather the reverse; particular care has been expended over the plastering and even more, over the fashioning of the marble threshold, jambs and lintel of the door. Finally the work on its two marble leaves is the best I know of in any Macedonian tomb.

In the interior of the tomb, in the earth which filled it, various marble and poros fragments were found, as well as the broken doors. Many of them came from a marble throne; they have all been collected together and positioned temporarily in place in the middle of the back wall of the chamber. The throne has no backrest, though this is shown in paint; that is, on the wall behind the throne the separate pieces which formed the backrest have been painted in red and between them, in white, are the projecting partitions.

We put the footstool in front of the throne, that is the stool on which the feet of the person seated on the throne rested. It is noteworthy that on its upper surface two heel-shaped incisions have been hollowed out, indicative of its use.

A small limestone larnax (casket) is one of the other notable finds from the tomb, together with a

15. The tomb with the wall painting and the throne from the "Bella Tumulus". The dead man is depicted in the middle of the broad surface of the facade; to his left is a female figure (? Virtue) wearing a wreath and to the right the seated figure of a young man (? Ares), sitting on a trophy of shields.

15

huge "pillar", and a limestone head. Because this is, as far I know, a unique instance in a Macedonian tomb, I am in some difficulty about its interpretation. If there had been no stone larnax we might have thought that the tomb was a cenotaph and that the pillar and the bust functioned as a "menhir".

The painting and the few sherds found scattered in the earth led us to date the tomb to the beginning of the third century BC.

The third tomb, much smaller (2.53 × 2.32 m.), is less lavish in its construction and plan. Its facade has almost no architectural feature; a small pediment has been constructed only above the opening of the door, with a light relief on the stones of the wall. About two-thirds of the interior was occupied by a vast sarcophagus which took up almost all the south (far) side of the chamber. Even though very few bones have been found inside it, I think a date towards the end of the third century BC will be the most likely.

These three tombs, their facades intact, their marble doors, and the couch-sarcophagus in one, the throne and even more particularly the well preserved wall painting in the second make up an extremely important group in the series of Macedonian tombs. In a most impressive fashion they supplement both the known funerary monuments and, more generally, the archaeological evidence for the first capital of the Macedonians.

16. The figure of a dead warrior from the tomb with the wall painting. Shown in heroic pose the whole weight of his body is supported on his upright spear and on his right leg. He wears a breastplate, a himation and high footwear.

THE PUBLIC BUILDINGS

THE PALACE

We noted in the first section that the existence of the palace was first recorded by the French archaeologist Heuzey. He was also its earliest excavator. By 1974 it had been completely excavated, but study of the finds for definitive publication still continues. Nevertheless, we are now in possession of an integrated picture, including the additional building to the west, so that we can evaluate the palace as an architectural unit. Taken together with the recent discoveries in the Great Tumulus its importance increases considerably.

The palace lies a short distance southeast of the village of Vergina. Both for the view it commands and for the protection it offers, its position on the northern slopes of the Pierian mountains which dominate the whole area of the Haliakmon river is outstanding. It is worth quoting the description of the site written by Heuzey in the poetic vein of nineteenth century archaeologists. "It would be difficult for anyone to imagine a better chosen site or one from which a more majestic horizon is to be surveyed. Beyond the thick belt of leafy trees which mark clearly the course of the Haliakmon river the entire Macedonian plain unfolds before the eye like an unending prairie. Towards the north Mount Paikon rises in a steep cone and it spreads eastwards in a long chain of descending hills, at the end of which the observer in antiquity would have been able to descry the high gables of Pella. Beyond them, still in the same direction, the low hills fall gently away, finally disappearing into the distance and leaving the nearness of the sea to be divined for it is nowhere to be seen. In more immediate contrast to the west, for they are closer to the observer, rise the stepped terraces of Mount Vermion, some forested, others cultivated. Over its lowest slopes spreads the large town of Veroia, successor to ancient Beroia, where the scent of roses in bloom and the cool streams of rushing water still mark the site of the Gardens of King Midas and of the ancient Paradise of the Phrygians."

The size and the splendour of the building led Heuzey to the conclusion that it had to be a palace. K. A. Rhomaios shared the same view as do we ourselves, its more recent excavators. After the War several objections from various quarters appeared in print, but as far as I know they have not met with general acceptance. Today, now that the identification of Vergina with the ancient capital of the Macedonians, Aigai, is strongly supported by the archaeological evidence, its interpretation as a palace may be regarded as certain. Further corroboration still derives from the unique inscription which was found in the most important part of the building, the "Tholos". It reads: *ΗΡΑΚΛΗΙ ΠΑΤ-ΡΩΙΩΙ;* in other words, it was a dedication to Heracles, the progenitor of the royal house of Macedonia.

From Heuzey's day we have known that the palace was not an isolated building in a lonely spot, but a building which formed part of some town whose acropolis must lie on the heights which rise immediately south of the palace. On these hills which today, as in Heuzey's time, are thickly tree-clad, the remains of the town walls survive. Heuzey even recorded a gate. Recent exploration of this sector proved rewarding. Careful observation confirmed that the walls of the acropolis followed the edge of the nearest hills above the palace and enclosed it on the east, south and west. The initial archaeological investigation uncovered the gate which Heuzey had marked on his topographical sketch as *Palaioporta* together with two stretches of wall running east and west from it, a total length of rather more than 250 m. It was 2 m. thick and had been very carefully constructed. Further excavation will certainly permit us to ascertain many details of both the defence walls and of the ruined walls which occupied the acropolis.

Besides the walls trial trenches cut in the fields east and north of the palace revealed considerable remains of houses of Hellenistic date. We had deduced from some of the finds from the excavation of the palace that it had not been erected on an uninhabited site. Amongst these finds were some pieces of architectural ceramics, some of which dated at the latest to 300 BC, others of which belonged to the fifth century BC. All these now acquire a particular significance, illuminating problems while at the same time they are themselves re-interpreted by the new facts brought to light by further excavation. Now that we believe that Vergina must be regarded as the site of the first capital of the Macedonians, Aigai, it is logical to suppose that there must have been an earlier palatial complex, either on the same site or somewhere else.

The palace which was dated first by Rhomaios and later by ourselves to the time of Antigonos Gonatas (276-239 BC) is more correctly regarded as having been constructed in the last years of the fourth century BC, as Charal. Makaronas suggested in 1971. It is certainly the most splendid Macedonian building we know of at the moment, not only because of its size, but also because of its architectural layout and its execution. Its length is 104.50 m., its width 88.50 m. The plan is marvellous in its simplicity. The necessary rooms were arranged with an organic indivisibility around the essential element of the ancient house, the courtyard; the plan made provision for their layout as a whole, with perspicuity and propriety while at the same time the existence of a central axis bisecting the eastern wing and the court divides the whole into two parts, the northern and the southern. On the north a narrow additional space (? a veranda) runs the whole length of the building, so that the northern part enjoys greater width and the centre of the palace coincides with the north wall of the propylon as Heuzey, the first excavator, called the three successive areas in the centre of the east wing which form the monumental entrance to the palace. The first room (Pr$_1$) is 10 m. wide and 6 m. in depth and seems never to have been enclosed. On its outer side (the east), doric columns form a stoa or colonnade. This colonnade probably extended along the entire length of the eastern side, left and right of the entrance. Its back wall would seem to have been lined with "benches". John

Travlos has suggested that on the facade, perhaps for the whole length of the eastern wing, there was a second storey with an ionic colonnade on each side. The stairway may have been on the southern, narrow end of the colonnade, with a second in the corresponding position at the northern end. This facade, the only one, I believe, in the entire Greek world to combine the two architectural orders, also has dark-blue and red colour on the architectural elements and other painted decoration. Visible from a long way off on the Macedonian plain, it would have been not only a magnificent sight, but would also have represented a tangible symbol of royal might.

Progressing to the "Propylaia" we come to a second room (Pr$_2$) which opens on left and right into two narrow halls lying behind the doric columns of the facade. At the far end of this second room there was a large doorway divided into three passageways by two columns; the central passage was much broader than the two side passages. The magnificent marble doorsill of the doorway is still preserved *in situ*. Through it one entered the third room of the propylon (Pr$_3$) which was larger and much grander than the first two. On its western side was an opening divided by two or three imposing double columns (columns which on the narrow capital had an ionic half-column). The three or four passageways thus formed led into the eastern stoa of the central courtyard.

As the reader may see by looking at the plan, the courtyard formed an open-air central space round which, on all four sides, ran an imposing colonnade. The courtyard was the heart of the plan, determining the layout of the building with perspicacious, simple and well-regulated order. It imposed on the palace the traditional shape of the Greek house as we know it from written sources (Vitruvius) and from excavation (Olynthos, Delos, Priene, Pella etc.), but infusing this also with a stately character because of its unique dimensions and the very high standard of the work which went into the architectural members. The square court has a side measuring 44.50 m. and is enclosed by

17. → Aerial view of the palace. In the centre lies the vast central court with its colonnade and on its southern side the mosaic which decorated one of the three most important rooms. On the right are the three large marble-paved rooms. The lower slope of the hill occupied by the old town of Aigai can be seen in the upper part of the photograph.

sixty doric columns, sixteen on each side. A notable testimony to the consideration and careful thought which underlay the planning and execution of the building is the open stone conduit to drain the rainwater which runs round the courtyard on all four sides immediately contiguous to the exterior face of the stylobate at the point where the roof of each colonnade terminated. Even more admirable is the carefully calculated slope of the conduit the highest point of which is at the southwest corner and the lowest at the northeast. From there, the water, by then in a closed drain below the north stoa, and also from a narrow space from the north wing, flowed away from the palace. There is plenty of material for an exact reconstruction of the stoa entire parts of the architrave, triglyphs and cornice have been found together with column blocks and capitals in the fill of the court. There is sufficient even to provide, at some future date, for a reconstruction of at least a part.

All the apartments of the palace communicated with the porticoes; ingress and egress were through the doors and openings. The most important place in the palace was certainly the circular hall (Th) which lay south of the third section of the propylon. Externally it is square; only the interior is circular. The entrance was on the west towards the east stoa. In the fill Heuzey found parts of a votive offering, and he also recorded the discovery of niches set into the walls as well as the base of the throne. In recent excavations a unique inscription was found on the floor – ΗΡΑΚΛΗΙ ΠΑΤΡΩΙΩΙ – which confirms that this room was put to a formal use. The "Tholos" (as Heuzey called it) may have been both shrine and court of judgement and we may also regard it as the "Throne Room" since we know that the Macedonian sovereigns were both kings and high priests.

Next to the Tholos, to the south, lie four rooms whose use is not yet clear to us since no portable object on which to base a hypothesis has come to our aid. Four other rooms existed in the corresponding position in the north wing of the palace.

Second to the Tholos, the official rooms next in consequence seem to have been located in the south wing. At the far end of the wing on each side was one room with a door giving onto the stoa. Between them lay the imposing group of three rooms (E-F-G) which we may regard as the "royal suite"; they form a unit. The two lateral rooms (E-G) were only accessible from the central one (F) and not from the portico. Almost the entire northern side of this room was open to the

stoa; three magnificent double-columns divided the space into four wide passages. Anyone wanting to enter either of the flanking rooms had first to pass through the massive antechamber and from there cross the marble threshold of the enclosed rooms. Both had mosaic floors, but only one (E) has survived. All four sides were bordered by red plaster 1.20 m. wide, which rises slightly higher than the mosaic floor. Couches probably occupied this raised platform, an interpretation supported by the position of the door which has been moved very slightly off-centre on the western side (the same holds good for room G) to create sufficient space to accommodate the length of a couch. This means that these two rooms, like many others in the palace, were the *andron,* suitable for the banquets.

The mosaic was made from small pebbles taken from the river in many shades of black, white, grey, red and yellow. The most glowing description – even the best possible photograph – can do no more than give the veriest hint of the beauty of this unique composition. Only the reconstruction drawing, executed with loving care and the precise and dexterous touch of a master by Christos Lefakis, unforgettable friend and erstwhile colleague in the excavations, can bring it to life. The design springs from the large rose with eight largish petals and the same number of sepals which is the heart of the design. From it sprout eight pairs of leaves which curl together and branch out regularly to frame the centrepiece and then shoot towards the border freely and symetrically. The gaps between are filled with blossom or flower-shaped decoration, leaves or spiralling tendrils. The entire central design is bordered by a circular band of composite meanders and spiral meanders. The triangular spaces remaining at the four corners are filled by a female figure who, below the waist, dissolves into a palmette-like decoration from which spring shoots, leaves, spirals and flowers which wend their way decoratively to the corners of the triangle.

The work reveals an uncommon sensitivity, a full consciousness of the means at the disposal of a craftsman, perfect mastery and experience born of practice. Everything is happily executed – the circular motif sits within the square, life breathes through the motifs executed with economy and discretion, while the linking of the integral development is assisted by the disciplined construc-

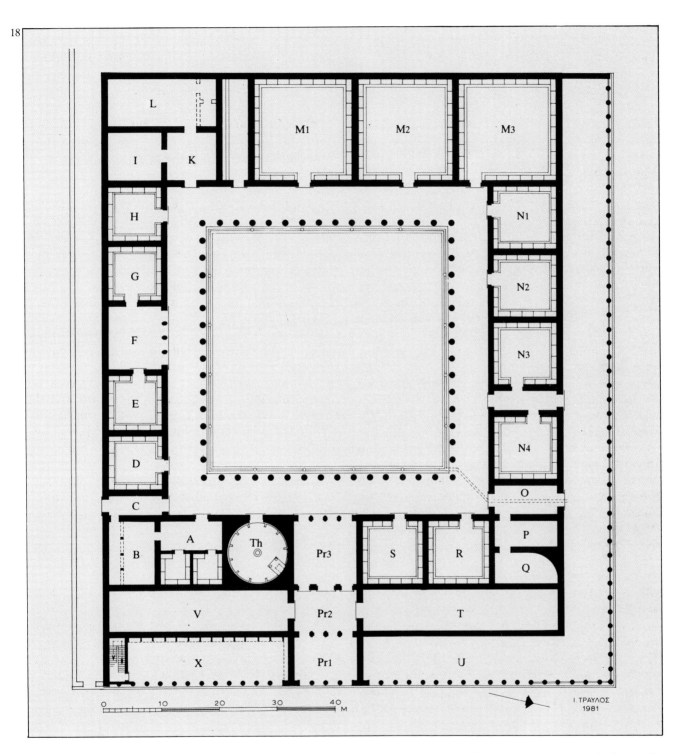

18. Plan of the palace drawn by John Travlos. The uncovering of this monumental building was begun in 1861 by the French archaeologist Léon Heuzey, was continued by K. A. Rhomaios (1938-1956) and was completed by Professor M. Andronicos and G. Bakalakis (1959-1974) with the cooperation of John Travlos in the last phase (1970-1974). The main rooms were laid out around the central court which is enclosed by a doric colonnade. The most important rooms were in the south wing; the chief of these was the suite of rooms E-F-G which contain mosaics. One of the most important rooms was the "Tholos" which lay to the south of the third section of the Propylon. The eastern side was two-storeyed. At ground level was a doric colonnade. The entire northern side formed a long veranda from which there was a view of the boundless Macedonian plain.

tion of the decorative scheme. In brief, the mosaicist recognized that the decoration must enhance the static nature of the floor, and his pleasingly aesthetic result was so created as to allow the pattern free and unimpeded movement across it.

The north wing of the palace which communicated with the north stoa has been almost completely destroyed, a process which had apparently been completed by men in recent times robbing the stone from the walls to a considerable depth, thereby obtaining a ready-made supply of building material. Nevertheless, carefully opened deep trenches permitted us to locate some few traces of foundations as well as the robber trenches from which the stones had disappeared. The information is sufficient for us to be able to reconstruct, with a reasonable degree of certainty, the plan of this section. In the north wing there were four almost square rooms, with the same measurements (10.55 × 10.85 m.) and a narrow space which was possibly used as a corridor for access to the veranda which extended along the entire northern side of the palace.

In the west wing – at its southern corner – there were three rooms of unequal size, possibly service rooms or perhaps store rooms. The entire remaining area of this wing was divided into three, equal, almost square rooms. They were unusually large, measuring 16.74 × 17.66 m., and it would not seem improbable that they had not been roofed. However, the floor of each, of carefully laid marble slabs, was covered by an undisturbed layer of tiles. Their existence disposes of any doubt, and it is now certain that the rooms were roofed even though there is no indication on the floor of the existence of intermediary supports as one would expect to find when such a vast span had to be covered. We must therefore conclude that the builders were capable of roofing such an expanse without the necessity for intermediate supports and on it we base both our appraisal of the architectural merits of the building, and of the knowledge and technical skill of those who erected it. A narrow mosaic border, very slightly raised above the marble slabs, borders the four sides of each room, suggesting that couches for the banquet probably stood on them. The only interpretation that can be put on these rooms is that they served for the banquets of the palace guards.

We mentioned earlier that a veranda had

stretched the entire length of the north side of the palace. Since destruction here is, as we said, comprehensive both in area and in depth, it is not possible for us to be absolutely certain of the configuration of the palace on its northern side. Nevertheless the archaeological evidence we possess leads us to the very probable view that the long unified space on this side, of which the foundations are well preserved, can only make sense as a long veranda with a low balustrade, while the parallel north wall acted as a retaining wall holding back the fill. If the interpretation of this space as a veranda is, as I believe, correct, we may imagine the reason behind the architect's forward-thinking solution which added a new element to the traditional plan of the closed house, opening it up on the outside and thereby bringing into being a model which was to have a brilliant and a productive future in the history of architecture. The reason for the creation of this space becomes obvious to anyone who stands on

19-20. Drawing of the mosaic in room E. The heart of the design is a large rose from which shoot eight pairs of leaves which curl together and branch out regularly towards the border. The spaces in between are filled with blossoms, leaves or spirals. The entire central subject is bordered by a circular band of composite meanders and spiral meanders. The triangular space in each of the four corners is filled by a female figure, (20).

19

its line today and gazes northwards to the seemingly limitless expanse of the refreshingly fertile Macedonian plain.

But on the southern side also there is a very narrow space running almost the entire length of the palace and continuing beyond it to the west, where it forms part of the building which extended adjacent to the west wall of the palace (it is not shown on the plan). I believe that the regular courses of the long wall which defines the southern limits bear out the suggestion that its chief purpose was to act as a retaining wall to protect the foundations of the palace from the pressures of soil slipping downwards from the higher ground which begins to rise a little way further south. My long experience of the area allows me to be sure that there is continual erosion and this I believe is the explanation for the curvature of the southern stylobate in the courtyard, which puzzled me for a long time before I could find a satisfactory interpretation.

Behind the palace, to the west, the foundations of a large building have been uncovered. Its eastern wall was the western wall of the palace. Its dating is not easy, for there seem to have been a large number of subsequent "interferences" though some may not have taken place so very much later. Certain details of construction, and the pottery which was found, are evidence that it can be dated to the third century, and indeed to the first half. It does not possess the magnificence of the palace, but nevertheless it is an imposing building with a central court and colonnade around which the rooms were arranged. The formation of the ground helped the destruction of the northern part, and so we cannot discuss its plan with any assurance. I think that it must have been erected to "house" extra ancillary services needed by the palace which did not have the space to accommodate them.

THE THEATRE

The theatre, which was discovered in the excavation season of 1981, lies a very short distance north of the palace. The first row of seats is separated by only 60 m. from the north wall of the palace, so that we may regard the two buildings as an integrated architectural unit. This makes it plausible to posit the existence of a number of other monumental public buildings in the same area, for example the largest temple of the city and the stadium. Indeed a small temple and a row of bases for votive statues have been found a little to the north of the theatre.

The natural contours of the ground where the theatre was sited were not ideal for a building of this sort, and especially not for the curving auditorium of a theatre for which possibly only the slope on the eastern and to some extent the southern sides could be turned to advantage. The western side, though it rose from north to south, did not fall from west to east as the eastern side did. One might imagine that these disadvantages were overcome by the construction of some kind of artificial revetment. I think however, that it is almost certain that this was not the case, because if it had been some part of the embankment would have remained, however small. A different kind of solution was found since in the end there was no need to construct rows of stone seats for the auditorium of the theatre above the first and lowest row.

The theatre lay open to the north so that the audience enjoyed an uninterrupted view of the vast Macedonian plain stretching in all directions. The corridors therefore were sited to east and west, one to either wing. I regard it as highly likely that on both east and west there was a broad street, that on the east leading to the palace, that on the west towards the area of the votive monuments outside the temple of Eukleia.

Excavation has uncovered almost the entire stone construction of the theatre, namely the first row of seats, the drain, the walls of the side passages, the eastern half of the foundations of the *skene* and the "thymele" (altar to Dionysos).

The first row of seats survives undamaged for its entire length (except for a very short section at the western extremity). Its curve is a little greater than the half-circle of the orchestra, while the two ends are aligned, thus forming a petal shape. The auditorium is divided into nine segments, the fifth being the central. The benches are well constructed, though they have a very simple straight profile, fashioned from square limestone blocks whose long sides curve to follow the shape of the orchestra with a simple straight face. Behind the surface on which the spectator sat (which was 0.33 m. wide) the blocks extend for a further 0.35 m., the surface three centimetres lower than the bench. This was the corridor along which the audience moved before and after the performance,

and where those seated placed their feet. The corridors between each block of seats were 0.74 m. wide.

In front of the first row of seats a wide deep drain (0.50 m. wide, 0.27 m. deep) runs round the perimeter of the entire orchestra to drain off rainwater. The drain, like the benches, is built in limestone; its eastern end was blocked, so the water must have flowed towards the western end where the fall of the ground would have helped it run away from the theatre (at the eastern side it must have drained either towards the *skene* or into the orchestra). So that the drain might work better it was built on a considerable slope, the western end being 0.32 m. lower than the eastern.

The careful excavation of two tiers of the au-

21. Aerial view of the theatre and the palace. About 60 m. north of the west part of the palace lies the theatre of Aigai where Philip II was murdered in 336 BC. The first row of stone seats, the eastern and western side passages and the whole orchestra can be seen. The corridors between the blocks of seats are also visible.

ditorium showed that there were no stone seats other than those in the front row. The corridors dividing the blocks of seats however were strewn with small irregularly shaped stones which created an uneven surface which helped those attending to climb up to the highest seats. In most of these corridors the pebbles have not survived over the whole length; in one, however, they have survived for a stretch of 20 m. so that we may say with certainty that this was their shor-

22. The theatre seen from the northeast corner. The foundations which form a corner are part of the *skene*; on the left is the eastern passageway and the seats of the easternmost blocks. In the centre is the orchestra with the thymele.

test possible length. I think therefore that after the first row of seats there was a wooden structure which has been destroyed. This is the way I would choose to explain the absence of a revetment on the western side where the benches would have been supported on scaffolding. Given that Macedonia was plentifully supplied with good timber I look upon this solution as the most plausible. But, on the other hand, the absence of thrones or of any other kind of individual seats is strange. Indeed, since we know that in theatres in Greek cities where democratic constitutions prevailed such seats were the rule, their absence from a Macedonian theatre which was directly associated with the royal family and the nobility becomes even more curious. The only possible explanation that occurs to me is that portable wooden thrones might have been brought out for the king and his retinue whenever they chose to attend the theatre. We know from the royal tombs that there were magnificent examples of such chairs in the palace. Alternatively, perhaps the kings followed the performance from the northern veranda of the palace in greater comfort and safety since, as we have noted, the distance was not especially great.

In the western side passage the foundations of the revetting wall were uncovered for a length of

20 m. In the eastern corridor the stones of the revetment wall, whose length is 14.60 m., rise in steps to the east following the natural rise in the ground, while another revetment wall at right angles to the first contains the earth from south to north over a length of 15.23 m.

The foundations of the *skene* have survived only on the eastern half where it forms an L-shape (12.40 × 2.50 m.).

Finally the stone on which the altar stood (thymele) was uncovered. This stone had an uneven surface on two sides, and thus it was plastered to cover up the roughness. This means that its upper part was visible. But over and above this fact, that such a stone was used while another, with flat even sides would have served just as well, implies, I think, that some special reason underlay the decision – either it had stood in the same place in an earlier theatre, or it belonged to some shrine of Dionysos and hence was consecrated as the altar of a new theatre.

It is not easy to put an exact date on this theatre. However, from such evidence as we have I believe that it can be dated to the fourth century BC. It is worth adding that, aside from its exact date, we may be certain that it was within the confines of this theatre that Philip was murdered in 336 BC since the site of the theatre did not change from one period to another. This alteration would not have been possible, firstly because there was no other area easily available which was suitable for the construction of such a building, and secondly because the site of a theatre was endowed with a certain sanctity linked with the worship of Dionysos.

THE TEMPLE OF EUKLEIA

About 80 m. north of the theatre the foundations of a small temple were discovered. It consisted of a small *prodomos* (4 × 2.50 m.) and a square *sekos* (4 × 4 m.). Since nothing of the superstructure survived, other than the roof tiles, it is difficult to pass any accurate comments on its shape. Nevertheless, I think it is very likely that the facade of the *pronaos* was open and that there was a door between *pronaos* and *sekos*. It is worth noting that the facade was on the northern side. In the two corners of the *sekos* bases of statues were found *in situ,* and between them two bases with slots into which a table might have

23. The stone seats of the western blocks; in front of the seats runs a stone drain to collect and carry off the rain water towards the western passage way. The entire construction was of limestone.

slipped; between the two statues therefore must have been the "sacred table".

Square solid foundations were uncovered a little north of the facade, measuring 4 × 6 m. The only possible interpretation I can offer is that this is the foundation underlying a large base on which a statue or statues would have been placed. Outside the temple, at regular intervals along the west side, three statue bases were found. The first, the most northerly, and the one immediately adjacent have preserved the limestone foundations, and the first low marble step. The south-

24. The temple of Eukleia. The small *sekos*, the threshhold of the door towards the *pronaos* and the *pronaos* can all be seen. To the upper right is the poros foundation which supported the base of a large sculptured offering. To the left are the bases of votive statues.

ernmost, however, had survived in better condition. As it is now we have its limestone foundation, the first low step and the main body of the base which is 1.43 m. long, 0.97 m. wide and 0.47 m. high.

On the face of the base, within a carefully executed sunken plaque surrounded by a curved border (0.88 m. long and 0.08 m. high) is the inscription – *ΕΥΡΙΔΙΚΑ ΣΙΡΡΑ ΕΥΚΛΕΙΑΙ*. The letters have been carved with extreme care by a very experienced and sensitive hand. It is not difficult to date it to the second half of the fourth century BC. The inscription reads "Eurydice, daughter of Sirra, (erected this statue) to Eukleia". We have now learnt, therefore, the name of the divinity worshipped in this small temple, because it would certainly have been to the deity of the temple that Eurydice dedicated her statue. Eukleia is not unknown in the Greek pantheon; as a "surname" the name sometimes accompanies that of Artemis (Artemis-Eukleia) while on other occasions Eukleia was worshipped as a goddess in her own right. Instances are known from many areas of Greece; Pausanias says that a temple to her existed in Athens.

If the name of the goddess is in itself a fact of more than passing interest, since it is the first time that we may add her to the deities venerated in Macedonia, and still more because we even know in which particular temple she was worshipped, the name of the lady who dedicated the statue is of still greater interest. The name Eurydice is found throughout Greece, and its incidence is particularly high in Macedonia where it was given to many queens and ladies of noble descent. On the other hand the patronym is extremely rare; it may even be unique. In the history of Macedonia there is only one lady who enjoyed this common name in conjunction with the uncommon patronym, and this is the wife of king Amyntas III, the mother of Philip II. Until recently historians and philologists were not even sure of its correct spelling, and many accepted the spelling "Irra".

We are thus assured that this inscribed base was a royal offering. I think it is logical that the offerings which occupied the two other bases may also have been made by members of the royal family. If we recall that the erection of the temple to Eukleia in Athens postdated the Athenian victories in the Persian wars and we consider the meaning of the name of the goddess and link these reflections to the date of the inscription, we arrive at the right to postulate that such an offering may perhaps be linked with Philip's victory at Chaironeia, in which his son Alexander distinguished himself. Finally one useful piece of information, though of less import, which derives from this find is the fact that Eurydice must have been long-lived and was certainly alive after 368 BC, the last attested date we have had until now in the wild and scandalous life this lady led.

More certainly still, the existence of royal offerings at this spot, together with the discovery of the theatre next to the impressive palace, come together to exclude the last lingering doubts about the identification of this area as the ancient capital of the Macedonians, Aigai.

25. The two marble bases for votive statues which were found outside the west wall of the temple of Eukleia. Only the first step of the lower one survives whereas the entire body of the upper one has been preserved.

26. The base on whose main face survives a votive inscription; the letters ΕΥΡΥΔΙΚΑ ΣΙΡΡΑ ΕΥΚΛΕΙΑΙ were cut within a sunken panel – that is "Eurydice Sirra to Eukleia". Eurydice Sirra was the mother of Philip II which means that the offerings which stood on the bases were made by royalty.

THE ROYAL
TOMBS

THE EXCAVATION OF THE GREAT TUMULUS

The first attempts

On the western edge of the Cemetery of the Tumuli rises a vast mound, a phenomenon wholly strange in the Greek world. Its diameter was as much as 110 m. and its average height exceeded 12 m. The first to record its existence was Léon Heuzey and, from his observations, it would seem that he gave it more than a passing glance. He wrote, "this man-made mound, diameter 110 m., is incontrovertibly the finest in Macedonia... the hollow in the shape of a crater which exists in the middle cannot have been created except by the collapse of a subterranean structure of very much greater importance than the two small tombs which we have excavated." (He meant Palatitsia and Pydna.) Prophetically he added "within these Macedonian monuments, as in the subterranean tombs of Egypt and Etruria, there is more than a selection of ancient objects for us to recover; there lies the life and a history of an entire people awaiting our discovery." The "crater" existed to our own time. The second excavator of Vergina, K.A. Rhomaios, believed that Heuzey's suggestion must be correct but, concentrating on the excavation of the palace, he did not seek, or perhaps did not have time, to explore it. And so it fell to my lot to endeavour to uncover the enticing but enigmatic secret of the Great Tumulus as the inhabitants of the area called it. I too believed that the "crater" had been formed by the collapse of the vault, or at least of the roof, of a building which was covered by the massive embankment, and so I decided to commence excavations at exactly that point.

The "crater" was a little to the east of the centre of the mound whose top surface had flattened out and was not conical even when I first visited it. This levelling-off was still going on in the first years after the War when, in the course of the Civil War, a military unit actually camped right on the mound, built their defences on it and dug trenches over the entire upper surface. These activities fulfilled the purpose of excavations which by chance produced the first really important finds – eleven marble fragments from grave stelai. Ten of these pieces matched at the edges and when they were stuck together they formed a relief stele with a relief depiction and a four line epigram. The eleventh fragment was the upper part of a smaller grave stele which bore only the name of the dead man, "Theukritos Theuphanous". Both could be dated a little later than the middle of the fourth century BC (350-330 BC). At that time nobody could have suspected their significance, nor did I ever imagine that the lower right hand corner of the stele then missing would be found thirty years later in the earth making up the mound.

The initial archaeological exploration of the crater had only limited scope. I opened a cutting, 5.50 × 4.50 m. and went down to a depth of between seven and eight metres from the top, without bringing any results. A second trial trench on the southwest side of the Tumulus was also sterile. I learnt nothing further from observation of the stratigraphy; no definite conclusions emerged. The very small quantity of sherds which were found in the soil confirmed that this large mound had been constructed in Hellenistic times; that meant that in all probability it covered a Macedonian tomb – i.e. a barrel- vaulted tomb. In the conclusion of the first archaeological report I wrote, "taking into account the dimensions of the mound it seems likely that a number of trial trenches of considerable size and depth will be required, since the negative results from the excavation of the crater implies the view that the tomb we seek does not lie at the centre of the mound."[6] This view betrays the belief that I then held, that the tomb I was looking for would be found actually in the overburden of the Tumulus.

A decade passed before I returned to the investigation of the Great Tumulus, in 1962 and 1963. This time I opened a large trench, 35 m. long, from the eastern side towards the centre. Once again the results were negative even though I went down to a depth 11.50 m. However, the experience of excavating the Cemetery of the Tumuli in conjunction with the sterile trench led me to think that the tomb I sought could not be in the overburden of the mound, but must be underneath it, that is in the ground itself and thus below the natural ground level. If however this new assessment was correct, exploration became even more difficult because the first task would be to remove all the earth, or at least a very large part of it. Only then could I proceed to the excavation of the tomb, that is to say at a depth of more than twelve metres below the top of the Great Tumulus.

I should explain that the description of the trench of 1962-1963 as barren is not entirely correct. A large number of fragments of grave stelai were found amongst the earth and stones of the fill. Some were limestone, others marble. Some preserved the names of the dead – Heracleides son of Archippos, Klesithera daughter of Lykophronos and wife of Kleitos etc.). Seven joined together to make a complete stele with a well painted scene.[7] All these, like those found by the soldiers, must have come from the Cemetery which surrounded the Great Tumulus and will have been brought there for use in the construction of the mound. Although there seemed to be no reason for their destruction, I had not yet grasped the problem I confronted; I thought that their presence could be attributed to chance circumstances, the more so because there were so few.

The excavation of the Great Tumulus was interrupted for a second time, in favour of the completion of the excavation of the palace and the publication of the results from the Cemetery. The final phase of the long-drawn out investigation did not begin until 1976. Despite my slender financial resources my long-term objective was the removal of a large part of the embankment of the Tumulus and the systematic excavation of the ground below so as to uncover the tomb I was

sure was there. The previous attempts, in particular the most recent large trench allowed us to make hypothetical deductions about this large mound and its composition. It was clear that its construction had demanded countless tons of earth which must have been brought there not just from the area close to the Cemetery but also from much further away. This was born out by the layers which were made up of red soil, sand, pebbles, stones and various other kinds of earth. I had already begun to reflect that construction on such a scale demanded both workmen and means of transport not readily available to an ordinary man. Even for an exceptionally wealthy person it would have been difficult to procure the hundreds of workmen required for the task. Without reaching any definite conclusions, I suspected that only the authority of a ruler could execute such an imposing construction. But for thought to range freely, the mind must be uncluttered by preconceptions; in my case the thought process was blocked by what I then considered an insurmountable obstacle. If the construction of the Great Tumulus was indeed the work of a ruler, then that ruler could be none other than the king of Macedonia, which implied that the tomb I sought would be royal. But I was well aware that the Macedonian kings were buried in the old capital of Macedonian, Aigai, and we all knew that Aigai was located at Edessa. And so my thoughts chased each other in circles, leading nowhere. Furthermore, my chief preoccupation was to locate the tomb of the Great Tumulus; I was not concerned with its nature, still less with the subsequent identification of its occupant. My strongest hope and greatest expectations lay in other directions. Since I had persuaded myself that the tomb lay underneath the twelve metres of earth heaped above it, I also thought it probable that it would have escaped the attention of tomb robbers, whether of antiquity or of more recent times; thus I began to dream of being lucky enough to find the first unpillaged Macedonian tomb, a stroke of fortune that every archaeologist would wish to have.

The excavation of 1976 had very limited objectives; specifically it aimed at the removal of as much of the earth as my financial resources would permit, so that the following year I could dig deeper and thus come closer to achieving my ultimate goal. The experience of the preceding years had convinced me that excavation only with

the help of workmen was impractical for two reasons; first because of the immense depth it was dangerous, and secondly it was ineffectual because it required endless sums of money and also a great deal of time. I therefore judged it a case for mechanical excavation carried out under increased and ceaseless supervision. I progressed in this way: a) deepening the trench on the east side to the level of the surrounding soil; b) widening the excavation at the centre, opening up a crater 35-40 m. in diameter and 5-6 m. deep, and preparing for the eventual widening out which would take place in subsequent excavation seasons. I did not foresee any immediate result from these preparations. At the same time I cut three smaller trial trenches on the south side of the Tumulus, equally without expecting to locate the tomb I sought. I was more interested in exhausting sources of information about the way in which the mound had been constructed and perhaps finding some indication of the probable site of the tomb. The work went exactly as I had imagined, the important deviation being that which led to success.

27. The Great Tumulus of Vergina from the east as it was in 1976 at the beginning of the last phase of the excavations which led to the discovery of the royal tombs. The trees planted on the Tumulus in 1958 made excavation difficult. The diameter of the Tumulus was 110 m. and its height (at the centre) was 12 m.

Almost at the centre of the mound, at a depth of 4 m. from the upper surface, and between the soil brought from elsewhere and the natural stones many fragments of broken grave stelai were found, as in the trench of 1962 and 1963 and in the cuttings of the military in 1948. But this time the pieces did not number four or five, nor ten nor even twenty. There were lots of them, mostly all together. Two of them were the upper parts of painted stelai, though the depiction had faded. The names of the dead, however, had survived because the letters had been incised and then painted. On one we read ARPALOS PEUKOLAOU two strikingly Macedonian names; the other read THEODOROS THEUPHANOUS. The letters and the shape of the latter recalled to mind the first stele found by the soldiers with the inscription THEUKRITOS THEUPHANOUS. Could the Theodoros of the new stele be the brother of the THEUKRITOS of the older one, both the sons of Theuphanes? Other marble pieces (more than thirty of them) turned out to be even more important; they were part of a large relief stele of exceptional workmanship which could be dated to around the middle of the fourth century BC. Its size is impressive – 2 m. high and 1 m. wide. The dead man is portrayed as an athlete standing upright and facing to the right; at his feet lies a hunting dog sniffing the ground; to the left is the slave who gazes at his master. On the upper left surface the incised epigram begins with the phrase "Ἡλικία μὲν ἐμήν..."; it has been destroyed at several points making its reconstruction problematic. We can decipher five lines, and in the sixth the name of the dead man, Antigonos A [deo]. The other pieces deserving of comment include a fragment from a marble lekythos, several pieces with a palmette and relief stalks and a small part from a relief horseman (? jockey). Altogether the finds of 1976 came from at least ten separate funeral monuments.

These finds brought the total number of funeral monuments found in the overburden of the Great Tumulus to at least nineteen. Amongst them were the two inscribed reliefs and the exceptional painted stele, while many others preserved the name of the dead man. The existence of these monuments, and the condition in which they were found, allowed me to form the following conclusions which I presented and published in the journal of the Archaeological Service:[8]

1. All these monuments come from the Cemetery which lay close to the Great Tumulus.

2. All were found shattered and had been used together with the earth and stones for the construction of the Great Tumulus.

3. The people who used them for this purpose would seem to have found them broken and thrown to one side.

4. The quality and range of the monuments testify that the Cemetery in which they had stood belonged to a rich and exceptionally well-developed town.

5. None of them is older than the mid-fourth century or more recent than the beginning of the third century BC.

The last, clinching testimony is that the Cemetery of Vergina was looted and destroyed at the beginning of the third century BC.

These facts invite two weighty questions which define the basic problem posed by the finds made up to then.

1. Who destroyed the Cemetery and why?

2. To what important Macedonian city had this Cemetery with grave monuments so rich in quality and quantity been attached?

Before we arrive at the answers I gave then, in 1976, a small digression is necessary so that the reader may appreciate all the aspects and dimensions of the problem.

As the reader may perhaps be aware, not all topographical problems of ancient Greece have yet been resolved. We know the names of many cities from documentary sources, though we may still not have succeeded in siting them correctly on a map. Conversely, archaeological research has uncovered ruins of towns and settlements which we can not identify with known towns. The problem becomes more acute in areas where written sources are scanty and the archaeological finds sparse. This is true especially for northern Greece – Epirus, Macedonia, Thrace – for which neither written testimony nor archaeological facts exists.

When therefore in 1861 Léon Heuzey recorded and excavated the ruins of the palace and the Macedonian tomb in the Palatitsia-Vergina area, he immediately came up against the problem: which ancient city was to be identified with this area? Basing his opinion on the meagre ancient evidence at his disposal, he thought that it should be identified with the city Balla, only the name of which has come down to us from antiquity. The next man to explore the area, K.A. Rhomaios, accepted Heuzey's opinion and repeated it in his own publications.[9] My personal interests never inclined towards ancient topography and I never became involved in it, accepting the conclusions of archaeologists who had preceded me in the exploration of the region, though not without hesitations and reservations. The very first excavation of the Great Tumulus and then of the Cemetery had convinced me that the settlement to which the graves belonged had had a long life and had enjoyed a lengthy period of civilization. In 1955, when I published the two first stelai found in the Great Tumulus I noted that we were in an area "exceptionally wealthy in Macedonian antiquities, but for which we cannot find an 'ancient' name"; in the footnote I observed that

Heuzey had identified it with Balla, but that "this hypothesis remains unproved and it awaits new archaeological findings before it can be fully accepted or wholly rejected."[10] I concluded the article with the observation that we are probably on the site of an unknown Macedonian town where life first started in the tenth century BC and continued for more than a thousand years.[11] Ten years later I published a more definite view; "we may even say with certainty that in the fourth century BC this region experienced an upsurge in prosperity and that the city – Balla? – was one of the most important centres of Macedonian Hellenism."[12] Finally, in the publication of the excavation results from the prehistoric tumuli I stated; "the conclusion must therefore be that the Cemetery belongs to the first phase of the settlement which endured for centuries before developing into the magnificent city which Heuzey identified as Balla, where the kings of Macedonia erected a palace but where several other buildings already existed, whose ruins await the archaeologist's spade."[13] However, lack of interest in topographical questions did not impel me to further discussion. Furthermore, if the archaeological discoveries bear witness to the fact that we find ourselves confronted by "one of the most important centres of Macedonian Hellenism", as I believed, our knowledge of the topography of ancient Macedonia was not such as to lead us to a solution of the problem. The few important centres, the large and notable Macedonian towns, were known and no one questioned their sites. And, though I knew that in 1957 Fanoula Papazoglou had expressed doubts about the identification of Aigai with Edessa,[14] nevertheless I would not have taken the matter any further, any more than she did herself. Nevertheless the time eventually comes when academic certainties regarded as fundamental truths are overturned. It seemed that the moment had come when we were to learn about the site of the ancient capital of the Macedonian kingdom, Aigai.

We know from written sources that the first capital of the Macedonian kingdom was Aigai (or Aigeai). A single reference in the works of the Roman historian Justin (VII.1) informs us that when Karanos, the founder of the Macedonian dynasty, led his men to the Macedonian city Edessa guided by a flock of goats (aiges) he called it Aigai. This single piece of information, and

this alone, was the basis on which Aigai was identified with the known city of Edessa. No historian had been perturbed by the fact that reliable writers, such as Plutarch and Ptolemy, record facts about Edessa and Aigai as two separate towns; indeed, the latter, as a geographer, gives different coordinates for each of them. It is not the only case where a widely accepted view in fact remains untested and is handed down through generations of scholars as established fact until the moment that a more sceptical mind examines all the available evidence methodically and without prejudice. So it was that in 1957 Fanoula Papazoglou demonstrated that the identification of Aigai with Edessa was mistaken. However, her suggestion that Aigai was to be located near modern Naousa not only undermined her position but from one point of view has allowed people to give her work less attention than it deserves. (The confusion may have been caused by the fact that her book is written in Serbo-Croat with only a brief summary in French, and the former is a language with which few scholars of the ancient world are familiar.) A little later, and independently of Papazoglou, the English historian N.G.L. Hammond while preparing his fundamental work on the history of Macedonia was faced with the same problem and reached the same conclusion, namely that Edessa and Aigai were two separate cities. Hammond's firsthand and more extensive knowledge of the archaeological material did not let him rest there. In 1968 he put forward his bold theory that Aigai should be placed in the region of Vergina where there stood the magnificent palace, the Macedonian tomb with its impressive marble throne and the Cemetery of the Tumuli. His original theory was supported by a detailed examination of the sources in the first volume of the *History of Macedonia*.[15]

The exploration of the region had reached this stage when I was made forcibly aware of the two questions noted above by the finds from the ex-

28. → The Great Tumulus of Vergina after the greater part had been excavated. A small section of the mound (still covered with pines) left unexcavated can be seen. The excavation trenches reveal the extent of the original mound. The royal tombs have been temporarily covered over with corrugated iron sheets. The long, narrow red-roofed bulding to the left is the laboratory where the organic material is treated.

cavations of the Great Tumulus. I am obliged to confess here that when I first read N. Hammond's theory I experienced considerable doubts, perhaps because I did not dare attribute such outstanding importance to the site and to the excavations on which I had been engaged for forty years. But the problem which the finds of 1976 brought into sharp focus obliged me to pay greater attention to sifting the arguments and delving into the ancient sources amassed by the English historian. Amongst them one in particular struck me as especially revealing; I considered that it not only solved the problem of the broken stelai found in the Great Tumulus, but deflected our thoughts into new channels, and provided a new basis for our reasoning. The information is contained in Plutarch's *Life of Pyrrhus* (26.ll). There Plutarch, after describing the Epirot king's invasion of Macedonia in 274/3 BC and the defeat of the Macedonian ruler, Antigonos Gonatas, continues,

"after the battle, however, he at once proceeded to occupy the cities. And after getting Aigai into his power, besides other severities exercised upon its inhabitants, he left as a garrison in the city some of the Gauls who were making the campaign with him. But the Gauls, a race insatiable of wealth, set themselves to digging up the tombs of the kings who had been buried there; the treasure they plundered, the bones they insolently cast to the four winds."

Plutarch's comment refers only to the robbing of the tombs of the Macedonian kings who, in accordance with ancient tradition, were always buried in the ancient capital of Aigai. However, it seemed obvious to me that such a sacrilegious act would not have stopped there. The rapacity of the Gauls would certainly have driven them to loot all the tombs from which they might anticipate valuable plunder – which would result in a general spoliation and plundering of the rich cemetery of Aigai. This piece of information may therefore provide us with the explanation of the wrecking of the cemetery which we had seen also in the Great Tumulus because of the existence of the many broken grave monuments. Moreover, the date of these monuments was far from inconsistent with their identification as the monuments which the desecration of the Gauls would have destroyed. Now the answer to our first question about the cause of the destruction also gives us

the answer to the second, since in a totally unforeseen fashion it reinforces the view that Aigai is to be located in the region of Vergina. "Over and above the identification of Aigai with the archaeological site of Vergina, new light is shed on all the finds from the area which thus acquire new dimensions of historical importance. The vast area covered by the Cemetery of the Tumuli and the vast wealth which accumulated there over a long period is no longer a puzzle; the palace of Vergina takes its rightful place – at the centre of the ancient capital. And, at this capital the presence of so many grave monuments of such magnificence becomes explicable." These then were my thoughts immediately after the excavation season of 1976, and they led me to the very optimistic conclusion, "if, as I believe, this view is correct, then the formulation of other conclusions becomes legitimate and especially tempting. Antigonos Gonatas succeeded in regaining Macedonian territory in a very short time, and he certainly recaptured the sacred capital of the Macedonians. He must have seen the pillaged royal tombs with his own eyes. His personal experience may have suggested two courses of action to him; a) the celebration of certain rites to rehabilitate the dead and to restore the graves which had been desecrated; b) to ensure the safety of both these and of his own last resting place. There was only one way to achieve this, and at the same time to maintain the very ancient shape of the burial mound; to erect a tumulus so large that it would discourage any tomb robber from undertaking its destruction. If these theories possessed the logical base that I believed them to have, then the Great Tumulus of Vergina acquires an interest wholly its own and its excavation may offer us the most unbelievable reward."[16] In another article I expressed my hopes more clearly still;[17] "now our expectations from its excavation (of the Great Tumulus) may be exceptional. Even the incredible hope that the vast mound of earth covers the tombs of Macedonian kings now acquires a foundation in fact. Nothing is to be ruled out."

The discovery of the Royal Tombs

Buoyed up by these theories and with a heartening glow of anticipation I recommended archaeological work on August 30th 1977. The

results were startling. In the first report on them, composed in February 1978, I wrote: "at the beginning of this brief preliminary report of the excavation of 1977 I am in a position to state that, without reference to any other hypothesis, the recent optimistic forecasts have been proved correct and have exceeded all expectations. The excavations of 1977 have given us the most unexpected rewards. This does not mean that the original hypothesis has turned into immutable and incontrovertible certainty. It has been substantially corroborated, it has not been given the lie, but it requires still more evidence, which we may anticipate from sustained excavation. Continuing excavation remains exceptionally seductive, especially for its director, whose goal has been, from the very beginning, the tomb for which the Great Tumulus was constructed. Only the rediscovery of this tomb can give any useful stimulus to the

29. The southeast part of the Great Tumulus, the last section to be excavated. The section shows the composition of the Tumulus with the alternating layers made up of sand and gravel, red earth and stones.

search and can throw light on the many problems of the two funerary monuments and the foundations of a third uncovered by last year's excavations."[18]

It is now time for me to acquaint the readers of this book with the finds and the results of the excavations up to this point. As I said earlier, work started on August 30th 1977. The aim of the large trench opened from the east side towards the centre of the Tumulus was to uncover the original ground level over a wide area. A second trench, opened from the south, was also directed to the centre. Both reached a depth of about 12 m., exposing a large area a little to the east of the centre of the mound at the original ground level. It was very probable that if the tomb were to be somewhere near the centre, deep exploratory trenches would pick up its traces or we would observe the ancient trench. But in five such trial trenches, each to a depth of 2.50 - 3.0 m. we encountered virgin soil without any of the signs we were anticipating. The disappointment experienced, both by myself and by everyone participating in the excavation, was terrific because the time, as well as the funds, at our disposal were limited. Both had been almost fully expended so that the margins of hope were shrinking. Nevertheless excavation to such a depth and over such an area had provided us with enough evidence to recharge our spirits. We had found still more broken grave stelai, and in the trench on the south side we discovered the most tangible sign that we were indeed close to a spot where a very important building had stood; "abundant breccia (as the chippings and dust which result from the working of marble and other stone prepared for use as building material is called) from marble and limestone covered a wide area in a thick layer over the whole width of the southern trench. It was obvious that the layer of breccia got thinner towards the east whereas it continued towards the southwest part of the Great Tumulus."

In a desire to save both time and manpower I left a segment of a circle untouched west of the southern trench and I opened a new trench from the southwest again towards the centre of the Tumulus. We had advanced some 10-20 m. from the edge of the mound to its centre when we suddenly and totally unexpectedly came on a strange wall; it was built of unbaked bricks. Its western face was bare, but the upper narrow surface (0.45 m.) and the east face were coated with a white, relatively coarse stucco. Such a rough and ready construction could not of course form part of the tomb I sought, but it was the first real structure which we had uncovered in the Great Tumulus after so many years. We had not completed uncovering the wall over its entire length and depth, when, at a distance 8-9 m. further north we came across another indication of human activity. Over a roughly circular area with a diameter of about 0.80 - 1 m. was a thick spread of burnt clay pottery fragments. Careful investigation of the area revealed traces of fire, the burnt bones of small animals and ash in plenty. Everything indicated

that some sacrificial ceremony for the dead man had been held on this spot. The vessels for these rites, (tall skyphidia, fish dishes, sauceboats "salt-cellars" etc.) dated to immediately after the middle of the fourth century BC, somewhere around 340 BC. When we cleared away the red soil on which these remains lay deposited, we saw the upper surface of a wall immediately below it. It did not take us long to realize that we were at the northern end of the brick-built wall we had encountered earlier a little further to the south. Thus this strange wall – plastered on its upper surface and eastern face, while its western was bare, showing the bricks of which it was made – came to light. It was 9.10 m. long. The style and the method of construction was unusual and reminded me of another grave which had been discovered in one of the tumuli in the Cemetery several years earlier. In this grave various clay vessels had been found which, without straining the evidence, dated to the third quarter of the fourth century BC (350-325 BC) – that is, to the same period to which we had ascribed the sherds of the sacrifice. These indications of date were extremely important, because even before we discovered this strange wall, and before even we were able to recognize its purpose, we were in possession of a date for its construction.

Continued archaeological investigation of the surrounding area soon revealed the remains of a second sacrifice a short distance west of the wall. The pottery fragments of this one also belonged to the same period. Practical reasons delayed the uncovering of the wall to any depth, since to achieve this it was essential to widen our trench to the east where the plastered face of the wall lay. This fresh operation led to the discovery of another impressive wall 10 m. southeast of the wall, that is to say at the edge of the Great Tumulus and at a depth of 0.20-0.50 m. below ground level. This wall was built of two rows of limestone blocks and was about 1.40 m. wide, a fact which revealed that it belonged to some extremely important construction. As excavation progressed it was clear that we had discovered a section of the foundations of an important building.

The prolonged and tiring waiting was succeeded by tension as we saw that from below the mass of the Great Tumulus the buildings we sought were emerging one after another. When we had uncovered the whole of the well-built wall we observed a very small distance north of its end a row of very large oblong limestone blocks which, as soon became clear, were the covering stones of a rectangular subterranean tomb. At the same time we were working to remove the mound east of the brick-built wall, so that we could begin to uncover its eastern face which also seemed to be the main facade. At this point, namely east of the strange wall, we discovered the remains of a third sacrifice. When we were finally able to uncover the eastern face of the strange wall we encountered the upper surface of another wall, which projects rather more than 0.80 m. from the strange wall at a very shallow depth. Our initial doubts about its purpose were soon resolved by further excavation; it was nothing other than the upper part of a cornice, the highest point of the facade of a tomb. We immediately observed that its sima bore painted decoration consisting of white palmettes on a blue background. At this point we stopped work, waiting for the specialist technicians who would carefully uncover the paint so as to preserve the colouring. Meanwhile we turned our attention to searching west of the strange wall for the vault of the tomb. We came across it at once; although we were expecting to see bare limestone, as in all the Macedonian tombs excavated till then, we saw, with a pleasant thrill of surprise that the whole expanse of the dome was protected by a thick, solid coat of stucco. All the indications were that the building we had discovered was of supreme importance.

We now had three buildings in front of us, the one adjacent to the other. Two of these were subterranean tombs; only foundations of the third remain and these were above ground. I know of no parallel in Macedonia where many magnificent Macedonian tombs have been found. There was also something else, of great significance. Two of the tombs were covered by a smaller, original tumulus formed by heaping up red earth, similar to the mounds in the extensive Cemetery of the Tumuli. It was clear that this tumulus, which had to be more or less contemporaneous with the construction of the tombs was later buried under the embankment of the Great Tumulus which at this point consists of sand and stones and can be distinguished from the original tumulus without difficulty. The foundations of the third structure lay outside this original tumulus.

The dimensions of this building (9.60 × 8 m.),

its plan and its well-built walls show that it must have been of considerable importance. This hypothesis is strengthened by the many broken pieces of marble from its superstructure (from cornice, architrave etc.) which were found in the foundations, covered with a layer of breccia. If we reflect that no architectural member was of marble except for the door sills, even in the nearby palace which was a magnificently impressive building, we may deduce that great significance was attached to this small building and that it was erected with particular care. But what purpose might it have served? Any thought that it might be residential is automatically excluded. Its plan, and its position belies such use. But equally, I think its location next to a grave tumulus and almost touching the small tomb excludes its interpretation as a temple. The only possible explanation is that it may have been a "heroon", that is a shrine dedicated to the worship of the dead whether one or more. A hypothesis of this sort leads naturally to the question of the relationship of the "heroon" to the adjacent tombs. If however rites for the dead man or men in these tombs were performed at the "heroon" this implies that the deceased were not ordinary mortals, but persons to whom worship was due.

At this point the picture suggested by the archaeological evidence is completed by some very specific written evidence which informs us that two kings were worshipped in Macedonia: Amyntas, Philip's father, and Philip himself. We may extract one other extraordinarily attractive fact from a documentary source. We should however note that historians regard this authority as one of the least trustworthy – the history of the Pseudo-Callisthenes. This mentions that Alexander, after burying his father with all due ceremony, "founded a temple above his tomb". But even without this unreliable source the remains of the "heroon", the sherds which were found amongst the sacrifices round the great tomb and the dating of these were sufficient evidence on which to pin the conviction that the hypotheses about the probable existence of royal tombs and my hope that continuing excavations would offer us the most incredible rewards would find their justification. I should add that what has materialized from the excavation of the last years (1977-1982) has so far surpassed even the most optimistic expectations as to bear out one more time the archaeologist's confidence that the fruits of excavation may sometimes be far more significant than his tutored imagination allows him to hope.

Close to the north wall of the "heroon" and level with the foundation stones, covering slabs of a rectangular tomb were discovered; on excavation it proved to have been plundered. The robbers had made two openings; one high in the western wall and the other in its upper part, breaking one of the covering slabs. I think it is very likely that the first attempt took place on the western wall from which a stone was removed; but when they had worked it free it seems that the robbers met some sort of obstacle, perhaps the shelf which ran the whole length of the wall on the inside, traces of which can still be seen. They therefore had to look for another point of entry, and so they came to break one of the horizontal stones which formed the ceiling of the grave. We found both these openings roughly covered over again – a stone had been used for the west wall and field stones for the roof but they were both placed with a care which cannot be attributed to the tomb robbers. Not unnaturally, quite a lot of earth fell into the tomb through these openings, most of it on the western side.

Entering it ourselves, we discovered it to be reasonably spacious, some 3.50 m. long, 2.09 m. wide and 3 m. high. Force of professional habit makes the archaeologist look first at the ground – our eyes automatically swivelled to the floor of the tomb – but not for long. It was immediately obvious that the tomb robbers had done their job thoroughly; but simultaneously, we could see they had left us the most precious item in the tomb; the magnificent and captivating painted decoration. Three of its walls, the north, the west and the south had a narrow frieze bearing decorative griffins and flowers – and above this an exceptional painting; on the south, there were three seated female figures and on the west another. But it was the north wall which held our gaze as we exclaimed over the sight in sheer amazement; its entire length was covered by a unique composition. The theme was easy to recognize; the rape of Persephone by Pluto (see the detailed description below).

We could, then, experience no disappointment because of the looting as we proceeded to the clearing and investigation of the tomb. The tomb robbers had struck the walls roughly at many points with some kind of metal object (a kind of crowbar perhaps). They had probably been trying to make sure they missed no passage to any other chamber there might have been. In the north wall they made an opening to the outside where they certainly met only earth; fortunately the opening was below the height of the wall painting. However, the damage they caused was limited to only a few points and was not comprehensive. The inevitable effects of time and damp had been much more destructive. The plaster on which the painting was executed was exceptionally friable and delicate; most of it was covered by a hard layer of sinter. The paintings were in dire need of immediate treatment. Fortunately the Archaeological Service maintains a team of some of the most experienced specialists and I knew the responsibility for the Vergina area lay with my old and dear friend Photis Zachariou. From the start he took charge of the work with his usual application. Today, we can see that under his wise direction, his dedicated and dexterous team not only preserved these splendid works but successfully exposed all that could be laid bare. The lower part of the walls was painted in Pompeian red, the colour usually found in Macedonian tombs. Most of it survived below the sinter.

When we removed the earth we discovered that the looting was complete. The only things left for us were a few sherds from clay pots and fragments of a marble shell together with a number of bones scattered from human skeletons, which were obviously not occupying their original position. Given that tomb robbers of antiquity only removed valuable objects – gold, silver and at most the bronze objects – it follows that the entire content of the tomb must have been exceptionally valuable. This, in conjunction with the absence of any trace of iron weapons, (not held in high regard by tomb robbers) led to the reflection that this was a woman's tomb. This was corroborated by the wall painting which depicts many female figures, as well as by the mythological subject of the rape of Persephone, none of them suitable for a man's tomb. The examination of the bones showed that this thought was not absolutely correct. As to the date, both the pottery sherds and the wall paintings suggest a probable date around the middle of the fourth century as the most likely.

A short distance to the northwest we had located the cornice and the beginning of the vault of a large Macedonian tomb. The sima which

30

crowned the cornice retained its dark blue colouring and its decoration of white palmettes. The specialist conservators who arrived immediately after the discovery of its top began by painstakingly removing the earth from the facade. Little time passed before we discovered, not without surprise, that directly below the cornice was a painted frieze, 1.16 m. high. As its uncovering proceeded from left (south) to right it was possible to distinguish the figures in the composition; the first to appear on the top left hand edge, was a running buck. When at last the entire surface of the frieze was free from earth we could admire the astounding wall painting which extended over a length of 5.56 m. It was not difficult to grasp that it was a hunting scene, in which the movement of men, mounted and on foot, hunting dogs and wild beasts unfolded magnificently across a landscape denoted by trees and rocks. We stood in front of a second major work of Greek painting of the fourth century BC, different from the first we had found in the "small" tomb, but just as impressive and certainly more sophisticated in its rendering and finish. Everyone was filled with a deep satisfaction, for the rewards of the excava-

30. The upper part of the facade of "Philip's Tomb" after the excavations of 1977. The upper part of the door, after the removal of the first porolithos in the "wall" which sealed it, is visible. A number of figures in the wall painting of the Hunt can be picked out, but at many points the earth had stuck to the painting along with the sinter. The cleaning and stabilizing of the whole frieze took three years methodical work.

tion were immense, and more, they were totally unexpected. Quite suddenly we had come to know two major works from the most brilliant period of Greek painting, hitherto considered irretrievably lost. Our first responsibility was to protect this inestimable work. It was immediately swathed in black cloth; next we rigged up a temporary roof so that from the instant of its discovery until today it has not been exposed to the effects of variations in climate even for one moment; equally, those working on its conservation were careful to take every possible precaution to ensure its survival.

Essentially the excavation season of 1977 had come to an end. Funds were available for only a few days further work; more to the point, autumn was so far advanced that the beginning of the rainy period could not be long delayed. Besides, we knew that we could not complete the uncovering of the entire facade and the vault, or even one of the two. All this had to wait for the coming year. The only thing we could do, indeed had to do, immediately was to uncover the entablature of the building. The procedure of course was based on one central thought which seemed to me to be self-evident after the excavation of the "small" tomb; that the large vaulted tomb had also been pillaged by the tomb robbers. I knew that in such a case the robbers would have entered by the rear part of the vault, but once inside, they would have destroyed every door they encountered to make sure that they had looted every possible space. I calculated that it would not be difficult to progress to the level of the external door and through it to have a quick look into the interior of the tomb and perhaps even to get inside, down a ladder.

On this assumption we continued the task of uncovering the entablature – first the triglyphs, then the metopes, and lastly the epistyle. Here also the architectural members retained their colouring unharmed – blue on the triglyphs, red on the *tainiai* with a pattern of white meanders. The shape of the ancient building appeared particularly well especially since damage was limited. Directly below the architrave we came to the capitals of two pillars at either end of the facade, whose painted decoration had survived in remarkably good condition; towards the centre, left and right of the position in which we had expected to find the door the capitals of two doric half-columns emerged. Immediately next to them appeared the marble jambs of the door, topped by the marble lintel. Two deep breaks at the edges and several cracks in the upper parts of the jambs showed that they had not stood up to the great weight of earth which had pressed on them for so many centuries, nor to various other forces of destruction, such as damp, the spread of oxidization from the metal pivot on the inside and the settling of the ground. Parallel to the facade and sited between the columns a large oblong limestone block emerged. Its significance was not difficult to understand. We know from most Macedonian tombs that after the burial a wall of such stones was erected outside the door, shielding its entire width. This was to stop the earth which would subsequently cover the tomb from

pressing on the doors and forcing them inwards; (in cases where the doorway was not closed by leaves, this wall prevented earth from filling the tomb).

This limestone almost reached the lower surface of the lintel; to be absolutely exact, it was a few centimetres shorter, leaving a tiny gap whereby we could look into the interior of the tomb. When we tried to do this we were completely taken aback; instead of the dark emptiness of the space we had expected, there, about half a metre in front of us, was the white marble surface of a door. It was almost unbelievable; the door of the tomb, two intact wide marble leaves, stood *in situ*. Had they never been forced? Had the tomb robbers left the tomb unplundered? Even though it seemed like a dream, it was nevertheless reality. Now when I reflect on it I think that this is still the most deeply moving moment of the excavation.

My conjectures of the year before led me to think that we might reasonably hope for the discovery of royal tombs. But these same surmises also led me to expect that the tombs would be found to have been robbed, just as we had found the "small" tomb. And then, seeking to confirm my conjecture, I had asked myself which I would prefer as an academic; to prove my supposition and its conclusion correct, or to disprove it and discover an unrobbed Macedonian tomb, even if it were not also a royal tomb. My answer, which did not come easily, was closer to the second half of the question; to find an unrobbed Macedonian tomb which would furnish much more new evidence and greater satisfaction than a correct guess. And now? The indications were that the dilemma was past. There was nothing to undermine my hypothesis. Moreover, we had discovered a large Macedonian tomb, probably intact.

Probably... Although everything indicated that it could not but be intact, I did not dare believe it. There remained, I thought, one distasteful possibility; that the tomb robbers had entered from the back, as always, but had baulked, for whatever reason, at the destruction of the external door. This we could check only when we uncovered the vault, and of course only its rear part. This was a task which should not be deferred for a whole year, not simply because of my own excusable curiosity but for reasons of security. Reports of a half-opened unrobbed tomb would be a terrible temptation to those who in their own fashion continued the ancient traditions of tomb robbing. And so I embarked immediately on the excavation of the rear part of the tomb with the aim of uncovering the whole area of the vault. The work occupied many days because there was a build-up of earth more than six metres deep at this point. We were nearing the level of the vault when an unexpected obstacle obliged us to proceed with great caution and at a very slow pace.

Square sun-dried bricks suddenly appeared in the earth at the western edge of the vault. As the clearing of earth proceeded further, we distinguished traces of fire on many of the bricks while on others were remains of white stucco. Finally, between the bricks and the ground where they were piled were two bent iron swords, a spearhead and many pieces of iron horse trappings, all showing clear signs of burning. The arrangement of the bricks led me to suggest that above the western part of the vault there had been a four-sided structure, some kind of altar on which libations would have been poured for the dead in the tomb. I now know that this was not the correct interpretation. The burnt iron objects must have been placed there after the cremation of the deceased and had been taken there from the site of the pyre. This means that horses (to which the harnesses had belonged) had also been sacrificed on the pyre. This fact recalls the funeral of Patroclos, to whom Achilles sacrificed "four high-necked horses" and it obliged us to regard the deceased for whom the tomb had been erected as no ordinary mortal. Furthermore, the wall painting on the facade conveyed the same message (see above). Lastly, scattered through the pile were three gold acorns (three others were found later), a fragment of a gold oak leaf, a bronze jug and many fragments of charred ivory.

Leaving the further scrutiny of the entire pile for later, we concentrated on freeing the area which interested us, the top of the vault on its western edge, because only from there could we enter, if indeed the tomb was unrobbed, or check if in fact it had been robbed. We know from all the plundered Macedonian tombs that the tomb robbers removed the last stone of the vault, the one which was supported on the back wall and which was nearly always short – the one which the craftsman calls the keystone. In construction it is the last to be put into position; its removal is easy and carries no risk. When we located the keystone and it seemed not to have been tampered with, the last shadow of doubt was removed; the tomb had not been pillaged. But only as we went deeper than the top of the western back wall and saw that that too was intact was I finally able to believe that I was to be blessed with the most unbelievable luck which awaits the archaeologist. I had found a Macedonian tomb, apparently an extremely important one, unrobbed. Stronger still than this satisfaction, however, was the burden of responsibility. I knew that from that moment on I had to have absolute control over all my actions and that there was no margin for error or carelessness: neither had I any time to spare, since we were already into early November.

The opening of the tomb was arranged for November 8th, the day the Orthodox Church celebrates the feast of the Archangels Michael and Gabriel. All the assistants who might be required were present, each prepared to help in his own field; my two archaeological colleagues, the two architects, the photographer, the conservator from the Museum of Thessalonike, the technicians from the Restoration Service who would remove the keystone from the vault and who would undertake any preliminary measures for reinforcement. Naturally officials from the Archaeological Service were also present – the Ephor, the Epimelites of the area and the archaeological staff of the University of Thessalonike. Besides our specialist selves, the Nomarch of Veroia, members of the gendarmerie and the Rector of the University of Thessalonike, which funded the excavations, were also in attendance.

The keystone was raised from its bed with only minimal effort, leaving an opening 0.34 m. wide; this was enough for us first to see inside the tomb and then to descend into it by means of a wooden ladder. I directed my eyes first to the back of the marble door which divided the main chamber from the antechamber and then to the walls. My first, immediate reaction, was one of sharp disappointment. The door presented a thick, coarsely worked surface; the walls were undecorated; they were not even painted in colour and it was obvious that they did not have the final thin, carefully applied surface which we had found in plastered Macedonian buildings. But the shock passed almost instantly as my gaze fell on the floor of the chamber. In the first official report of the excavation I attempted briefly to sketch my state of mind at that moment. I wrote: "this is not

31. The objects which were found in the southwest corner of the main chamber of "Philip's Tomb". The large bronze cover of the shield, the bronze vessels for the bath, the sponge, the greaves and the lampstand are visible. At the bottom right the Macedonian helmet and the diadem can be seen.

the appropriate place to relate what went on in the excavator's mind during this unparalleled moment in his career as an archaeologist. The reader will readily imagine that although it was imperative to remain cool, calm and collected in order to live up to the responsibilities of the situation the excavator was deeply stirred and awe-struck at the sight of a rich burial chamber which had remained untouched over the centuries from the moment when the marble doors had been shut after the last rites for the dead. The long years spent studying burial customs far from dulling his

sensibilities had sharpened them to such a degree that he lived through the thrilling, never to be recaptured moments, when it was granted him to travel back through the millenia and come close to the living truth of the past, as a direct experience. The excavator felt a scientist's elation and a desecrator's guilt; of course, the first cancelled the other out."

My gaze was fixed on the rear part of the chamber, exactly below the opening. Here all the objects provided for the after-life of the dead man were piled together. To my right, in the southwest corner of the chamber, bronze and iron objects lay one on top of the other; the bronze items had acquired a beautiful dark green patina from oxidization; the iron ones had turned black. To the left, next to the north wall, was the gleam of silver vessels. At the centre of the back wall, directly beneath our opening, was the

70

square covering stone of a marble sarcophagus; next to it, in front of us, the spreading remains of blackened, rotting and disintegrating timber, amongst which twinkled some small fragments; gold leaves glittered over its whole area. Beyond was the black-red of an oxidized cuirass. The rest of the floor was bare.

We had to find an empty space where the wooden ladder which was ready to hand could rest so that we could descend. Themis Kardamis tied a rope around his waist and swung into the void; he stepped carefully onto the lid of the sarcophagus and reconnoitred. We were lucky; next to the sarcophagus was the only spot where we could site the bottom of the ladder without danger of destroying anything. When it was in position I descended the almost vertical rungs; I had no leisure for sentiment, however human this would have been. Although it was hard, even for

32. The silver vases as they were found heaped close to the north wall of the main chamber of "Philip's Tomb". One of them had knocked against the plastering of the wall and the limestone is visible. Handles which had come unstuck from some of the vases were to be seen on the floor.

me, to believe it, the minute I found myself inside the chamber I had the cold eye of the anatomist and the rigid logic of the mathematician. The first and most immediate problem was the structural condition of the building. I needed no specialist knowledge to ascertain that there was no danger either from the walls or from the plaster work. Everything was in very good condition, even though tree roots have grown down between the stones of the roof. The marble door seemed to be securely in its place. However, no one could be sure that the change in conditions, and vibrations from footsteps or from whatever tasks we had to undertake would not create the danger of collapse. It had therefore to be shored up. The second problem was the finds. The metal and pottery objects appeared to be in very good condition, although the iron objects, some of them at least, such as the cuirass, helmet and a sword were at risk from deep and advanced oxidization. Only the decayed remains of organic substance made it clear that we should touch nothing before the arrival of other specialists, particularly of a

chemist, in addition to the conservator from the Museum of Thessalonike. Finally, but not immediate, was the problem of how we could enter the antechamber.

With these considerations in mind the course of action I had already mapped out had to be executed with great care but also with some speed for two reasons; a) from the moment that the tomb had been opened and it became known that it contained a number of valuable objects there was no advantage in these remaining there for longer than was strictly essential, even if they were well guarded; b) because we were into November and the unseasonably favourable weather could not hold much longer.

My first charge was to ask for the chemist from the National Archaeological Museum and the Director of the Antiquities Centre to be sent immediately from Athens. Until such time as they

33. The iron cuirass, which had fallen to the floor, as it was found. It had apparently been placed on the couch and broke when it fell on its right shoulder. In the lower part of the picture the two gold lion heads which were attached to the right side of the cuirass can be seen. At the edge pieces of the "pectoral" which
protected the neck and chest of the warrior are visible.

33

could arrive we had to progress in our tasks. First came the photography; this is difficult and delicate work, essential and of great value as a record of research. The condition of the tomb and of the finds had to be recorded as well as could possibly be managed. Spiros Tsavdaraglou, the photographer who was longing to get to work, was ready. The results of his labour and of his experience may be judged by everyone, so further comment from me is superfluous. Then at last we could buttress the door so that we could continue our work in safety. When this was achieved it was the architects' turn. Anna Xenariou (now Mrs Manasi) and John Kiagias drew up the first plans and marked the location of the finds on them. Next my two immediate assistants, Miss Styliani Drougou and Mrs Chrysoula Paliadeli numbered the finds and filled in all the essential information on the plans so that we were ready for the objects to be packed up and taken to the Museum of Thessalonike. This work would not begin until our photographer notified us that the films had been developed successfully. Only then could we touch the objects and alter the situation which we had found. This change, in reality signified the destruction of much scientific evidence which could never be recovered; for this reason the archaeologist, who is also a treasure hunter, proceeds gingerly in this ever necessary operation, and never before he has made sure that everything he has been lucky enough to find and to see has been photographed, planned, looked at carefully and described in his notebook.

We had yet to open the marble sarcophagus. Even though the assumption that therein lay the most valuable object awoke an ungovernable curiosity in me – a feeling with which an archaeologist is well acquainted though it is dangerous – my sense of academic responsibility imposed patience. When eventually I judged us ready for this final act, I descended into the tomb with two assistants, the technician-conservator from the Museum of Thessalonike, Demetrios Mathios, and the excavation foreman, Costas Pavlides. Forseeing that the content of the sarcophagus would be especially valuable, and wishing to keep it a secret for reasons of security, I ordered that the opening of the tomb should be closed. Overcoming the unavoidable difficulties caused by the organic material scattered over the floor we managed in a short time to raise the lid. And then we saw a sight which it was not possible for me to have imagined, because until then such an ossuary had never been found; an all-gold larnax with an impressive relief star on its lid. We lifted it from the sarcophagus, placed it on the floor and opened it. Our eyes nearly popped out of their sockets and our breathing stopped; there, unmistakeably, were charred bones placed in a carefully formed pile and still retaining the colour of the purple cloth in which they had once been wrapped. In one corner lay a very heavy gold wreath, now folded, which had covered them. We shut the valuable casket, covered it, and placed it in an inner corner of the chamber.

We felt the need to return to the light and to take deep gulps of fresh air. When I was once more outside I moved a little apart from my colleagues on the excavation, the visitors and the police and stood alone to recover from that unbelievable sight. Everything indicated that we had found a royal tomb; and if the dating we had assigned to the objects was correct, as it seemed to be, then... I did not even dare to think about it. For the first time a shiver ran down my spine, something akin to an electric shock passed through me. If the dating... and if these were royal remains... then... had I held the bones of Philip in my hands? It was far too terrifying an idea for my brain to assimilate.

Together with my colleagues who knew the secret we made our way to the house, inviting also the Epimelete of the Archaeological Service, Mr Pantos, so that he could be informed. Shortly afterwards I also told the acting Ephor of Antiquities, Mrs Mary Siganidou. So far, only seven people knew that in the tomb there was a uniquely valuable treasure side by side with other magnificent finds. I took an immediate decision; the treasures had to be moved as fast as possible to the Museum of Thessalonike without anybody realizing what was happening. We descended into the tomb again, packed up the larnax with the utmost care, removed it from the tomb without anyone suspecting the significance of the box and, with the technician, Demetrios Mathios, got into my car and drove away from the site. Escorted by the Archaeological Service car, we set out for Thessalonike. Mathios cradled the box in his capable hands; we drove in silence. We had told the Museum to expect us. When we arrived we went to one of the safest store-rooms, opened the box and displayed the treasure we had brought to the delighted gaze of our colleagues

34. The west part of the main chamber of "Philip's Tomb". At the centre is the marble sarcophagus which contained the gold larnax. In front of the sarcophagus are the remains of the wooden couch and table. Left of the sarcophagus is the sword, to the right in the background is the torch. Above left are the bronze vessels and weapons, below is the cuirass. To the right, by the wall, are the silver vases.

who had meantime assembled.

Sleep that night was impossible. It had been the most fantastic day of my life... until then. For the next few days held other surprises both for me and for my team.

Help started arriving from Athens; the engineer from the Department of Restoration, Nicholas Kavoulakos; the chemist from the National Archaeological Museum, Constantine Assimenos; the supervisory conservators S. Baltoyiannis and T. Margaritov and the master technician G. Petkousis. They examined the ob-

jects, took samples and established a plan of campaign. From then on I trusted their knowledge, their experience and their capable hands with the rarest materials ever found in an archaeological excavation. Now I know, as indeed we all know, that this trust was fully justified. Each performed his allotted task; the packing of the finds progressed; the iron objects required special care – the cuirass, the helmet and the sword. We decided not to touch the remains of the organic material and of the ivory, but once the other essential work had been completed to temporarily seal the opening of the tomb. We had, nevertheless, observed that among the other pieces of ivory some parts of the human body were to be distinguished – heads, hands, legs. Because I wanted to have a more careful look at some of these I very cautiously lifted a small head; I could not find my voice. The bearded middle-aged man it depicted bore an amazing resemblance to Philip as we know him from the gold medallion from Tarsus. I

74

put it back where I had found it and picked up another, very close to it. By now I thought I was dreaming. Unless it was a hallucination I held in my hand a very lifelike portrait of Alexander the Great. It was incredible – but true. Three other heads lay close by; one was not unlike Alexander, the two others were also obviously portraits but I did not recognize the features. I deemed it essential to pack them as carefully as I could and remove them from the tomb. That night was the second most agitated night of my life as I stared fixedly and speechlessly at the five faces. (Today I know that these were not the only ones there).

Because of the excitement of the work, we lived in our own fairy-tale world. However, the real world around us was in the grip of its own fever. Greeks were preparing for the second elections to be held after the seven year dictatorship. The technicians had to leave to vote in their own villages. The newspapers were filled with pre-election speeches. Even so, the news from Vergina began to occupy front page space. Greeks, always absorbed by politics, now divided their interests between the elections and the archaeological discoveries. The Rector of the University of Thessalonike had sometime previously arranged a press conference for November 24th, four days after the elections, at which we, the Professors of Archaeology, would announce the results of our excavations.

It remained only for us to enter the antechamber. The inner marble door could not be opened until the objects in the tomb had been removed. I judged there to be only one way – carefully to remove a stone from the wall right or left of the door. The technician from the Museum of Thessalonike, Sideris Karalis, patiently sought and found the joints of the second stone in the wall south of the door of the chamber. He freed them and we were ready for its removal. In the afternoon of November 21st we moved it and could see into the antechamber. Exactly in front of us, next to the south wall, was a second marble sarcophagus. None of us had expected that, for none of us knew any Macedonian tomb where signs of burial had been found in the antechamber. I raised my eyes to the vault; a wonderful Pompeian red covered the upper part; lower down the walls were white. The plastering was very smooth, totally different from the main chamber. High up, at the spring of the vault were painted rosettes and there were nails from which

ornaments for the deceased had once hung. Now all that remained of these lay decomposing on the ground which was covered with rotting organic remains forming a very much thicker layer than in the main chamber. Even on the sarcophagus there was a very thick covering of grain or ferns. I could not be sure which for their ashen colour was of no assistance to comprehension. Next to the sarcophagus, on the floor, lay a broken gold wreath (we now know that it is a most delicate object, made up of myrtle leaves and flowers). Carefully I put my hand into the hole and then, head first, I wriggled into the antechamber. I was able to tiptoe into the centre where the floor was clear, on fallen lumps of plaster. I looked towards the outer door; the weight of the lintel had made the upper part slope inwards, at an apparently dangerous angle. I turned back towards the inner door, whose lintel was also cracked. My eyes turned to the floor and I was taken aback by

35. The gold larnax found in the main chamber with the burnt bones of Philip. On the left, folded is the heavy gold wreath of oak leaves and acorns. The bones, all of which show that they had been carefully washed, were wrapped in a purple cloth. Traces of the deep blue colouring left when the cloth rotted were found on many of the top-most bones.

35

36

37

38

36. The inner marble door between the main chamber and the antechamber in "Philip's Tomb". In the left hand corner the gold sheathing of the gorytos can be seen and next to it the gilded greaves. The alabastra and a "Cypriot" amphora can be seen amongst the fallen lumps of plaster.

37. The gorytos and the greaves against the inner door of "Philip's Tomb". Left, below the gorytos, lies its base which became detached and a wide gold hoop. Next to the greaves are alabastra.

38. Arrows were found inside the gorytos; when we lifted the gold sheathing 74 arrow heads and remains of their wooden shafts were discovered in their original position. Gold bands which secured the sheaves are also visible.

39. The marble sarcophagus in the antechamber of "Philip's Tomb". In front of this and to the left the disintegrated remains of wooden furniture with ivory and gold decoration can be seen.

everything I saw. The threshold was packed – a spear, alabastra, a Cypriot amphora and, in the left hand corner, between the jambs and the door, a curious gold object with dainty decoration and relief scenes. Next to it was a pair of gilded greaves. Suddenly an image rose in my mind; the gold artefact was exactly like the Scythian *"gorytoi"* – a kind of quiver – which had been found in Russia. When I moved it a little I saw a bundle of bronze arrowheads; even parts of their wooden shafts had been preserved. My colleagues in the main chamber could not see

this, for everything was concealed by the jambs. I decided it would be prudent not to mention anything to anybody until the next day. Beyond this lay a pectoral, which looked at though it were of iron, though its decoration made me suspect immediately that such decoration would not have been executed on such a hard metal; we later discovered that this too was of gold.

The work continued next day. We attempted to guess the content of the sarcophagus, but only by opening it would we have the answer. Although there were more obstacles than in the main chamber, we set about opening it with care and we saw, not without surprise, a second gold larnax, a little smaller than the first and more plainly decorated. We lifted it from the sarcophagus and placed it on the plank on which we stood. Our previous experience blunted the edge of our curiosity about its contents. We knew that we would find the charred bones of a second dead person. Calmly and carefully we opened it – to experience yet another shock, one which overshadowed all the others, as though the tomb was only yielding up its remarkable secrets stage by stage. What we saw in front of us was not the bones of a dead man, but the wonderfully decorated gold and purple cloth which covered them. Next to it, squashed against the side of the larnax, was an elegant woman's diadem (it was impossible indeed even to imagine, in that first glance, that we had found the most beautiful piece of jewellery in the ancient Greek world). Immediate photography was something more than a necessity, for no one could tell whether that wonderful glimpse of the fabric might not be the only one afforded to the human eye. No one could judge the state of the material.

The transfer of this larnax to the Museum of Thessalonike finally brought the excavation season of 1977 to an end. After twenty-five whole years working at Vergina, I felt I deserved to enjoy what, as an archaeologist, I could never have allowed myself to dream of.

I arrived in Thessalonike, prepared the slides and rose in the morning to go to the University to announce the results of the excavation to the Press. But before I made them public, I regarded it as my duty to inform the most senior members of the government, the President of the Republic and the Prime Minister. Only as I entered the amphitheatre of the old building where many years before I had attended my first university lectures did I again come into contact with reality. And it was then that I understood that what we had achieved in the isolation of Vergina was not of concern only to the archaeologist. The entire Greek people had taken to their heart what started as an academic discovery. Today I know that there is no satisfaction and no honour which can compare with the love of those who said to me "thank you for what you have given us. Health and long life be yours."

The end of the excavation

Excavation could not be continued before the spring. However, all the indications were that we had to be ready for radical changes both in the

40. This elegant myrtle wreath was found on the floor where it had fallen in the southwest corner of the antechamber; many flowers which had belonged to it were found scattered round it which means that originally it must have hung somewhere high up on the wall.

rhythm and in the conditions of our life and work at Vergina. Up to this time we had worked with limited financial means, for short periods of time and without any distraction from visitors. We had been undisturbed in the isolation of a remote area, to which only a few well informed lovers of antiquity came to peer at the ruins of the palace and Rhomaios' tomb as the magnificent Macedonian tomb discovered before the War by my teacher is called. But now the news of the striking finds had spread not just throughout Greece, but over the whole world. The most enthusiastic had even begun to arrive on the site in the rainy days of winter, while journalists continued to write about it, thereby keeping up the world's interest. But the heaviest emphasis on the importance of the excavation came with the visit of the Prime Minister of Greece, Mr Constantine Karamanlis, first to Vergina and then to the Archaeological Museum of Thessalonike to which all the finds had been transferred, and with his public announcement that the Greek government would make a generous subsidy available to the University of Thessalonike for the continuation of the work.

Now that the essential finance had been secured, we could plan the continuation of the ex-

cavation over a long period and thus we resumed work in April 1978. The vast mass of earth demanded sustained and patient effort. But a much greater problem was created by a curious stone construction which extended over the entire central section, 4-5 m. below the top of the Tumulus and reaching to its northern edges above the surface. Its careful excavation uncovered a huge horizontal surface of rough stones which showed that they had been placed with orderly care. Its depth ranged from 20-30 cms. to 4-5 m. at the centre. There was not the slightest trace of sand or earth in this entire mass; it was large heap of stones. I knew of no previous example – even on a smaller scale – which would have helped understand the reason for the construction of this stone mass. Three possible interpretations could be regarded as satisfactory; a) this stone construction formed the core of the tumulus and was made to hold the earth mass together, both around and above it; b) this stone construction served to

41. When the marble slab which covered the sarcophagus in the antechamber was moved the gold larnax which had been placed inside was revealed; on its lid was the relief twelve-pointed Macedonian star.

41

drain the rain water towards the edges of the Tumulus; c) this stone construction hindered possible tomb robbers from sinking a shaft in the centre to explore the depths, from which they could also deduce the existence of a tomb because any such bore hole would fill up from the stones of inner walls. The second two explanations seemed to me to be the more probable; this meant that we should expect another, or other tombs at the centre and to the north, and certainly the tomb for which the Tumulus had been constructed. This indeed was the ultimate goal of the excavation.

We worked for more than two and a half months to remove the overburden of the mound from the central area. When we had achieved this we began the archaeological exploration proper. The smaller, earlier mound which covered the two tombs which we had discovered the previous year showed certain disturbances in its northern section, a little way away from the large Macedonian tomb. In the attempt to ascertain their significance, we cut a trench at a deeper level. It was not long before we noticed an ancient trench filled with sand and gravel; the chance that it could be the trench for a Macedonian tomb seemed to be entirely justified and the proof came much sooner than we had expected. The very next day (5.8.1979) continuing the excavation of the trench to the west we encountered the top corner of the cornice and the frieze of the tomb. Everything showed that the shape of the facade resembled the earlier one; the colours on the *tainiai* and on the sima were preserved in good condition. Even before we had got as far as uncovering the entrance, we located the vault and removed the earth from the rear (western) end. Once again, luck was with us. The tomb had not been violated by tomb robbers. We continued the excavation in preparation for the opening of the new tomb, with the experience of our earlier work and with greater patience, but with no less joy and satisfaction. The uncovering of the frieze – from which we expected so much after the two previous examples – ended in bitter disappointment. Nothing of the five metre surface had survived even though the traces of colour testified that the whole frieze had borne a large painted composition. Disintegrated fragments of wood and perhaps leather suggested that in this instance the painting had not been executed on the stucco of the plastering but on a portable surface

– either of wood or leather – which had then been attached to the frieze. It was of course natural that these organic substances had rotted in the earth so that we were deprived of one of the most valuable features of the tomb.

Everyone connected with the excavation was present when, for a second time, we loosened the keystone of the vault and saw into the inside. One of the two leaves of the inner marble door had fallen into the main chamber; it had broken and covered part of the floor. It had perhaps also smashed some of the objects; however, this misfortune solved two important problems for us. Firstly, we could easily balance a wooden ladder on the leaf. Secondly, we had direct entrance to

42. The inside of the gold larnax found in the antechamber. The burnt bones of the dead woman were wrapped in a magnificent gold and purple fabric and her gold diadem had been placed against one of the narrow sides of the larnax.

42

the antechamber through the half-open door. For a second time I descended into the funerary chamber which had remained untouched from the moment the burial had taken place and the outer marble door of the tomb had been closed. The space was smaller than in the other tomb, but the entire floor area was covered with decomposing organic material amongst which lay assorted objects. In the northwest corner were two large bronze vessels and next to them a tall iron lampstand; in the northeast corner there were lots of silver vases; other silver vases lay in the centre of the chamber where a rectangular sheet could be discerned, probably a stretched-out skin. Beyond was a pair of gilded bronze greaves and close to them a huge bronze wreath with gilded leaves; beyond this were two gold bands. In the middle of the western side, close to the back wall, was a rectangular structure rather like a table; in a hollow at the centre of its upper surface stood a silver ossuary-hydria; a gold wreath rested on its shoulder.

I went forward into the antechamber – where a totally unexpected and happy surprise waited me; on every wall below the spring of the vault was a narrow frieze painted with chariots. The destruction of the external frieze was redressed by this other painted composition, even though it was only decorative. Here too the floor was thick with objects; to my left – the northern half – the remains of a gold-trimmed skin or fabric spread in folds over the floor. I could not be sure what material it was – something which resembled a most sumptuous uniform. To my right – the southern half – there was something similar, but simpler and next to it, upright on the floor, the lower part of a gold-sheathed spear; its wooden shaft had disappeared and there remained only the gold leaf which had covered it. Close to it were many strigils, of iron and bronze; the latter looked as though they had been gilded.

While it did not possess the wealth of the larger tomb, this tomb also offered us a completely unusual burial and objects the like of which had never been found elsewhere before. One other happy discovery; the structural state of the building was extremely good and offered no serious problems. My colleagues each performed his task with care and intense diligence; photography, planning, the immediate stabilizing and fixing of the objects. After the objects which it was essential for us to remove had been taken out, we closed the opening again and sealed it so that it was air-tight.

The uncovering of the facade had proceeded to the point where it showed us an imposing facade of a building which preserved the marble door *in situ*, undamaged and intact. On the upper part of the walls, right and left of the door, two relief shields were still to be seen, which retained some coloured decoration.

Continued excavation in the middle of the Tumulus brought no results. There was nothing below the point at which the stone construction was at its deepest. The work proceeded to the west and north of the Tumulus. The only finds were the broken funerary stelai which, discarded, lay chiefly in the upper layers.

The next excavation period commenced in May 1979 and ended in November. The overburden of the Tumulus was removed completely from the western and northern parts.

Even if the exploration below the original ground level had not been completed over the entire area, we could consider it almost certain that no other large Macedonian tomb existed in this area. This piece of information ran counter to our forecasts and indeed to our hopes which had been founded on the safest archaeological logic. We had excavated a large section of the eastern side of the Tumulus; in the southeast area, where a smaller, earlier tumulus which had suffered disturbance was clearly visible three tombs built in sun-dried brick were found. Two had not been robbed. The offerings in them showed that they were the tombs of ordinary Macedonian citizens, and could not have had any connection with the southwest area of the Great Tumulus. The most important find from the excavations of 1979 was the large number of broken grave stelai which were found, like the others, in the overburden.

After all this, and even though part of the Great Tumulus still remained, it seemed probable that this huge mound was constructed for the three rich tombs we had discovered and in particular for the largest of these. I shall try to answer the questions this conclusion raises later on in this book. The only piece of information which I should add to this brief account of the excavation is that in the natural soil below the Great Tumulus five human skeletons were found, at different spots, without any grave offerings. But in two of these bronze coins of Philip II were found.

The excavation of the Great Tumulus was completed in 1980. The only finds of this year were a few more fragments from funerary stelai and the burial of a young child on the northeast edge above the original ground level. Thus we ascertained that the Great Tumulus was raised to cover the three tombs we had uncovered in 1977 and 1978, along with the foundations of the destroyed "heroon".

Surface indications had led me to think that in the small garden which lay north of the tombs it was probable that some other monuments existed. I had therefore opened a small trench a few days before the close of the 1979 season. The watchful eye of our foreman, Costas Pavlides, immediately spotted a difference in the soil which might signify the existence of an ancient trench. The weather conditions forced us to stop, but we continued our efforts in the summer of 1980. In a short space of time his observation was proved correct; we really had discovered a broad trench sloping sharply to the north, that is towards the Great Tumulus. Following it, we came to the point at which the tomb should have been. However, though we continued to excavate to the depth at which we calculated the vault should be we were still shifting earth mixed with other, later refuse. At a certain point a piece from a limestone cornice turned up, and next to it other smaller fragments from the same cornice. It was obvious that the tomb had suffered severe damage. Our surprise was therefore considerable when the smooth circular surface of a column drum stuck up from the earth; and the surprise increased when we realized that we had found the greater part of a column *in situ*. The first was followed by a second, then a third and fourth. Until now, we had known columns of buildings which stood above the ground; for the first time we had columns belonging to a subterranean structure which could be nothing other than a tomb. The rest of the excavation was compounded simultaneously of discovery and disappointment. Certainly we had found the only Macedonian tomb with free-standing columns on the facade, but apart from the columns, the stylobate and a few stones from the walls, the rest of the building had been dismantled probably so that the stones could be reused. The damage was indeed great. Nevertheless, we suceeded in planning the facade with considerable precision and I hope that we shall be successful in reconstructing it in a drawing.

THE GRAVE STELAI

As we noted in the preceding section hundreds of broken pieces from grave monuments were found in the overburden of the Great Tumulus, waste material used for its construction. Most of the fragments were of marble and had been grave stelai. Some came from funeral monuments of other kinds, such as marble hydria; while others were limestone blocks from the bases of grave monuments. Quite a number of the stelai bore relief decoration, but the majority were painted. After the pieces had been stuck together forty-seven complete, or nearly complete, stelai were reconstructed. All can be securely dated to the second half of the fourth century BC (350-300 BC) and to the beginning of the third century BC except for one relief stele which belongs to the close of the fifth century BC. Almost all have inscriptions recording the name of the deceased. I believe that their dimensions and quality support the conclu-

43. Detail of one of the first grave stelai which was found in pieces in the overburden of the Great Tumulus.

43

sion that these are the monuments which decorated the graves of ordinary Macedonian citizens, not of the nobility or other members of the ruling class. We are thus in possession of a very useful collection of everyday Macedonian names both male and female; the list reaches the very respectable total of seventy-five. The following are typical; *Alcetas, Alcimos, Antigonos, Berenice, Drykalos, Euxeinos, Theocritos, Theodoros, Heracleides, Cleagoras, Laandros, Lysanias, Menandros, Nikostratos, Xenocrates, Peukolaos, Proxenos, Pierion, Philistos, Philotas* etc. It is obvious that the majority of these names are Greek, or, more accurately, that they have an unequivocally Greek root (only one, *Amadocos,* has a Thracian root). It is worth pointing out that many of them are typically Macedonian and almost unknown in Attica, a sign that they spring from Macedonian tradition. If then we accept a date of about 330 BC for many of these inscriptions, and an average age of thirty to forty years for the deceased, we have to conclude that these were the names of people alive in the decade 370-360 BC. If we add to this the fact that on most of these stelai the name of the deceased's father is also recorded, we arrive at a dating of 410-400 BC for this second group of names. This means that we have epigraphic evidence for the names of ordinary Macedonian citizens of this period and, in other words, that at the close of the fifth century BC the Macedonians who inhabited the original capital of the Macedonian kingdom, in the heart of the Macedonian state, had Greek names. In the most unambivalent way this evidence confirms the opinion of those historians who maintain that the Macedonians were a Greek tribe, like all the others who lived on Greek territory, and shows that the theory that they were of Illyrian or Thracian descent and were hellenized by Philip and Alexander the Great rests on no objective criteria. So the first important and historically significant find from the excavation of the Great Tumulus consists of this collection of humble fragments preserved in the overburden. The sacrilegious pillaging of the Galatian mercenaries who destroyed the cemetery of Aigai was the means by which this valuable evidence for the nationality of the desecrated dead came into our hands.

44

45

44. One of the grave stelai from the Great Tumulus with the names of the dead: Xenokratis Pierionos and Drykalos Pierionos (they must have been brothers). The names Drykalos and Pierion are typical Macedonian names.

45. The most beautiful of the painted stelai found in the Great Tumulus. On the left is an armed man standing; on the right a man seated on a backed chair. In the background, between the two, was a standing female figure; below, to the right, a young child. The inscription gives four names and the patronyms.

"THE TOMB OF PERSEPHONE"

The smallest tomb, found on the edge of the Great Tumulus adjacent to the foundations of the "heroon" is a rectangular structure built in the limestone common in Macedonia;[19] its clear internal measurements are 3.05 × 2.09 m. and it is 3 m. high. There is no opening in any of the four walls which enclose it. The burial must therefore have been effected from an opening at the top and after the ceremony the tomb would have been closed forever when narrow oblong limestone slabs were positioned over its upper part. We may assert, with little fear of contradiction, that before these closing blocks were laid in place the tomb had been covered with a temporary roof of planks, shown by the indentations which exist in the topmost row of stones in the wall. This means that after the tomb had been closed and covered over the possibility that it would have been opened again for a later burial is ruled out.

As we noted above, this tomb had been robbed. Traces of the tomb robbers of antiquity were visible from the outside; they had made an opening in the upper part of the west wall and had smashed enough of the central closing slab to permit a man to wriggle through. It is almost certain that they first attempted to enter through the western wall; when, however, they had lifted away the top stone at the northern edge they came up against a shelf firmly fixed along the whole length of the wall. Traces of its position remained visible on the two adjacent walls. This forced them to seek another point of entry, and so they broke part of the upper section. It is worth noting that both these openings had in some way been sealed again; a limestone block had been crudely positioned in the western wall while stones and broken bits of limestone had been piled up over the upper part. This "protection" was not of course the work of the tomb rob-

bers, whose sole interest lay in the loot. It is safe to say that both holes probably remained open for quite a long time, because the considerable amount of earth which had slipped in was far greater than could possibly have fallen in during the few hours needed by the tomb robbers for their sacrilegious activities.

Traces of the bungling, barbaric methods of the tomb robbers were visible also inside the tomb. The most typical are the gashes they left a little below the middle of the north wall, made with some sort of crowbar, piercing its thickness and creating a small hole. The only reason behind their action must have been the hope that at this point there would be some kind of treasure, or another area worth investigating. I believe that this, however, bears witness to the fact that the culprits were inexperienced, and were ignorant of matters of which organized tomb robbers were well aware. Signs of minor destruction are to be seen everywhere; the most obvious are at the western ends of the north and south walls to which two rows of shelves or some kind of cupboard had been fixed.

Little of the contents of the tomb survived. The bones which lay in disorder below the earth show that the pillaging took place when only the skeleton, or skeletons, remained. The few sherds found belonged to stamped black-glazed pots dating to around the middle of the fourth century BC. The only offering left behind by the tomb robbers was a marble shell – and that was broken. It was an exceptionally rare object, forming in all probability part of a woman's toilette.

We know that the tomb robbers of antiquity, whether professionals or amateurs, only removed objects of value and left the rest – for example pottery vessels and iron weapons. The very thoroughness of the plundering leads us to the virtually

The interior of the "Tomb of Persephone" from the west. The lower part of the wall is red; next there is a blue band painted with griffins; on the upper part are three paintings; to the left, the rape of Persephone, to the right the Three Fates, opposite, Demeter.

certain conclusion that the contents of the tomb had consisted of gold, silver and bronze objects. This means that it was the last resting place of a very wealthy person. The absence of iron weapons led us to think that it might have been the tomb of a woman. The examination of the bones showed that some belonged to a woman, others to a man while still others are probably of a newly-born baby. Moreover, we may deduce that none of the removed objects was bulky, because if they had been, it would have been impossible for the looters to extract them through the two relative small openings.

The tomb robbers then left us only this funerary building. Nevertheless, this building, small and unassuming in its externals, preserved on its interior walls a most magnificent find; the wall paintings.

The lower section of all the walls is painted in glowing red, (Pompeian red). 1.50 m. above the floor is a narrow frieze (0.22 m. high; it narrows to 0.19 m. on the south wall) which runs around three of the four walls – it is absent from the western side where there were "shelves". The same decorative theme, two griffins facing each other with a flower between them, repeats itself against a blue background. Above this frieze the plastering of the walls was white and on that were the paintings. On the long southern wall were three seated female figures. They are not very well preserved, the central

one having suffered most. The first, to the right (west), is a mature lady seated turned very slightly to her right. She is an austere and venerable figure; we may discern part of her himation which retains its violet hue. While some colour is preserved on her face, little has survived over the greater part of the body. If we look carefully at the remaining traces, the central figure was painted in a similar pose. The figure on the left (to the east) is much better preserved – at least in outline. Also seated, she is depicted in profile; her left hand is raised in a courtly gesture, her fingers are stretched out to about the height of the head in a gesture of tenderness. A necklace encircles her throat. The drawing of the figure conveys her tranquil beauty; she is the youngest of the three, and her fresh happy face is in clear contrast to the serious, almost melancholy, expression of her elders. The lack of examples of Greek painting of the classical period forces us to look back to the delicate figures of the white Attic *lekythoi,* and to search there for likenesses to her, or to the good Roman copy of the work of Alexan-

47

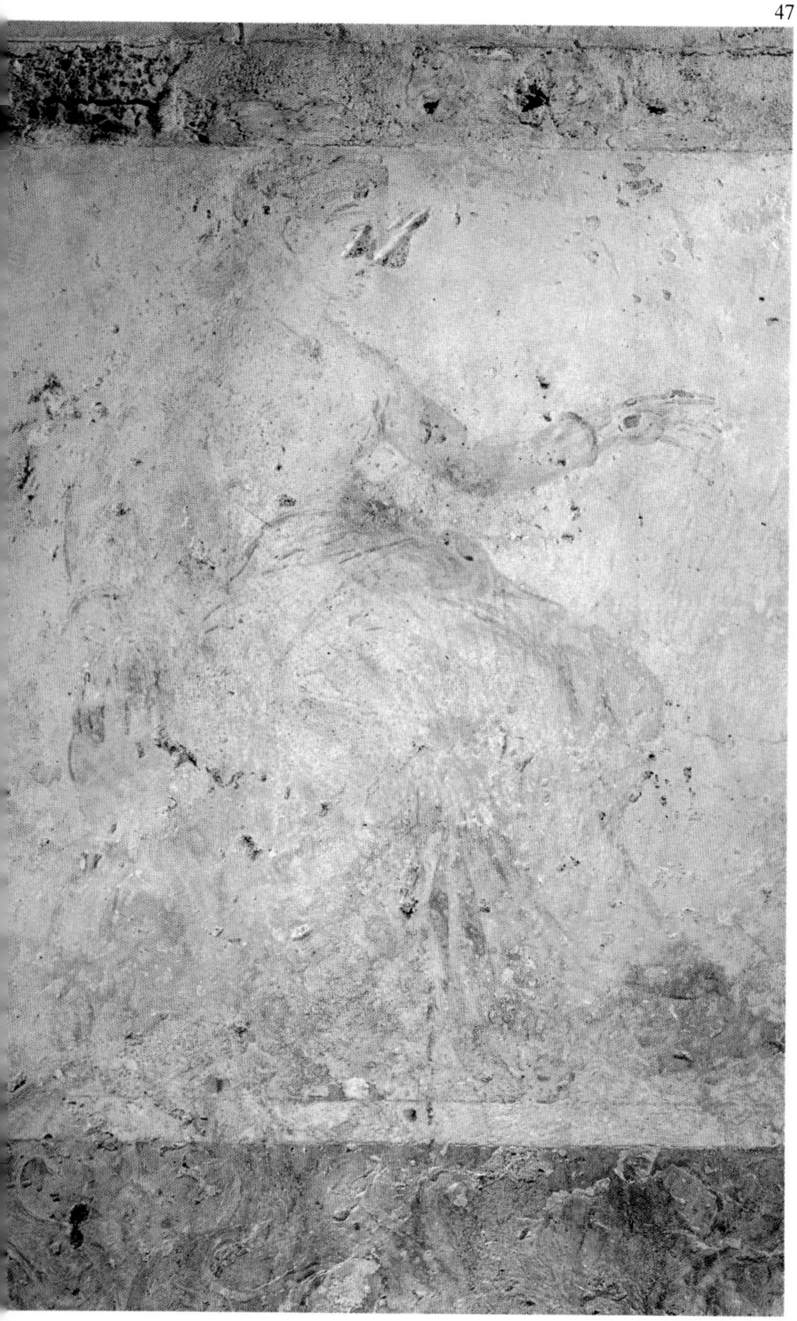

der of Athens found at Herculaneum which depicts Leto and Niobe with other girls playing knucklebones. I consider it highly probable that this trio represents the Three Fates.

The centrepiece of the narrow eastern wall is a female figure depicted seated alone on a rock. It is very well preserved, even though the colours which filled in the outlines of the drawing have almost disappeared. This figure too turns slightly to her right. Her expression is less harsh than that of the first of the Fates, but nevertheless she has a pained severity and her venerable figure shows that she is "not of this world". This severity is intensified also by the himation which swathes not only her entire body but also, rising at the back, covers her head. One's first reaction might be to take this female figure as a portrait of the deceased. But the rock on which she sits, and even more, the composition which occupies the north wall gives us, I think, the correct interpretation; she is Demeter, sitting on the "mirthless stone", deeply mourning the loss of her daughter, abducted by Pluto the god of the Underworld.

This is exactly the scene which covers the long north wall. Here we are confronted not by a magnificent depiction of isolated figures, but by an absolutely unique dramatic composition. Luck was particularly favourable to us, for almost all the figures, together with the colour, were preserved in exceptionally good condition. The subject, the rape of Persephone by Pluto, spreads comfortably over the surface, 3.50 × 1.01 m. Broken orange-red lines burst forth from the upper left corner, representing Zeus' thunderbolt. Beneath these and a little to the right is the first figure of the composition; Hermes with his wand in his right hand runs, or perhaps flies, towards the left. His right foot is stretched out, the toes turned down though they do not touch the ground; the left is bent at almost a right-angle, leaving a strong impression of speedy motion. The sandals are quite clearly visible, tied with thongs to about one third of the way up the calf. The head of the young god, who is wearing the characteristically Macedonian headgear, is turned to the right and so we see him almost full face. His purple cloak is also visible. In his left hand he holds the reins of the four horses of the quadriga which gallop in pursuit of the "conductor of souls". The horses' heads and the surrounding area is the least well preserved part of the composition. Nevertheless we may pick out their shape, the one differentiated from the other, and the wonderful movement.

47. The "Fate" at the eastern end of the south wall, preserved in better condition than the other two. She is depicted in profile, lifting her left arm on which a bracelet can be seen in a noble gesture. The calm beauty which pervades the figure is reminiscent of those on white Attic lekythoi.

48. The eastern wall; Demeter, seated on the "mirthless stone". Her himation swathes both her head and her body. Her pose, turned to the left, leads the viewer's eye towards the north wall which depicts the rape of her daughter whose loss she is mourning.

The remaining part of the composition, the major section, is preserved in a state which we might well say is near miraculous if we consider the conditions of its preservation and the time that has passed since its creation. The white horses' rumps appear above the the red breastwork of the chariot. The right wheel has suffered some damage, but the left is marvellously preserved, a strong oblique perspective emphasizing its fast movement. On the chariot itself stands the impressively dominant figure of Pluto, whose right hand grasps his long sceptre and the reins of the horses. His left hand is round Kore's waist; her body leans desperately backwards, her arms thrown upwards, dramatically emphasizing the hopelessness of any attempt to escape her unavoidable abduction. Careful observation shows that only the god's right foot is on the chariot, while his left is still suspended in the air, the sole only just off the ground. On the ground can be seen the flowers the young goddess was gathering in the company of her friend (?Kyane) when she was abducted. Her friend, wearing a yellow chiton and a mauve himation, is shown kneeling behind the chariot. Her frightened face is turned towards Persephone and her right hand is raised in distress and despair.

In words it is difficult to convey the visual impression left by this creation, particularly of the implacable god and the beautiful Persephone. The wild look on Pluto's face, the disordered hair rendered with swift, sure, short strokes of orange-red, stand out from the whole composition. The god's left hand has a firm grip on the young girl's body, her clothing dishevelled by his violent movement. He stands out almost tangibly as he leaps on his chariot because his mauve himation billows out, dominant and disturbing. The tension in Persephone's body gives the painter the opportunity to describe, in one unbroken, undulating curve, the contour of her body from the hip through the arms to the fingers. The ripening swell of the breasts, the noble face with the frightened, half-closed eyes and the fine mouth, the shapely, braceleted wrist – make one forget the tragedy portrayed and marvel at Kore's exquisite beauty.

The entire composition is based first and foremost on the drawing. The artist, one of the greatest in his own time, drew with a sure hand, a meticulous eye and great feeling. I consider it almost certain that in this wall painting he was not reproducing some work known to him, but creating his

48

own composition on this wall. Moreover, he himself has left us not only valuable traces of his art, but of his technique. After the picture had been cleaned the lines he had incised in the fresh plaster before proceeding to the final design with the brush showed clearly. For every figure, and for each member – heads, hands, feet etc. – he cut a preliminary sketch; he did not stop there, however; next to the final drawing, successive small variations, "studies" one might say, bear witness to his attempts to find the right expression. The comparison with Leonardo da Vinci springs readily to mind; his sketches, preserved in his famous notebooks, show infinite variations in his search for satisfying "formulae". But these incised lines reveal something else as well, or so I believe; namely that the painter was either forced or was accustomed to painting quickly over the surface which he

was to decorate. If it were not so he could have carried out all his preparations at his leisure in another preliminary sketch before finding himself in the cramped space of a subterranean tomb.

However, the merit and the strength of the drawing in no way diminish the colour values of the work. The sparing, but especially delicate and expressive use of colours confirms that the artist had wide experience and thorough knowledge of the tricks of his trade. A wall painting demands not only accurate design but also well matched clear colours, sparsely applied. Over and above that, the subject itself and the space in which it will unfold cause the true artist to shun all superfluous detail; by warding off all rhetorical flourish or dissipation of colour it obliges him to deliver his message "calmly and simply".

Of course it is not easy to name the painter of

these wall paintings, since, as we know, all the examples of large scale Greek painting have been lost to us, and this is the first time we are lucky enough to have such a unique creation. If, however, we take our stance on certain literary references we may go by what Pliny tells us about one of the most famous painters of the fourth century BC , Nikomachos. "He painted a rape of Persephone, a picture formerly on the Capitol", he wrote (*Hist. Nat.* XXXV,108) adding "no other painter was ever a more rapid worker" (*Ibid.* 109). Furthermore we know that this subject (the rape of Persephone) was very rare in the iconography of the fourth century BC and that subsequently we encounter a series of renderings which must originate from an identical magnificent original. Certainly some of the later works obviously copy the difficult pose of the goddess and the shape of her friend.

Linking the quick brush strokes of the Vergina painter with Pliny's second statement, I venture to suggest that the wall paintings of the "small" tomb of Vergina were executed by the atelier of Nikomachos and indeed that it is very probable that he himself painted the large composition on the north wall.

49. The magnificent wall painting depicting the rape of Persephone. On the left Hermes with his wand flies in front of the chariot. It is drawn by four white horses and in it stands Pluto, reins and sceptre in his right hand while his left clutches Persephone firmly, though she is trying to escape. Behind the chariot is a friend of Persephone, perhaps Kyane.

51

52

50. Pluto and Persephone in the chariot. Both the perspective depiction of the wheel and the rendering of the god and Persephone is outstanding. The force and facility of the drawing rival the expressive intensity of the colours.

51. The head of Persephone. As she is carried off Persephone's arms and body tauten in resistance and her hair blows out in the wind, framing the frightened features of her youthful face.

52. The awesome face of the god of the underworld is rendered with unparalleled strength; short sharp strokes depict the ruffled hair and beard and emphasize his piercing eyes.

93

53

54

53. Hermes, who guides Pluto's chariot. Above, to the left, are the ends of the wavy lines which represented Zeus' thunderbolt. The young god holds his wand in his right hand while in his left he grasps the reins. He wears a cloak and the Macedonian *petasos*. The movement of his legs is important for it emphasizes his haste.

54. Persephone's friend (Kyane) shown still kneeling as she was when gathering flowers with Persephone, her eyes turned up in an agonized gaze, her right hand raised in a gesture of fear as she witnesses the abduction of her friend. The colour combination of the white body and the yellow and purple clothing is magnificent.

"PHILIP'S TOMB"

THE STRUCTURE

A short distance northwest of the "tomb of Persephone" is a large Macedonian tomb which for the first time, and even now in inverted commas, I shall call "Philip's tomb".[20] Like all large Macedonian tombs it consists structurally of two basic elements; the building itself and the facade which covers the entire structure. The tomb building consists of two large square areas, the antechamber and the main chamber, each covered by a barrel-vaulted roof. The antechamber is 3.36 m. long × 4.46 m. wide, the main chamber 4.46 m. long × 4.46 m. wide. The height reaches 5.30 m. If we add the thickness of the walls to these measurements (3 × 0.56 m. = 1.68 m.) we have the total length of the facade, namely 9.50 m. This means that this is the longest and the highest of all the Macedonian tombs known to date, the second largest being the other tomb at Vergina which K.A.Rhomaios discovered before the War. This difference is created by the length (i.e. the depth) of the antechamber (3.36 m.) which is exceptionally large and thus creates an adequate space for the second burial. These are not the only constructional anomalies of the tomb. I regard it as certain that its construction was carried out in two stages; the chamber was built first and afterwards the work of building the antechamber continued. This is revealed equally by the construction of the vaults and that of the walls. The vault of the main chamber ends above the dividing wall which separates the two chambers. In a later phase the construction of the vault of the antechamber was carried out, clearly shown at the point where the two adjoin where there is no sign of the essential and customary bonding which is also a factor in constructional safety. Moreover, the walls of the main chamber

end at the same point against the dividing wall and from it the new coursing of the walls of the antechamber starts.

The way in which the vault is covered externally by a layer of stucco must be added to complement the picture of these observations. As far as I know, it is the only example of a Macedonian tomb in which the external surface of the stones of the vault has not been left bare, but has been covered by a strong protective coat of stucco sometimes as thick as 0.10 m. This plastering was quite clearly applied in two stages, for over the top of the dividing wall one layer from the side of the main chamber comes to an end, while a new layer for the antechamber begins. Moreover, the fingerprints left by the workmen as they tried to smooth the coating of the antechamber to meet that of the main chamber are quite clear. They did not succeed for any length of time, because the time difference in the construction did not permit perfect bonding and so the crack is still apparent today.

The most strikingly unexpected feature about the tomb was the heap of bricks above it on the west side of the vault. The traces left by the bricks on the stucco of the vault show that they were placed there even before the plaster was dry. This, together with other evidence, allows us to assume that the work was executed in great haste. There being no other parallel, we have to find an explanation for the bricks from the archaeological evidence. The first interpretation I placed on them immediately after the discovery of the tomb (and printed in my first reports) was that this was the funerary altar intended to receive the libations and the sacrifices in honour of the deceased. However, when we proceeded to careful examination in the following years and the removal of the upper layers of the bricks, I found that my explanation was incorrect.

55

It was quite certain that this was not some construction over the tomb, but sun-dried bricks which had been positioned above it, the first in some sort of order, the rest piled up in a heap. As I have already said, traces of fire were clear on many of these while on others the narrow sides showed the remains of plastering. These indications lead me to think that all these bricks were taken from the funeral pyre where it would seem that there had been a brick-built construction on which the logs and then the body were placed. Furthermore, as we have noted, in the pile of collapsed bricks, we found two burnt iron swords, an iron spearhead and many bits of iron from horse trappings. Quantities of pieces of burnt ivory were also found; some had been decorative elements (cymatia, astragals etc.), but there were also microscopic pieces of human figures executed in relief. I believe that all these objects must have been on the funeral pyre, were burnt along with the body, and were collected up after the cremation and the interment of the deceased when the flames were finally extinguished. These remarks lead to the conclusion that in addition to the other objects which had belonged to the dead man (for example his weapons) that were placed on the pyre and burnt, that is "sacrificed", there were also horses; this custom is brought to mind by the Homeric description of Patroclos' funeral (*Iliad*, 23, 171, ff.)

"and four horses with high-arched necks he cast swiftly upon the pyre, groaning aloud the while"

Such a sacrifice, regardless of the Homeric parallel, implies I think that the dead man in the tomb can have been no ordinary mortal; this view is reinforced by the existence of a "heroon" adjacent to the tomb.

Amongst the finds in the pile of bricks were six gold acorns and a small piece of a gold oak leaf. I do

55. Reconstruction drawing of "Philip's Tomb" (the actual stratification of the mound is not represented). Behind the impressive facade with the wall painting there is a vaulted building made up of an antechamber and the main chamber; communication between the two rooms was effected by an internal marble door. Close to the southern wall of the antechamber is a marble sarcophagus with a small gold larnax; the large gold larnax was found in the sarcophagus close to the west wall of the chamber.

98

99

99

not think that there can be any doubt that these came from the large gold wreath which was found in the gold larnax in the main chamber above the burnt bones of the deceased. Their presence above the tomb, is , I believe, unexpected and weighty testimony. These too must have come from the pyre after the cremation; this implies that when the dead man was laid on the pyre he was wearing the impressive wreath which, when the flames began to rise higher around the body, was removed – traces of fire are to be seen on some leaves of the wreath. It is highly likely that at this moment the bits we found broke off from the wreath and with others, fell in to and round the pyre. As many as had not been destroyed must have been gathered up very shortly afterwards, within a few days at the most. The fact that they were put on the tomb and not inside it must mean that the burial had taken place and the door of the main chamber been closed in such a way that it was impossible – or at least very difficult – to open it to reunite these fragments with the bones of the deceased. This conclusion, virtual-

56-57. The impressive facade of "Philip's Tomb". Two end pillars and two doric half-columns support the entablature and the triglyphs with the metopes. Above this is the cornice and higher still the frieze with the painting of the Hunt. A second cornice crowns the structure. The painted decoration of all the architectural elements is impressive, as can be seen from the detail of the corner of the cornice (56).

56

ly forced upon us, leads us to a second; that the construction of the chamber and the burial were carried out with special haste. Even though this may seem unexpected, it is confirmed by another piece of evidence, equally unforeseen. The stucco inside the main chamber is very crude and only half-finished; in some places it is limited to a first thick layer and over a large area to a second. Nowhere has the final plastering with the third, thin coat been carried out – the coat that would eventually take paint. Such plastering, which is uncommon in much more humble constructions, is inexplicable in a tomb whose facade carries the most magnificent wall painting of the fourth century BC that we yet know, and in which the plastering and the painting of the antechamber are perfect. The only possible explanation is that there was some reason which made it imperative for the burial to be carried out and the door sealed with such speed that there was no time to even finish the construction of the dead man's chamber. What could that reason be? Elsewhere, I will try to set out the theory that I regard as possible.

There is one further peculiarity to be noted in the shape of the tomb. We noted in the preceding section that the first sign of human activity uncovered by excavation was a curious mass of sun-dried bricks. It was 9.10 m. long, and had a direct connection with the tomb although it was not a constructional feature. In reality this wall extended left and right of the facade of the tomb and was a few centimetres higher above and behind it, acting as a parapet which, up to a point, held back the overburden covering the tomb and the earth banked up against the sides. It is worth noting that this flimsy construction was brick-built to right and left, while in the centre the uneven stucco which covers its eastern face (the one visible from the facade of the tomb) and the narrow upper surface was slapped over a core of sand and gravel. As we have noted, the only purpose this construction could have served was the retention of the earth which covered the vaulted chamber in the first phase of the tomb's construction. But if this is the reason for its erection, this means that the vault of the tomb was buried in earth before its facade was covered up. This makes it plausible to suggest that the facade remained exposed for some time while work continued on it, although the main body of the tomb had been completed with great haste.

58-63. The frieze with the painting of the Hunt; overall picture (58); line drawing of the whole (59); sectional photographs 60-63 →. Within a sacred grove, denoted by the broad garland which decorates the first tree from the left and the tall pillar with the "statues" on the top (between two trees), three mounted men and seven men on foot hunt wild animals. From the left the figures are; above, a deer pierced by a javelin, below, a young man who has seized a deer (above him can be seen a hunting dog); a naked horseman with his back turned to the viewer; a second tree, a young man with a spear seen from behind, and a second youth with a spear both attack a boar (the dogs can also be seen); a bare tree, an imposing young horseman with a spear (? Alexander) and another leafless tree; two youths and a mature man on horseback (? Philip) attack a lion (together with dogs), a standing youth with a spear; to the right above is a wounded bear; lastly, a youth carrying a net.

58

59

103

60

61

62

63

One last notable peculiarity of the tomb is the existence of two lateral walls to right and left of the facade extending 3.55 m. in front of the tomb to the east. These walls were built of square sun-dried bricks generously coated with stucco on the side of the facade and on the upper, narrow surface; only the southern wall was found (to the left as we enter the tomb), still standing to a height of 4.20 m. The corresponding wall on the north had collapsed even before the facade was covered over; the bricks of which it was built were found as they had scattered over the whole width of the facade. It seems that the collapse took place as soon as the filling in of the trench associated with the facade was started; there would therefore have been no reason to re-erect it and so the work of concealment continued, burying also the fallen bricks.

The facade of the tomb is easily the most impressive part of the structure. It is one of the two absolutely complete facades from an ancient building that we know (the second is that of the third tomb which lies a few metres further northwest). A pillar at either extremity protrudes – to be exact, half a pillar since the rest is sunk in the wall. The decorative colours are marvellously preserved on their carefully executed capitals. Right and left of the doorway rise two doric half-columns. Pillars and columns together support the entablature which is composed of the epistyle, the triglyphs with the metopes and the cornice. The original colouring and decoration has been preserved on all the parts in very good condition; deep blue on the triglyphs, regulae and guttae, red on the *tainiai* below the cornice, white meanders on the *tainiai* of the epistyle, white palmettes on the front surface of the lower cornice and alternating deep blue, red and white on the cymatia which run across the different parts of the entablature. Finally a permutation of the three colours emphasizes the different elements of the capitals on which very delicate decoration of white palmettes can be seen. But the preservation of the colours is eclipsed in importance by the survival of the two-leafed marble door, undamaged and in its original position. Now, instead of only in drawings, we have the complete facade of an ancient building before our very eyes for the first time; we are now able to judge for ourselves its impressive reality.

Above the doric frieze one would expect the usual termination of the building, as we have in almost all the large Macedonian tombs. But once again this tomb is different from all the others; above the cornice a frieze extends over the entire width (5.56 m. long and 1.16 m. high). The upper edge of this frieze is protected by a second cornice which projects over it and forms the upper edge of the facade. We shall find this idiosyncrasy also in the third tomb where again a frieze takes the place of the pediment. Heuzey's tomb, near Palatitsia, was completed by a related solution – the horizontal upper termination – but it lacked the frieze. Perhaps this style – without the pediment – is the older solution to the problem of the facade of the Macedonian tombs which must have exercised the "architects" in their efforts to tie together the vaulted building with a monumental architectural front. It should be noted that only these three tombs can be dated with certainty to the fourth century BC.

The painting

The last, and the most important, idiosyncrasy of this tomb is the painted composition which covers the entire frieze. Its burial in earth – quite literally, in sand and gravel – for twenty-three centuries might well have destroyed it entirely. We should therefore be satisfied that anything at all survived, and that the damage, which is not inconsiderable, is not such as to destroy the totality of the picture nor to impede our enjoyment or our appraisal of the painted composition in detail.

The subject of the composition is a hunt in a forest. Seven men on foot, three on horseback, five or six wild beasts and nine hunting dogs move against a landscape denoted by four trees, a high pillar-like stele and rocks. All the elements which make up this painted composition are welded into a thoughtfully structured arrangement. The painter has calculated the space and the figures which are disposed therein to a nicety; without sign of artificiality he succeeds in ordering the thematic elements to match the principles of composition de-

64. The first mounted man from the left. The drawing of this figure is striking and the daring stance impressive. Seen from behind in a 3/4 pose he moves diagonally to the left towards the background while his horse raises his left front leg, rearing up on his bent hind legs.

manded by a painting. Centrifugal and centripetal forces create the essential tension which balance the whole. From the three or four different vignettes, drawn from moments in the chase, he produces the unified theme of the hunt, while at the same time the fatal and dramatic moment on which the whole composition centres and concentrates is isolated. Although still maintaining the severity and balance of classical tradition, the painter is free from its conventions of layout, forms and most important, of space. The outer edges of the com-

65-66. The central horseman. Between the two bare trees, exactly at the centre of the composition, is the figure of a young horseman who dominates the whole painting. His spear raised he moves purposefully from the left towards the lion which is on his right; on his head he wears a green wreath (65). He is the only youth whose face is possessed of definite features, (large eyes with a steady gaze). It is very likely that this depicts Alexander.

65

position constitute the critical area where the painter is testing his talents and is in turn tested. On the left, at the top, a buck, a javelin in its side, plunges wildly to the left behind the rocks, ready to escape beyond the bounds of the painting; below this, in front of the rock a man on foot, turned towards the right (the inside) seems to have seized a deer which is also attacked by a dog (the damage here is considerable). To the right, at the top behind the rock, a bear turned towards the left (the inside) tries to rid itself of the twisted javelin which has transfixed it. Below, in front of the rocks, a man, slightly turned towards the right (the outside) grasps a net ready to ensnare some wild beast. Thus while on the left the animal leads us out of the space and the human figure below it forces us to look towards the centre, on the right it is the animal which directs our gaze to the centre and the human figure which opens up the vista to the outside. The ingenuity of the artist, however, has not spent itself on this simple and separated cross-shaped arrangement, as one might describe it. The opposing – and up to a point contrasting – setting of man and beast is continued by the figures placed immediately next to them towards the centre. Left, beyond the deer and the man on foot follows the bold and breathtaking drawing of a horseman. Seen from behind in a 3/4 pose, he moves diagonally to the left, towards the background (i.e. away from the viewer) while the horse lifts its left foot and turns its raised neck and head to the right, unmistakeably, even stubbornly. Thus by a technical masterstroke the artist leads us adroitly to the centre of the composition. On the right, immediately in front of the man on foot with the net, the body of the second youth on foot, firmly balanced on his left leg while bending his right sharply, leans forcibly backwards; his left arm is stretched out, but protected beneath his cloak spread out like a shield, while with his right hand he prepares to hurl the javelin upwards to the right, the direction of his gaze. The tension in his stance and the marvellous drawing of the body in motion rival the expressive force of the horseman on the left side. Both the stance and the twist of the man on foot lead the eye upwards to the background, thus creating a sideways current which links the movement of the bear towards the centre of the composition with that of the last man on foot towards the outside.

These four human figures form the framework

66

for the rest of the composition. It is not difficult to distinguish the point at which this intensifies in dramatic fashion; immediately to the right of the centre where the lion is the quarry two men on foot and a rider are grouped together; the latter gallops forward from the right to the foreground, his pike high in his right hand ready to plunge it into the enraged beast which has already trodden a hunting dog underfoot though two others still attack it. The way in which the lion stands, his head raised defiantly but in despair, the calculated attack by the dogs, the solid strong movement of the foremost man on foot whose spear already grazes the beast's breast, the decisive, strenuous action of the second man on foot whose body tautens as his two hands lift the axe to strike the lion in his turn – all this, rendered with an unparalleled strength of line, create the artistic excitement which reaches its peak in the horseman who rides in from the right, his raised spear that which will, apparently, deliver the mortal wound to the trapped animal. The figure of the rider, high above the rest, dominates the entire composition, even though a large part of his face is hidden by the neck of his horse whose forelegs are raised and whose head is turned to our right.

Behind the horseman can be seen a tree, the last to the right in the composition; this entire scene is bounded to the left by another, leafless, tree. This bare tree and its counterpart which stands a little way further left, frame the central figure of the composition, a young rider who gallops towards the right. In terms of composition this is the most impressive figure as it occupies the centre of the painting and is separated from all the others because it is framed by the two bare trees. His movement directs our attention to the group around the lion, but a certain distance and the tree between permits the painter to isolate him and impress his presence on the viewer. It should be noted that a wreath of green leaves crowns his bare head.

Further left are two more men on foot; one is almost on top of a boar (?) the other, a little further away, has his back turned to the viewer. They reveal quite clearly how towards this side of the picture the composition has thinned out and the tension has slackened. It might indeed be more correct to start one's appraisal of the work from the left, where by gentle preludes we are prepared for the scenes where feeling intensifies, both in the subject matter and in the style of painting.

In trying to follow the elements of composition presented by the painter we have necessarily also taken note of his expressive talent in the drawing of specific figures. I consider it useful to examine certain aspects more carefully and to help the reader and the viewer to a more accurate appreciation of his artistic ability.

Six of the seven men on foot have survived in a condition good enough to permit us to discuss the drawing and moulding of their bodies with confidence. Starting from the left, the first man on foot has suffered considerable damage; there follows a horseman and immediately to the right, between the first tree and the tall column the next man on foot is depicted in an unusual position. He stands firmly on his right leg, his back to the viewer, while the toes of his left foot – as far away from the right as he could move it – only just touch the ground. He grasps his spear with both hands, and, bending slightly at the waist, he turns slightly to the right, that is towards his quarry there. With immense skill the painter depicts the supple young body so that the viewer may see it at work not in a moment of violent action but in a glimpse which suffices for him to visualize the movement both of the muscles and of the entire body.

The stance of the next man on foot is totally different. Turned full face, he balances his weight on his left foot, his right bent sharply to rest on a rock. His whole body curves, poised for action; he leans hard to the right and, with his right arm raised and bent at the elbow, he clutches his javelin firmly to lunge at his prey (? a boar) which is shown in front of him. His left hand holds his cloak spread out protectively like a shield. He is placed a little higher than the preceding figure and this shows distinctly that his action takes place on a different plane, further from the foreground.

The two men on foot to the right of the horseman at the centre in front of the lion are presented in positions different again. One, shown sideways on,

67. Two youthful figures participate in the lion hunt alongside the mature mounted man. Both are ready to strike the ensnared animal, towards whom the hunting dogs are rushing; one has his spear extended, the other has his axe raised on high. The youth with the spear wears a curious hat and the figure recalls that of a warrior beside Alexander in the well-known mosaic from Pompeii.

stands with his left foot bent against a rock while his right leg stretched behind him meets the ground; it is a wide stride, eloquent of an intensely aggressive stance as he grasps his spear with both hands, its tip close to the lion's chest. His stride and movement have made his cloak spread round him, and, open in front, it leaves the youthful body silhouetted against its purple background. A little higher, which means on a deeper plane, the second man on foot appears in an exceptionally dynamic depiction; his left leg is extended with some force, his right is bent and his body is twisted to the right at the moment when he raises his axe which he grasps tightly in both hands ready to strike the lion. In contrast to the body his head is turned to the left so that he sees his target. These violent movements make his cloak billow out behind him and to his left, leaving his body quite uncovered. He is the boldest of all the figures of the men on foot in the composition.

The pair of men on foot who close the right edge of the composition display two more positions of the human figure in action. The last but one, his left leg stretched out, his right bent, his body leaning backwards, his head turned to the left, his right hand with the spear down by his side and his left tucked within his cloak has a dignified easy bearing, emphasized by his spreading cloak falling in pleasing folds. We might well say that this is the most "statuesque" figure in the composition, the parallel in painting to the Apollo Belvedere. The last figure, bent to his left, is depicted in a 3/4 pose; he is completely enveloped by his clothing and holds a net in his left hand.

The six figures thus provided the artist with the occasion and the opportunity to paint the youthful male body in six different poses and positions, to study and render its movements and display the working of the limbs. He exploited the clothing to depict above or next to it the nude human body and even employed it to complete the shape and bulk of the human figures.

The rendering of the horsemen demonstrates the dexterous skill of the artist to even greater advantage. The three mounted figures in the composition demonstrate the three possible characteristic positions which a man on horseback can adopt, as well as the handsome animal itself. The first rider from the left is depicted, as we have noted, from behind; the horse, as it moves diagonally towards the back-

ground presents its left side 3/4 on; its hind legs, slightly bent, show its rump and its curved tail on the same plane while its body rears up in the middle and its raised left leg cleaves the air; the magnificently sensitive rising curve of its neck which turns to the right completes the marvellous depiction of the animal. Naturally, the young rider too is viewed from behind; his right arm, very clearly turned back from the shoulder, holds his spear. Thus we have an undisturbed view of his back and his left leg extended loosely against the animal's left flank. It would be difficult to render the noble figure of horse and rider with greater fullness in a stance so

68-69. The last but one youth in the painting has a dignified and easy bearing emphasized by his spreading cloak which falls in pleasing folds. We might say that this is the most "statuesque" figure in the composition, the parallel in painting to the Apollo Belvedere attributed to the sculptor Leochares.

69

characteristic and comprehensive which, however, is not often visible to the human eye.

More common, though no less typical, is the depiction of the mounted figure which dominates the centre of the composition. The rider is in an almost completely sideways pose galloping towards the right; nevertheless, his movement is not absolutely parallel to the borders of the frieze, because the horse is shown in a pose 4/5 from left to right so that its hindquarters fall somewhat to the inside of the space while the forequarters are close to the viewer. Thus we have a complete view of the rear quarters and almost all of the right side; at the same time the rider's body twists to the right so as to pull his right arm with the spear backwards, clearly displaying his fully expanded chest.

It is unfortunate that the damage to the third horseman prevents the viewer from immediately and effortlessly perceiving the wonderful picture there once was. Here the artist brought all his talents into play and succeeded in drawing one of the most daring and most memorable pictures of a horseman in the history of art. This rider moves from the background to the foreground, for his legs are astride the horse. The animal, startled by coming on the lion, abruptly raises its right leg while turning its head left, the opposite direction. The rider leans towards the right and, bending his head towards the enraged beast, readies himself to strike it with the spear he grasps in his bent, slightly elevated right arm. In this position we can distinguish only part of his face, the left cheek above the jaw and the right arm with the spear. The rest of his body is obscured by the horse's raised head though some part of the violet-purple cloak billows out beyond his left side. This figure gives us the opportunity to admire the magnificent grasp of perspective the painter possessed; it is perhaps no exaggeration to say that here he sets out to display his full power in this field, not unlike Mantegna's impressive figure of Christ in the Descent from the Cross.

The same dexterity, artfully and emphatically presented, is evident in the figures of the dogs, most markedly in the three attacking the lion. One is in a clear side view; the second in a 3/4 view with its head close below the lion's claws, the third is shown from behind and sideways on; this one has even bitten his fearsome opponent. The crowning achievement in the drawing of the animals is the rendering of the lion; viewed sideways, his proud head raised to the left, he fights bravely to the last minute which is now upon him.

A painter with such drawing and compositional abilities is naturally also a master of the essential technique of painting; colour. Though the damage to the surface creates several blank spots and may even perhaps mislead us as to detail, we may confidently say that the whole range of colours was almost entirely built around warm tones: – orange, brown, reddish-brown and violet purple. The background is white, flecked with muted hues of red or sometimes grey. As they are today, the rocks too retain various shades of grey and the same tones are found repeated in both the bare trees and in the pillar-like stele. It is nevertheless worth observing that some details are picked out in dark blue (such as the spearheads) and there are some small areas in green, for example the chaplet worn by the central horseman while the tree behind the lion seems to have had dark green foliage. The time is not yet ripe for an exhaustive study of the juxtapositions of colour. We can do no more than say that there is a careful and far from coincidental play of light and dark colours, sometimes complementary and at other times contrasting which completes and emphasizes the restraint or the explosions of the linework.

It is also too soon to discuss the various technical problems posed, or solved, by this painting. It suffices to say that, according to expert opinions, it is executed in water colours; this does not mean that the entire composition is a fresco; it is very likely that the work started *a fresco* and continued *a secco*. It remains only to answer two other questions: 1. exactly what does the theme depict? 2. who was its painter?

Conscious that any attempt to provide a specific answer to these two questions carries with it the danger of reaching conclusions with little to support them and small likelihood of acceptance, I shall nevertheless essay, albeit with reservations, to provide an answer. For I am sure that if I desist from the attempt, there will be those amongst my colleagues who will not be proof against temptation. I shall base my hypotheses on facts and observations which are, as far as possible, objective.

First then, the theme. As I noted above – and it must be obvious to the meanest intelligence – the

70. Drawing of the central horseman of the wall painting. His face, with the large piercing eyes, is reminiscent of the youthful figure on the Alexander sarcophagus which is identified as Alexander. The features, the pose (recalling that of Alexander in the mosaic from Pompeii) and the wreath on his head make it possible for us to identify this figure as Alexander.

subject of the wall painting depicts a hunt in a forest, or rather in a sacred grove. A roebuck, a lion and at least one boar (or a bear?) are to be distinguished without any doubt. There are ten huntsmen, seven on foot, three on horseback. It would be logical to suggest that the horsemen are the more important personages. Moreover it is significant that two of the three are associated with the lion hunt; the third has his back turned and he is moving away from the area of the main scene. All the people participating in the hunt are young, I would even say very young, except for one, the horseman above the lion whose face is half hidden. One other youth stands out; the mounted man in the centre. First of all, his is the dominant position in the composition; secondly, he wears a chaplet. Thus the rider above the lion and the central horseman are the two prominent figures in the scene. If we look carefully at all the other figures we may note an absence of any specific individual characteristics; all are handsome, supple youths, almost children, but without personality. The face of the central horseman, however, is possessed of definite features. He too is little more than a child, but not only does he wear a chaplet, but his face is stamped with highly personal traits; it is not difficult to observe the particular expression which his eyes, large and wild, confer. Thus these two horsemen are to be picked out because the painter elected to endow them with individual characteristics; in other words, he sought to present their portrait. I think therefore that the first reasonably safe conclusion must be that out of the ten figures of the wall painting only two were names to the painter (or to the man who issued the orders for the decoration of the tomb); one a young boy, the other a mature man. If we next consider that the tomb contained an ivory head which we may almost certainly regard as a portrait of Alexander the Great and a second which I have identified with great probability as a portrait of Philip the next step, to venture a link between the ivory heads and the two portraits in the wall painting, is justifiable. Again, starting from the better known figure we observe a similarity of the central horseman with the portrait

115

of Alexander which is not coincidental. The most typical facial characteristic which the later portrayals of his face have passed down to us on the coinage of his immediate successors, on the familiar mosaic from Pompeii (now in Naples), on the sarcophagus from Sidon etc., are undoubtedly his large sullen eyes. The viewer may discern them without difficulty in the figure of the young horseman of the wall painting which is distinguished from his companions who move around him. If this identification is correct, then that is the explanation of the chaplet he wears on his head and his dominant position in the middle of the frieze. One would expect the figure of the occupant of the tomb in this position; but we know now from the anthropological examination of the bones that the dead man in the tomb was a mature man, more than forty years old. Now, linking the information supplied by the finds in the tomb and my hypothesis about the figure of the central horseman, I venture to recognize in the face of the older horseman that of Philip himself. In terms of painting, his position dominates the entire composition, for it towers over all the other figures and above the space of the fatal scene on which the whole episode is focussed. This curious position, which simultaneously reveals and conceals him, is I believe one further strategic de-

71. Drawing of the mature horseman striking the lion with his spear. The spear is visible on the left, the mounted man's fingers clenched round it. Immediately to the right his bent head is shown in profile, and further right still is the horse's head. The facial features permit us to identify this figure as Philip.

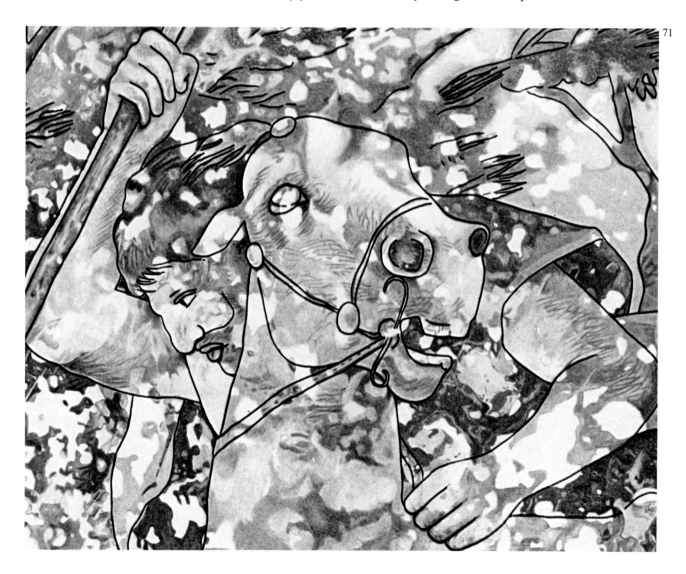

71

vice on the part of the painter, not without connotations. The young ruler appears in all the splendour of youth; the dead man overcoming the lion is almost heroized; ascending to the heights there is something ethereal in his face.

Of the other young huntsmen we may simply say that they are the indispensable followers of the royal hunt. Arrian, however, gives us one specific piece of information (*Anabasis of Alexander*, 4.13.1) which casts considerable light on our theme; [21] he writes,

"it was a practice going back to Philip's time that the sons of Macedonian notables who had reached adolescence should be enlisted for the service of the king; and besides general attendance on his person, the duty of guarding him when asleep had been entrusted to them. Again, whenever the king rode out, they received the horses from the grooms and led them up, and they mounted the king in Persian fashion and were his companions in the rivalry of the chase."

The young followers then, the youths, in the wall painting depict the *paides* who were his "companions in the rivalry of the chase." Thus there is no clash between the conclusions which emerge from the depiction on the frieze (which even force themselves on us) and the other finds in the tomb; on the contrary, they form one more piece of corroborative evidence.

There remains the very pertinent and essential problem of the painter. Whereas for the "rape of Persephone" in the preceding tomb we were lucky enough to possess some support from documentary sources which allowed us to formulate a hypothesis which in my opinion is very plausible, there is nothing similar, as far as I know, for the wall painting of the "royal hunt". Equally, surviving examples of ancient painting which might have come to our aid are virtually non-existent. I do not consider that the paintings in the tomb at Kazanlak (Bulgaria) which can be dated to the fourth century BC offer us a firm basis for any comparison because their quality puts them into a different category of works, while their dating, to years later than the Vergina period, is one further factor disallowing comparison. Historians of Greek painting have regularly sought help from Greek vase painting from earlier periods (the fifth century BC) and for later periods (fourth – second centuries BC) in Ro-

man works which "are inspired by", "imitate" or "copy" Greek originals. I am afraid that in both the first and the second case the help afforded by these pictorial sources – valuable in all other respects – has usually proved misleading. We may pass this comment today, now that Luck has decided to acquaint us with two products of large scale Greek painting from the fourth century BC.

Confronted for a second time with this problem we would again be helpless but that Luck came once more to our rescue; had it not been for the survival of the magnificent mosaic from Pompeii (now in the Naples Museum) depicting the combat between Alexander and Darius we would have been left stranded. It is beyond doubt that the mosaicist of the second century BC copied some splendid work of art of the fourth century BC. It is indeed very probable that the copy followed its model as faithfully as possible. The mosaic is 5.12 m. long and 2.71 m. high; it is therefore almost the same length as the wall painting in the tomb, though its height is rather more than double. It is not possible to linger long over a detailed comparison in this book useful and enlightening though this would be. We can only say that a historian of ancient Greek art has no difficulty in seeing that the distribution of space was more daring in the original of the mosaic than in the Vergina wall painting, that the display of perspective was bolder and more boisterous, the unrest in the composition of the structural elements greater and the exploitation of artistic contrivance and psychological discovery more intense. This, as K. Schefold has already hinted, testifies to an interval of time separating the two works, and suggests that the Vergina composition is indubitably the earlier in date.

On the other hand, there are certain similarities which cannot be coincidental; firstly there is the composition; the position of the two protagonists in the mosaic, their placing and inter-relationship simply as artistic figures immediately recalls the two central figures of the hunt at Vergina. Secondly, there is the overall balance of colour; the dominance of the reddish-brown and darker hues has almost the same intensity in the two compositions. More striking still are the common features of certain specific figures. The mounted Alexander of the mosaic is shown in the same stance and in almost the same movement as the "Alexander" of the hunt. The motion of the horse towards Darius'

chariot bears a meaningful affinity to the horse of the left-hand rider of Vergina, while its two hind legs are so depicted as to constitute the corresponding "rendering in reverse" of the legs of the horse belonging to the Vergina "Alexander" though this is drawn from in front. Furthermore, an even more striking similarity exists between the sole tree of the mosaic and the two central trees of the Vergina painting. The wholly strange shape of the bare trees and the same dark colours cannot be chance. In my opinion, the spear snapped off at a right angle to the lower right in the mosaic and the similarly broken spear which struck the bear in the Vergina painting are examples of correspondence which point to close direct links between the two works.

We may draw certain useful conclusions from this brief comparison. The first, which is almost certain, is that the Vergina painting is earlier than the original of the mosaic by not less than fifteen to twenty years. If therefore we accept the almost unanimous agreement of scholars on a date for the original of the mosaic around 320 BC or 317 BC, then we must date the picture with virtual certainty to the decade 340-330 BC. The second conclusion, more tenuous, at least for the time being, is that the two works are the product either of the same artist, or of a common atelier. Personally, I incline to the belief that the wall painting of Vergina is an early, still youthful work of the painter to whom we owe the original of the mosaic. If this is Philoxenos, as Karl Schefold maintains, then our interconnections become quite extraordinarily seductive, since I have earlier supported the view that I do not regard it as improbable that the "rape of Persephone" should be ascribed to Nikomachos himself. And we know that Philoxenos of Eretria was a pupil of Nikomachos. Would it therefore be strange if both were found at the court of Philip in the last years of

72-73. The objects in the main chamber as they were found when the tomb was opened; the northern part of the chamber with the silver vases piled against the wall (72) and the southern part of the chamber (73); the fallen cuirass, the bronze vessels for the bath and the weapons can be seen in the southwest corner. The sponge in the mouth of the bucket can be seen, a little to the right is the iron helmet and next to the sarcophagus is the sword. The circular cover which protected the chryselephantine shield is propped against the wall; above left an iron spear head has stuck to the wall; its wooden shaft had rotted and had completely disappeared.

the reign of this surprising ruler whom we know took pains to surround himself with the most brilliant representatives of art, thought and learning of his time?

THE GRAVE GOODS
IN THE MAIN CHAMBER

It is well known that the ancient Greeks placed many items in the tombs of their dead which they believed would be essential for them in the next life. These are the objects described by the term grave goods. It is not always easy for us to distinguish which of these, and how many, were the personal possessions of the deceased and which were only offerings laid in the tomb for use in the hereafter. All of course were considered to be serviceable to the dead man in his new life in the other world. This means that in every case the offerings were commensurate with the sex, age and social standing of the deceased. The objects which have been found up to now in tombs covering the whole period of Greek antiquity are innumerable, from the poorest and the humblest to the richest and most impressive. Nevertheless, for the first time Luck succeeded in preserving such a tomb unplundered, in which all the evidence permits us to regard it as royal. Thus, for the first time since the discovery of the royal graves at Mycenae we have before our eyes the tomb of a king. The important aspect is that this tomb belongs to the historical period and the deceased – whoever he may be – does not originate in the mythical world but is a historical figure. The permanent dwelling place of this historic personage with the full complement of vessels for the after life swam into our ken when we entered the tomb. Because no one had entered the tomb since the burial all the objects were naturally found untouched; that does not of course mean that they were exactly in the position that they had been left or that they had remained completely without change. It is not possible for us to be specific about the natural phenomena which, in the course of 2,300 years could have caused some alterations (earthquakes and floods for example). The only effect that we can actually see is the oxidization of the metal objects and the decomposition of organic matter which in most cases is complete or nearly so. However, bearing these preliminary observations in mind, we may say that the objects were found either in their place or that it is possible for us to imagine their probable position.

The point of reference for all the grave goods is certainly the marble sarcophagus in which the larnax with the burnt bones of the dead was deposited. This stands clear of the back – west – wall of the chamber and at its centre. Thus all the objects were found "around" the sarcophagus at the rear of the chamber. In the southwest corner were the bronze items and the weapons, and roughly at the centre of the north wall were the silver and pottery vases. Only the iron cuirass had fallen upside down and lay approximately in the middle of the chamber, a little south of its axis. In front of the sarcophagus (towards the door of the chamber) were the decomposed remains of some wooden piece of furniture. The east half of the chamber (towards the door) was completely empty.

The first problem we had to solve was to what piece of furniture the remains in front of the sarcophagus belonged. The authoritative solution to the problem will only be reached after the final treatment and study of the innumerable fragments which will, of course, take a long time yet to come to fruition. However, from the facts already in our possession, we may safely say that these came from a wooden couch with very sumptuous decoration. The question nevertheless remains; are these only from the couch, or were there perhaps other wooden items or some other construction? And I believe that this question leads immediately to the problem produced by the position and condition in which the silver vases were found. Anyone looking at the photograph taken of the arrangement of the objects as they were found when we opened the tomb can see that the silver vases were piled up against the north wall in a peculiar way; it looks as though they had rolled there from somewhere higher because of some external force and had collected where they were found because the wall blocked their further movement. This general impression is strengthened by the position in which the deep silver crater was found and the way in which it lay and that of the long narrow "amphora". It was not possible for the crater to have been found with its base towards the wall unless it had slid there from a distance, knocking against the wall on its way and then staying as it fell. This impact had destroyed the plaster of the wall – which might have been blis-

74

74. Behind the circular bronze shield cover in the southwest corner of the chamber the remains of a gold and ivory shield were found. Some of the ivory parts can be distinguished (the leg of a male figure) part of the gilding at the centre and the gilded silver sheets from the inner face of the shield. After some five years labour this unique shield has been reconstructed from hundreds of such fragments.

tered at this point – exactly where the crater struck it. The position of the "amphora" also shows that it must have either been upright on the floor and simply tipped backwards, in which case it would have been completely separated from the other vases or, alternatively, and which I think more likely, that this too slid until it stopped when it came in contact with the wall. If however this deduction is correct, then we must suppose that these vessels had been on some kind of "table" towards the middle of the chamber a little in front of the sarcophagus. But in that case we must look for the remains of a wooden "table" as well as of a wooden couch and so we have returned to our original question about the existence of a second piece of wooden furniture. Certainly, as the reader may ascertain from the photograph which shows the entire area in front of the couch, there are clear traces of decomposed planks in the foreground of the picture. The way in which they have spread open like a fan towards the northern part allows us to reconstruct the probable stages of decomposi-

tion. Let us suppose then that in front of the couch there stood a wooden "table". At some point the wood began to rot; if we accept that the first to go were the two legs on the northern side, while the two opposite on the south were still intact, the picture of a fan presented by the four planks at the top of the table is explicable; still supported on the southern side they opened and fanned out to the north when they lost the supports that had held them together. In this case they would have collapsed suddenly, and thus the vessels on the table top would have slid towards the wall. We may even suggest that the northwest leg of the table gave way first, so that most of the vases slipped and fell in that direction.

In contrast to the problems posed by the silver vases, the position in which the bronze vessels were found seems to be that in which they were placed during the burial. As we noted above, all these were concentrated in the southwest corner of the chamber. Only two or three show any sign of having been moved, and we may take it as certain that this movement was of the slightest, consisting basically of only a small slide from their original position; it might be due to a minor tremor or simply to natural sliding on their smooth curved bases. Once again, this too is easily observed in the photograph taken of the state in which they were found when the tomb was opened. Beginning at the left, touching the south wall, there was an iron tripod; I think it beyond doubt that this has stayed in the position in which it was laid during the burial. Above this must have sat the bronze cauldron which tipped and which we found supported on its side by the tripod's crown. Adjacent to the iron tripod was a second tripod, of bronze. Between the two, placed on the floor, was the bronze lantern, I believe in its original position. Next to this, fallen with its side onto the floor, was a bronze situla (bucket). I think it is very probable that it fell from the bronze tripod on which it had been placed. There followed a bronze jug and a bronze phiale (a deep saucer). A bronze basin had been placed below the bronze tripod.

A large shield-shaped bronze object, dominant because of its size, was propped up against the west wall. Next to it, again leaning against the wall, was a pair of bronze greaves. Very close to these and to the bronze phiale was a circular silver-gilt object (? a diadem) and touching the phiale an iron Macedonian helmet. Not far from it – towards the short side of the sarcophagus – a pair of bronze greaves lay sideways on the ground and above them was a rotted remnant of leather.

On the floor, behind the shield-shaped object, a mass of ivory fragments, gilded silver sheets and pieces of (?) iron were found. As I guessed from the beginning, all these were the remains of a shield unique in its sumptuousness and skilful execution. The cleaning of the remains showed that they were mixed up with the remains of a second shield. It seems therefore that the bronze object which covered them was the protective cover of the first shield which, as we shall see, was exceptionally delicate.

Six iron spearheads and one butt (the metal capping for the bottom of the wooden shaft) were found amongst the bronze vessels. It is probable that the spears had been placed upright next to the wall, and when the wooden shaft rotted the heads fell to the ground. One head was found stuck into the plastering of the west wall; the position in which it was found is important, for it tells us about the exact original placing of the spear.

As I noted above, these objects do not seem to have moved – or if they have, their movement is of the slightest – from their original position. But this is not true of every object; three which raise doubts demand more careful examination. I refer to a) the greaves found lying sideways on the floor; b) the iron helmet and c) the circular diadem.

1. I regard it as thoroughly improbable that the diadem had been placed on the floor, for it was one of the most valuable and most important objects in the tomb. Irrespective of its interpretation and of its significance, its shape and the material of which it was made would have imposed a rather different positioning. One possible suggestion is that it was hung somewhere on the west wall from which it fell. In this case, there ought to be a nail in the wall, but at the point where it should have been suspended, there was neither nail nor sign of a nail. Moreover, the diadem bore no sign of rough contact with the ground which its fall from a height would have caused.

2. It is equally improbable to my mind that the helmet should have been placed on the ground, at least at the spot it was found. If it had indeed been placed there, care would have been taken at least to see that its front was turned towards the entrance of the chamber and not to the wall. This is a simple matter of logic, but we also possess an objective piece of information which bears out the fact that it was somewhat violently transferred to the floor; the cheek pieces of the helmet, even oxidized as they are, show that they were turned down in the original position they occupied; this means that the helmet, as one would expect, had stood on some kind of wooden support, and certainly not in the position it was found next to the bronze vessels. In all likelihood it was close to the cuirass.

3. It is even more important to comment on the position of the greaves, for it is impossible that they should have been placed on the floor (all the others – three pairs – had been placed upright against the wall or the door; so too had the pair in the antechamber.) It is also improbable that they had leant against the short sides of the sarcophagus and had fallen from there onto the floor.

The cuirass poses the same problem. As we have said, it was found with its front face flat on the floor; with it, at the neck, was a pectoral. As can be seen in the photograph, its fall threw it further to the east than all the other remains of the wooden furniture. The fact that the left shoulder is broken shows that this must have been the point of impact and that the cuirass fell from some height; it also leads us to suggest that even when it fell there was some oxidization of the iron and its resistance had been weakened. The foregoing observations are strengthened by the finding of two gold lion heads which had been attached to the left side of the cuirass. That they became detached means that the oxidization and disintegration of the organic material was already advanced and the intervening space suggests again a fall from a height and a sharp bump against the floor. It is very probable that it stood on some kind of wooden support which rotted, as the traces of wood preserved on the inner surface of the shoulder pieces show.

We have therefore four objects found on the floor and for which there are strong reasons to believe that they arrived there somewhat abruptly from their original position. Three of these form part of the armour of the deceased, and I think the fourth, the diadem, probably ought to be linked with the helmet. But before I formulate any theory about their original positions, I think it is relevant to continue with this descriptive account of the grave goods as they were found.

To the left (south) and in front of the sarcophagus above the remains of the wooden couch, an iron sword was found; it was in its scabbard, only the ivory part of which had survived. The lower edge of the sword and of the scabbard projected beyond the remains of the couch towards the west, and consequently protruded beyond the straight line of the front surface of the sarcophagus. Towards the north end of the remains of the couch and below a heap which the chemist described as the remains of feathers, was a second, shorter sword. Both swords appear to have been placed on the couch, the former on its left, (southern) edge and the latter on the right (northern) edge. With the disintegration of the bed the larger sword slipped somewhat towards the back wall (the west) and moved slightly from its original position.

(I shall describe later the finds which probably form part of the decoration of the couch in an attempt to reconstruct and describe its shape.)

The few clay vessels, the "salt-cellars" and the askos were found scattered about the northwest part of the chamber. In addition to these a little way from the west wall and parallel to it a cylindrical bronze object lay on the floor. One end of it was a hollow iron socket into which another, wooden, rod could be inserted. I think this is almost certainly a torch.

Having now listed the grave goods we must try to reconstruct the appearance of the funerary chamber as it would have been after the interment.

The bronze vessels and the weapons of the deceased had been deposited in the left corner, the southwest, the spears stacked upright leaning against the wall. The torch had been propped somewhere against the sarcophagus. Immediately in front of it was the wooden couch whose wooden side touched the sarcophagus. The swords were laid on the couch. On some kind of wooden support standing on it hung the dead man's cuirass; the helmet was probably on another such support, while the gold circular diadem and the bronze greaves were placed somewhere next to these. Thus on the couch were all the deceased's defensive weapons except for the shield. Because of the disin-

75. Tentative reconstruction of the couch in the main chamber. This drawing is a preliminary and provisional attempt to locate the positions of the decorative elements which embellished the couch and to acquaint the reader, at least on general lines, with the shape of the legs and the relief frieze between them.

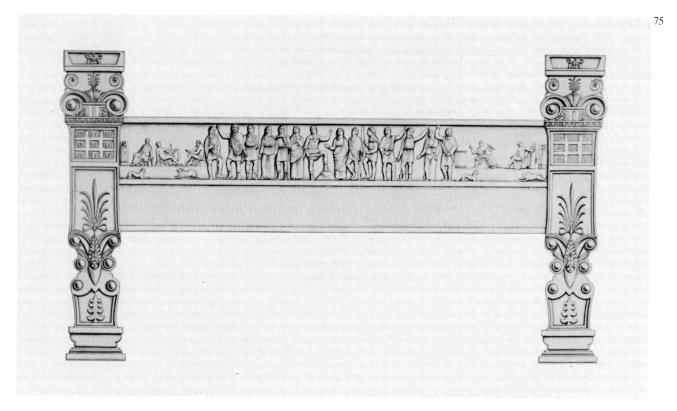

tegration of the couch all these were found on the ground, shifted violently from their original positions.

In front of the couch there must have been a "table" with all the silver, bronze and clay vases needed for a banquet; a situla (bucket), a "crater" a large "cup", two "amphorae", two oinochoai, two kantharoi, two stemmed kylixes and two without stems, two kalyxes, a small jug, a skyphos and a strainer, a spoon and a ladle – every one of them of silver. There was one oinochoe and a patera of bronze; one oinochoe, one askos and four "salt-cellars" of clay.

It is clear that all these objects, both vessels and armour, were the personal possessions of the dead man which would be as essential to him in the after life as they had been in his earthly existence. They testify to unusual wealth, though they are still in measured good taste from which exaggeration and *hubris* are both excluded. I would regard the characterization as sparingly sumptuous which I suggested in the first days after the discovery of the tomb as the most accurate to render this uncommon combination. To whatever degree we may be impressed by our first sight of them, there is nothing superfluous and nothing ostentatious. A preliminary comparison with the finds from the tombs of the Thracian and Scythian princes permits us to perceive this distinction which reflects a different level of civilization, something we shall perceive even more clearly and convincingly when we carefully examine the standard of the works. We may deduce without any risk of misinterpretation that the contents form a historic witness to real life and are not a collection of objects envisaged and then made only for the world to come where the dead were the superiors of the living. In other words, they denote the real world, not one dominated by the ideology of religious imagination.

The couch

It is still premature to attempt a reconstruction of the couch. Its entire wooden frame has been lost and only the decorative elements have remained, scattered on the floor themselves in fragments and not all in good condition. We may estimate the length and breadth with tolerable approximation and formulate some provisional thoughts about the shape based on the disintegrated material of its decoration by making comparisons with other similar models in stone or with couches shown in paintings.

Its length will not have exceeded 2 m. and is not likely to have been less than 1.80 m. Its most probable breadth may be estimated at ± 0.80 m. The whole couch was wood without the decorative elements in metal which we know of from other couches (see for example Pella). The two legs on its main face must have been in the shape we know of, either from thrones or from exceptionally sumptuous and well fashioned couches. Until recently the best and most closely related example which could supply us with a complete picture of the leg was the marble leg of a couch which came from a Macedonian tomb near Kerdyllia, now in the Kavala Museum. (See *The Search for Alexander, An Exhibition*, colour plate 7, cat. 47). Now however we also have the stone couch from tomb I in the "Bella Tumulus" at Vergina. In these we have not only an exceptionally carefully shaped foot bordering even on affectation, but also one where the craftsman faithfully rendered all its decorative elements with very skilled carved detail on the surface. It is unquestionable that these craftsmen were copying another material. It is not difficult to posit that the original was wood, but it is not easy to guess the other materials used in the decoration which here are rendered by carving and paintwork.

On the basis therefore of the two legs, one from Kerdyllia and the other recent find from Vergina, we can reconstruct the couch from "Philip's tomb". An ivory sheath encased the flat surfaces of the wood. The carved spirals on the lower part of the leg and on its upper part directly above the capital were also of ivory. The eye of the spiral was of transparent glass under which was a very thin circular sheet of gold. The leaves of the palmette were also of glass, inset within an ivory plaque. On the Kerdyllia foot an acanthus leaf sprouts from between the lowest spirals; the corresponding leaf on the couch from "Philip's tomb" was probably ivory. On the Kerdyllia capital was a grid-like decoration made up of small square protrusions, the central one of which is semi-cylindrical. Without the find from "Philip's tomb" it would be impossible for us to guess what this curious grid represents. On the couch from "Philip's tomb" these squares are all glass pieces which cover small scenes cut out from a

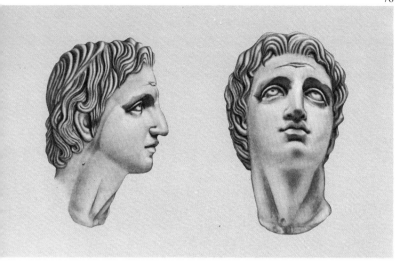

sheet of gold (these are rendered in paint on the couch from the "Bella Tumulus"). This means that the glass plaques were transparent and contributed as much to the appearance as to the protection of the delicate gold elements. Immediately above the capital are two identical plaques between two spirals, whose outer side is curved to follow the inner curve of the spiral. These, on the couch from "Philip's tomb", were also of glass and covered gold figures (Cupids in flight etc.) from a cut sheet. To all this we must add bands of ionic and lesbian cymatia which embellish the horizontal surfaces linking the vertical parts of the bed.

This valuable find from Kerdyllia is unfortunately in fragments. Nevertheless it allowed us to reconstruct the shape of the entire front face of the couch with a considerable degree of certainty because parts at least of the essential pieces survived. When they were extended, the full picture was obtained, more or less as we see them intact on the couch from tomb I in the "Bella Tumulus".

A narrow band, bordered above and below by two projecting regulae springs from the level of the capital. This forms the border of the horizontal area of the couch on which lay the mattress. As we know from other stone couches (and from their depiction on vases) cross-pieces between the legs formed the framework of the couch. Sometimes this narrow bordered band was decorated with painted or relief scenes. The most notable such relief decoration is offered us by the marble couch found in the Belevi tomb near Ephesus where the frieze between the legs is embellished with relief "Sirens".

There was, apparently, such a frieze on the Vergina couch which had ivory relief figures and very thin sheets of gold. It will take many years before we succeed in finding – if indeed we do succeed – the place of each of the different figures on this frieze and before we can attempt a probable reconstruction. For the moment I shall confine myself to describing the pieces we have at our disposal and to a provisional appraisal.

Two groups of ivory reliefs were found at the spot where the couch stood. The first was made up of figures carved in very low relief, depicting mythological beings or objects associated with religious rites. The figures of the second group are in very high relief; some of the limbs are even ren-

76-78. Ivory head, 3.4 cms. high (78). The long neck twisted slightly to the left while the head is turned in the opposite direction is characteristic, as too is the rendering of the eyes whose gaze is upward combining strength and tenderness. The nose is thin and hooked. Each of these features make the identification of this face as Alexander's almost certain. The side view of Alexander's head confirms the identification (77). Fig. 76 is a sketch of Alexander's head, full face and profile, completed by hair. The addition of the hair makes it easier to compare the Vergina head with the other known portraits of Alexander.

79-81. Sketch of Philip's face, with the addition of hair (80). Ivory head 3.2 cms high (81). It is that of a mature bearded man, 40-45 years old. Strength and decision stamp the face though there are signs also of suppressed exhaustion. The nose curves right from its top. The eyes have a strange gaze. The right eye, which is wider open than the left, seems to be sightless; a scar can be seen in the brow above. Its identification as a portrait of Philip can be taken as certain. Fig. 79, view of Philip's face in profile showing his strongly hooked nose.

81

82

83

dered in the round. Only the heads, hands and legs of the figures in this group have survived because they were of ivory; it is certain that the rest of the body was made of wood or stucco, which decomposed. This is the same technique as was used for chryselephantine statues, where the exposed limbs were made of ivory while the clothed parts were of wood encased by a gold sheet. Finally, all the heads in this group depict real people, not mythological beings; we therefore have portraits of specific historic personages.

I regard it as certain that not all the figures belonging to the relief decoration of the couch have survived undamaged. There are examples from both groups where either the damage is very great or an entire part has completely disappeared; it follows therefore that several figures have been lost or at the very least have altered beyond redemption so that an exact knowledge of all the figures which decorated the frieze of the couch is no longer possible. Many reasons have contributed to decay; excessive damp, the effect of other rotted substances found near the couch, some original integral weakness in the ivory, since not all the pieces could have been of the same quality or could have been equally durable. The difference in colouring and the degree of preservation of various parts of the same figure is significant, and depended on whether they were found together or separated from each other by even a small distance and contact with other substances.

The relationship between the two groups is problematical – at least for the moment. I think that the solution is one of two; a) the low relief representations of mythological beings decorated a certain section of the frieze while the high reliefs, of historic personages, embellished a different part; b) the low reliefs decorated the back-ground and the figures in high relief were set between them. From my knowledge of the material acquired by looking at it and studying it up to now I regard the first solution as the more probable for two main reasons.

1. It is difficult to understand the juxtaposition of the seated Muse and the seated Dionysos, for example, to the live portraits of the second group.

2. The figures of the first group make it obvious that they were placed in pairs, i.e. one facing left, the other facing right. The existence of two identical hermaic stelai facing in different directions is

characteristic. This latter observation leads me to the reflection that one possible solution may have been that the low relief ivories were placed at either end of the frieze while corresponding paired figures and the historic personages occupied the centre. However, this solution is not without its difficulties because in some cases the figures of both groups were found at almost the same point or with only a small space separating them. I hope that when the treatment of this material has been completed and we can embark on its exhaustive study we shall be able to reach more certain conclusions.

I am still not in a position to say with any certainty what the shape of the narrow sides of the couch may have been. Did these have corresponding friezes or not? I shall therefore confine myself to a preliminary presentation of the most important figures from this magnificent group of miniature ivory sculptures, leaving open the question both of the overall composition and of the rendering of the different limbs of the particular figures. (In consequence, I shall not attempt to define the exact placing of each figure.)

Fourteen portrait heads have survived; at least seven of these are preserved in very good condition though none has its hair; this means that the hair was probably rendered in some other perishable material. I imagine that it may have been gilded, an opinion based on the very slight remaining traces and on the ivories of the third tomb. Its absence somewhat alters the faces and demands considerable efforts of imagination on the part of the viewer to reconstruct their original appearance.

Two of these heads are outstanding, and I think both can be identified with known historical figures. The first is 0.034 m. high and depicts a very young person, not yet out of his teens. His long

84

85

82. An ivory head, probably that of a woman; the pronounced features and a certain resemblance to the head of Alexander leads to the thought that it may depict his mother, Olympias.

83. Male ivory head, that of a young man. His eyes look upwards, filled with pain and tension.

84. An ivory head, perhaps that of a woman. The eyes deep in their sockets and the half-open mouth express grief.

85. Ivory head of a young man, whose face, turned definitely to his left, is stern and thoughtful.

neck slightly turned to the left while the head turns in the opposite direction is characteristic; so too is the rendering of the eyes, their gaze fixed upwards and filled with resolution as well as with a veiled tenderness. The flesh of the face has been rendered with great dexterity, successfully modelling the youthful cheek with a smooth and simultaneously firm structure. The nose is thin and slightly crooked. I believe that we may without difficulty recognize the face of Alexander in this small head, taking into account only Plutarch's well known de-

86. Ivory head of a bearded man (the nose is slightly damaged). The impeccable sculptural workmanship successfully conveys the noble and commanding personality of the subject. At first glance it brings the face of Philip to mind, but a more careful look confirms that it is a different face, perhaps of a relative, (? Amyntas).

86

scription – ..."namely the poise of the neck, which was bent slightly to the left, and the melting glance of his eyes... (*Lives* 4, 1-666 b); Plutarch, *Moralia*, "with his face turned towards the heavens (as indeed Alexander often did look with a slight inclination of the head to one side..."); *Moralia*, 335 b "the others wished to imitate the flexing of his neck and the melting and liquid softness of his eyes, but were unable to preserve his virile and leonine expression." If we compare the Vergina portrait with the innumerable works which depict the legendary conqueror we may easily discern facial resemblances. All the other portraits depict Alexander at a more advanced age, when he had become king and had begun his campaigns in the East. Most of these portraits, which are later renderings of his face, attempt to retain, usually clumsily, the characteristics described by Plutarch; they rarely succeeded in capturing a faithful picture of his face. The only true portrait to be found is, I believe, that in the famous mosaic in Naples where the painter of the original has preserved the truly fascinating figure of the young warrior. A comparison between the Vergina head and the Alexander of the mosaic convinces us of the authenticity of both.

The second head which can, I think, be identified is 0.032 m. high. It depicts a mature bearded man, aged forty to forty-five; his face shows strength and determination, but is nevertheless suffused with a suppressed exhaustion. His nose is characteristically planted firmly on his forehead, developing an immediate hook. But a still more characteristic element of this face is the eyes. His gaze has a curious expression, simultaneously strong and yet deficient. Closer observation reveals that his left eye is narrower and more alive; in contrast, the right is open over-wide, betraying a sightless gaze, but without destroying the proportions of the face. In his right eyebrow a scar is to be seen at the point where the brow rises at a strange angle, its curve like that of the left. This unusual line of the brow adds a personal touch to the individuality of this face.

It is not difficult for anyone to trace the close facial resemblance of this head with the portrait of Philip on the gold medallion from Tarsus in the Bibliothèque Nationale, Paris. Moreover, the comparison of the ivory head from Vergina with the marble bust in Copenhagen which is considered to be a portrait of Philip produces several si-

gnificant resemblances, the most important of which is the identical shape of the eyebrows. But, in addition to these similarities between the two familiar portraits of the Macedonian king, the Vergina head presents the very features which lead to the conclusion that it does indeed portray Philip; the blindness in the right eye and the scar in the eyebrow above are the most convincing characteristics, since we know that Philip lost the sight in his right eye because of a wound received during the battle of Methone in 355/4 BC. Lastly, the presence of a portrait of Alexander may constitute indirect corroboration of the authenticity of the identification as Philip.

If these attributions are, as I believe, correct, then we have two unique portraits of Philip and Alexander, executed while they were still alive. This means that the subjects themselves knew about them and accepted their authenticity. Even if this had been our only gain from the excavation of the Great Tumulus we could have been exceptionally satisfied.

Next to the portrait of Alexander another head was found; its left side has been destroyed, though rather more than half the left eye and forehead, the greater part of the lower jaw and part of the cheek remain. The face is framed by a head-dress which falls to the throat. The deep-set eyes, the sharp, slightly crooked nose, the harsh bony cheeks and the defiantly raised chin, confer an arrogant hardness and testify to a character of inflexible determination and purpose. Although it is difficult to decide on the sex, I believe it is a woman's face; I also believe that the facial resemblances are such as to permit us to suggest that it depicts Alexander's mother, Olympias. But the absence of other genuine portraits of her oblige me to make this suggestion with due caution.

Two other heads, found together, are totally dissimilar in their structure, in their facial characteristics, their sculptured moulding and their expression. One depicts a young man with an unu-

87. Relief hermaic stele in ivory. As a contrast to the figures which depict particular people (the portraits) which were worked in high relief, the decoration of the couch also had a group of mythological and religious subjects in low relief. This sculpture is a typical hermaic stele with the head of the bearded Hermes and the archaic features.

sually thick neck, an almost spherical face, a half-open mouth and deep-set eyes looking upwards with compassion. The second, which probably represents a woman, has a pronounced twist to the left, while the neck is stretched and turned to the right; the eyes, deep in their sockets, turn upwards and the mouth is half open from grief. It is however, difficult to recognize particular individuals for we are completely ignorant of the faces of the Macedonian court.

Two further heads were preserved in perfect condition. One depicts a young man with a stern and, I would say, thoughtful countenance looking to his left, while his long neck is stretched and twisted in the opposite direction. His expression,

though not without intensity, does not compare with the emotion which stamps the two preceding heads. The second, its nose very slightly damaged, represents a mature bearded man, and at first sight it brings Philip's face to mind. More careful observation, however, assures us that this is a different face. The perfectly modelled finish successfully conveys the noble and lordly personality of the subjects. These two heads perhaps come closest to the classical tradition, still retaining many elements from the structure and the moulded shape of the world which had already passed away, even if many others were not immune from the spirit quickening the art which the Hellenistic world was to create.

The co-existence of these two tendencies, of the classical tradition and of the newer mannerisms, is instructive from many points of view. It becomes clear not so much between the different heads in the "portrait group" as in their comparison with the "mythological group" of reliefs. In the latter the craftsman rendered shapes in a long establish-

88. Relief ivory of Muse playing a lyre. The seated Muse holds her lyre in her left hand though her head is turned to the right, perhaps towards another figure which existed there and to whom she gestures with her right hand. The upper part of the figure is well preserved whereas the lower has been badly eaten away.

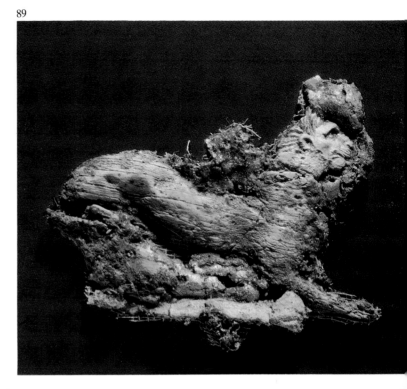

ed tradition, whereas in the "portrait group" the same man blazed a new trail and felt his creative instincts much less tramelled. Nevertheless, in both the first and the second the revivifying tendencies of the age and even more the creative and inspired work of the artist are clear.

The two hermaic stelai, one of which is magnificently preserved, are important. The craftsman conveys the archaic shape of this idiosyncratically shaped monument, and was careful to maintain the impression of antiquity without letting it become sterile and archaic. He succeeded in transform-

89. Ivory lion in relief; parts of the gilding which decorated the surface of the background have been preserved around the body.

90. Ivory Dionysos and a Silen in relief. The youthful god has spread a panther's skin over a rock on which he sits nonchalantly, his body supported on his right arm, his left hand stretched in front of a small altar. An aged Silen sits opposite him, the brutish features of his body pronounced.

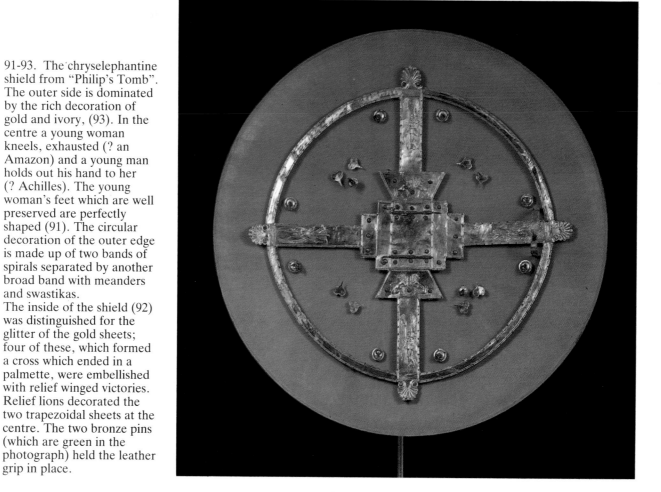

91-93. The chryselephantine shield from "Philip's Tomb". The outer side is dominated by the rich decoration of gold and ivory, (93). In the centre a young woman kneels, exhausted (? an Amazon) and a young man holds out his hand to her (? Achilles). The young woman's feet which are well preserved are perfectly shaped (91). The circular decoration of the outer edge is made up of two bands of spirals separated by another broad band with meanders and swastikas.

The inside of the shield (92) was distinguished for the glitter of the gold sheets; four of these, which formed a cross which ended in a palmette, were embellished with relief winged victories. Relief lions decorated the two trapezoidal sheets at the centre. The two bronze pins (which are green in the photograph) held the leather grip in place.

134

94. A small rectangular sheet with a relief representation of the club of Heracles was attached somewhere on the inside of the shield. Heracles was the progenitor of the Macedonian kings and it is certain that here the club was employed as the emblem of royalty.

ing the venerated and stylized elements of the figure (the hairstyle, the beard, and the genitalia) into the language of contemporary sculpture. In contrast to the realistic faces of the portraits, those of the divinities are unwrinkled and idealistic, tinged with the delicate bloom of the new age; the Muse playing her lyre and even more of the youthful Dionysos seated nonchalantly on a panther's skin next to his own altar; facing him is a perfect Silen whose enchanting, expressive ungainliness underlines the simple, almost feminine beauty of his master and his god.

It is no exaggeration to say that this couch is a work of art of very high standard which combines luxury with unique delicacy and decorative finesse.

As we shall see later this comment is borne out by both the furnishing of the antechamber and the remains of the couch in tomb III (the "Prince's tomb") where the ivory decoration rivals the artistic standards of the objects in "Philip's tomb". The justifiable conclusion is therefore that these furnishings must have been the products of a very important workshop, directed by some very well known master where very skilled craftsmen were employed. And certainly this furniture was not constructed within the very narrow limits imposed by the need for a funerary couch; it had stood in the royal palace and had been in daily use. These reflections may, I think, receive confirmation from another object which was found in the main chamber of the tomb. Although it is not part of this group of finds I shall separate it from the group to which it really belongs since I judge it useful to describe it at this point; I believe it is a creation of the same artists who fashioned the ivory with such great skill.

The ceremonial shield

I refer to the "ceremonial" shield which was found in a state of disintegration in a corner of the main chamber. As we noted above, all that remained of the shield was a mass of broken ivory and silver gilded sheets. In the first report which I wrote after the excavation of 1977 I commented; "until this mass has been transferred to a laboratory and studied, no accurate description or tentative reconstruction is possible." Nevertheless I essayed a hypothetical description which turned out to be not far from reality and I concluded; " I believe that if, as I hope, this shield can be restored, even if only partially, it will prove to be one of the most beautiful and precious finds in our possession." (Ἀρχαιολογικά Ἀνάλεκτα ἐξ Ἀθηνῶν, X, 1979, p. 24). Today (1983) after nearly five years effort, the reconstruction of the shield has progressed to a degree which no one, not even I myself, could have hope for. And my first appraisal has been far surpassed by reality. The shield from Vergina is a marvel, unique in the art of the fourth century BC.

Its skeleton must have been of wood; above it more than one layer of leather was stretched. On its outer face it had such rich and magnificent decoration that very little of the leather surface was left visible.

At the centre, the entire, slightly curved circular surface of the shield was gilded, thereby creating a glittering background for the main, centrally positioned decorative feature which occupied the place of the emblem; an ivory relief group ± 0.35 m. in height. A young man, his body bare as his cloak falls in thick folds to his left side, stands on the outcrop of a rock, stretching his hand to the female figure on his right. She has disintegrated; her knees which have been destroyed must have rested on the rock, and her legs, passing underneath the legs of the man, extended to the right where we see their perfectly preserved extremities (below the ankle); her right arm bent at the elbow and raised towards her head, holds her hair or her himation. The erosion of almost the entire surface of the ivory is very extensive and only certain parts, such as the young woman's extremities, permit us to assess the magnificence of the modelled finish correctly. However, it is not difficult to pick out the overall moulding, the structural merits of the figures and their perfectly balanced interlocking. It is still premature to formulate any suggestions about the subject of the composition. A first reaction, that it represents an episode from the Amazonomachy, now seems less probable.[22]

The circular edge of this gold surface was decorated by light relief palmettes, their tips placed alternately one to the inside, the next to the outside. There must have been a bare circular area immediately surrounding this gold band. Immediately beyond, the outer rim of the shield was decorated with a circular ivory border of extraordinary artistic merit. Its main theme consisted of a relatively broad band with a complex meander motif alternating with swastikas and squares. Inside, these squares had a very thin silver sheet while the four which marked the top and bottom of the shield and its two horizontal extremes were decorated with a gold star, the familiar emblem of the Macedonian dynasty. Thinner sheets of silver covered all the other empty spaces (that is, the background of the meander theme). Lastly, all the silvered parts were covered by thin transparent pieces of glass.

This broad band was bordered by two narrower bands, which delimited its inner and outer edge; their decoration consisted of spiral meanders in whose empty spaces were gold sheets covered by transparent glass. Lastly, the outermost circle of the shield, the rim, was encircled by a tongue pattern executed in very light relief in gold (like the edge of the central circle). The leather folded back against this edge of the decorative circle thus forming its own protection against destruction by rubbing.

The inner side of the shield was also unusually decorated with gilded silver sheets. At the centre was an almost square sheet with four additional sheets attached to its four sides; the two which lie on the vertical axis are large and trapezoidal in shape; on these is a relief scene with two lions placed heraldically. To the edges of each of the four sheets was attached an oblong sheet which ended in a palmette, embellished with a relief winged Victory in flight holding in her hands a ribbon with which to crown the victor. These elongated sheets formed a cross. The ends of four narrow bows were fixed to the bases of the palmettes, thus forming a circle and delimiting the inner curve of the shield. In the central square sheet two bronze pins have survived, which secured the shield grip which was certainly of leather. Another very narrow sheet, elliptically shaped (broader at the centre), with holes at the ends which show that it must have been attached somewhere, must have covered the leather grip, by which the shield could be held.

Eight ivy leaves were found scattered amongst the remaining fragments together with eight circular little "shield-bosses" with a ring at the centre (all were silver gilt). It is almost certain that, in pairs, they decorated the four sections of the shield formed by the sheets placed cross-wise. Coloured ribbons probably hung from the rings of the little "shield-bosses" as we see on depictions of shields on vases.

Lastly, one more small rectangular sheet (0.06 × 0.04 m.) with a relief depiction of a club was found. This must certainly have been attached to the interior of the shield at some point. It repre-

95-96. → The iron cuirass from "Philip's Tomb". This unique breastplate was hinged at the sides and on the shoulders; it was lined with cloth and leather. There were leather flaps on the lower edge covered with gold platelets. The gold decoration, on each side, is impressive. The shape of the cuirass worn by Alexander the Great in the famous mosaic from Pompeii is absolutely identical.

sents the royal emblem, the club of Heracles, mythical forebear of the royal family of Macedonia.

It is superfluous to add that this shield was the most unexpected find and quite unparalleled. Archaeology has so far offered us nothing comparable. Only poetic fantasy soars to description of such magnificent works – Homer of the Hephaistean shield of Achilles, the author of *The Shield* which has been handed down to us as Hesiod's work, of the shield of Heracles. Nevertheless, the existence of such rare creations, intended for especially cultivated people, is borne out by Athenaios, that invaluable treasure house of miscellaneous information. In his *Deipnosophists* (XII, 534e) recording various wonders about Alcibiades, he added;

"and even when he was a general he wanted to be a dandy still; he carried, for example, a shield made of gold and ivory on which there was the device of Eros with a thunderbolt poised like a javelin."

I do not think it is necessary to amass arguments which would justify the characterization of this shield as "ceremonial". It is obvious that this exceptionally delicate work had itself a need for protection, and was completely unsuitable to ward off the blows of battle. The reflection from the gold surface, the glass and the white surface of the ivory would certainly have astounded whoever had to face it, but its owner would have known his need for a less magnificent but more serviceable shield for his protection. (The remains of such a shield were found alongside the fragments of the former.)

I believe that the existence of this shield alone must lead us to the conclusion that the tomb was that of a king. I would even make so bold as to add; to a king who had a special love and affection for his weapons and their shining appearance. And the last man who could conceivably have had in his lifetime, or in his grave, this outstanding shield was the peaceable and intellectually backward Philip Arrhidaios (see below).

97-98. The Macedonian helmet from "Philip's Tomb". The tall crest is typical. A relief head of Athena, protective deity of the Macedonians, decorates the forehead. The cheek pieces bear laminated decoration. We must imagine that, like a helmet we know about which belonged to Alexander, it had a polished surface, the colour of silver.

97

THE WEAPONS

It is not only the "ceremonial" shield which assures us that the dead man was a warrior in life who not only needed his weapons but who loved their beauty. The entire panoply which accompanied him to the grave contained works of unusual elegance and artistry. The "real" shield, the cuirass, the helmet, the sword, the spears and the greaves all bear witness to an extraordinarily rare quality.

The cuirass

The cuirass is perhaps the most outstanding. It is the only cuirass of this type to have survived from antiquity and the only iron cuirass older than the Hellenistic period; it is certainly the only example to have such brilliant gold decoration. As it is today

the iron plates and the gold decoration have survived; at several points on the inside the remains of leather are clear and there are even traces of cloth. It is therefore certain that the inside was lined with these materials. A similar covering may have existed on the outer surfaces, although deep oxidization has obliterated all traces. Treatment in the laboratories of the National Archaeological Museum and gamma ray photography have enabled us to make certain both of its shape and of its technical details which are invisible below the oxidization.

As one might imagine, the cuirass is made up in sections, hinged together by means of small tubular projections on either side of the parts to be joined, through which passed a separate pin. The body of the cuirass is made up of four sheets, one covering the chest, one on either side and one over the back; a fifth section which however consisted of only a metal border and which must have been covered with cloth and leather was found on the underside of the part which covered the chest. The shoulder pieces were each made up in two sections and thus had a double joint, one at the top of the shoulder to the sheet covering the back, and the second to the front plate. There was therefore a total of eight joints so that in practice the cuirass could open out flat; it is obvious how practical this was both when the warrior had to gird himself for battle and then when he was in action since its many joints left the fighter free to move in any way he needed. A leather piece was attached to the lower edge which has left traces on the oxidized edge of the iron. One part of it, found on the floor, we managed to save. Lastly there were the flaps at the bottom, probably of leather sheathed in gold; fifty-eight oblong gold sheets, each decorated with three palmettes, were found. As the reader may see in the photograph the edges of all the iron plates are decorated with a narrow strip of gold, itself decorated with a relief lesbian cymation. A wider band of gold sheeting with a double lesbian cymation, placed in opposite directions, passed across all four parts about one third of the way up from the lower edge. Gold lion heads provided the finishing touch to the glittering gold decoration; six on the front side and two on the left side. Gold rings which passed through the mouth of the lion heads were used to fasten the shoulder pieces and the front to the side plates. Through them passed leather thongs tightly tied as

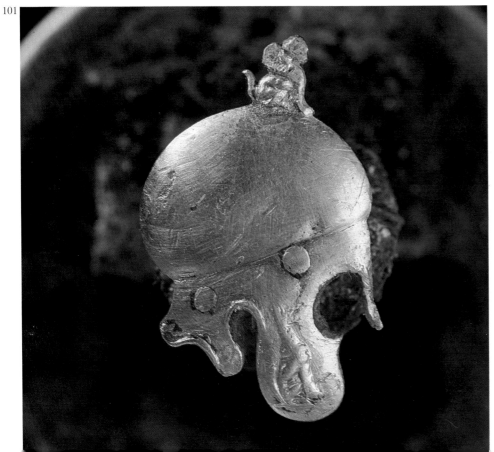

99-101. The large sword from "Philip's Tomb". It was found in its scabbard from which only the ivory parts, the bottom and the hilt survived. The hilt of the iron sword bore shining gold decoration. A miniature gold helmet (101) was attached to the upper circular surface of the hilt. The decoration of such a minute object – a sphinx at the top, a lion on the cheekpieces – is breathtaking.

we may see from the similar type of cuirass worn by Alexander in the Naples mosaic. Lastly, there was a small square gold sheet with a relief depiction of Athena on the right, the unprotected side. I should add that the formation of the curve of the back is amongst the most admirable features of the whole piece, while the care taken to protect the nape of the neck by the elongation of the back piece is specially noteworthy. If this cuirass invites our wonder even in its present state, it is not difficult to imagine its splendour when the glitter of the gold was complemented by the brilliance of the silver

102. Three of the iron spear heads from "Philip's Tomb". It should be noted that each of those found has its own shape and has been fashioned with exceptional care. It is no exaggeration to describe these weapons as outstanding works of art.

sheen of the gleaming iron and the polished surface of the leather. We are now in a better position to understand why the Cypriots considered that the two iron cuirasses which they brought as a gift to Demetrios Poliorcetes would be something which this king, famous for the elegance and ostentation of his attire, would particularly appreciate.

The helmet

The iron helmet is no less magnificent; it is the first and only Macedonian helmet to have come down to us. Indeed it is not just chance that up to now no other iron helmet has been found, but it is certainly due to the fact that such a helmet was exceptionally rare. We may deduce this without trouble from a revealing line in Plutarch's *Life of Alexander*. Recounting the story of the battle of Gaugamela he judged it worth noting that Alexander wore an iron helmet which glittered like silver; he added that it was "a work of Theophilos", i.e. the creation of some renowned craftsman.

Gamma rays show that it is made up of smaller parts which were hammered into their curved shapes and then put together. We may say with certainty that there was even a leather lining on the inside which has left a few, but unmistakeable traces. The two cheek pieces, whose entire surfaces bore laminated decoration, were joined to the main body, while on their lower sections there was a small ring. A leather thong will have passed through this ring and both thongs will have been tied under the chin, thereby holding both the cheek pieces fast against the skin and the helmet firmly on the head. The lower edge of the forehead of the helmet was decorated by a low ridge, originating in a spiral over the ears (in imitation of a band) while right at the centre of the base of the crest is a relief head of Athena, the protective deity of the Macedonians. But the most impressive feature of the helmet is the peculiar high crest with its high griffin-like termination.

The sword

The same high quality and restrained luxury are to be discerned in the sword; its handle was preserved reasonably well although the entire length of the blade had suffered heavy corrosion. It is certain

144

that it had been placed in the tomb in its wooden scabbard which has decomposed, leaving only streaks on the oxidized iron. However, the top and bottom edge of the scabbard were decorated with ivory, large sections of which survive. The hilt of the sword was decorated in gold; the spine of the horizontal arms of the hilt was encased in a gold sheet held in place by a gold nail which pierced the iron. From the centre of this sheet, on both sides, sprang a thin rod whose tall stem rose towards the pommel where it blossomed into a delicate palmette. The upper edge of the handle was encircled decoratively either by ivory or, more probably, by a precious wood which has been lost. Two gold rings decorated the base and the upper end of this part. But the most unexpected and elegant decoration was at the top of the handle where the iron shaft narrowed and ended in a nail-like point. This was covered by a miniature helmet no larger than 1.5 cms. and yet, crowning the helmet is a sphinx; the craftsman showed the wings by engraving the feathers and decorated the cheek pieces by engraving the figure of a lion. Thus this unimportant decorative feature was transformed into a marvellous miniature work of art in its own right, to which nothing comparable exists, at least as far as I know.

As we have seen, there was a second sword besides the first one on the couch – smaller, also of iron, which suffered much greater damage from oxidization.

Two iron swords found not in the funerary chamber but above the tomb amongst the sun-dried bricks also belonged to the armour of the dead man. Only their blades were preserved in good condition because they had been placed on the pyre and the heat apparently toughened the iron. Their hilts, wooden or ivory, were missing. It is worth noting that on the upper part there was a small projection from the same sheet as the sword in the shape of a palmette; it certainly decorated the hilt.

Spears

In the southwest area of the chamber six iron spearheads and one spear butt were found. Each of these was a different shape and size from the others; the smallest was 0.332 m. high, the largest 0.553 m. We might postulate that the largest came from a sarissa and the smallest from a javelin, the rest from normal spears. However, not only must such a hypothesis remain non-proven, but it might even be incorrect as certain other facts lead us to conclude (for example the diameter of the socket, the cylindrical hollow into which the wooden shaft fitted). Leaving detailed examination aside, for it has no place in this general account, I shall confine myself to the observation that probably these spearheads do in fact belong to the three types of offensive weapon we have mentioned, without proceeding to make any more definite attributions. There are

103. One of the three pairs of bronze greaves found in "Philip's Tomb". The greaves, except for the gilded pair, were the least impressive of all the weapons, offensive or defensive, found in the tomb. A bit of leather, which must certainly have been from a lining for the inside, was preserved on one pair.

103

145

three important facts a) the large number; b) the exceptional artistic quality; c) the magnificent shape which in at least two instances allows us to regard them as works of a very high standard.

The removal of the oxidization on one of the spearheads revealed the original surface, on which there were small, very well-designed engravings; it had a silvery colour and a texture identical with that of modern steel. All these spearheads gleamed like silver; each had its individual outline; the central

104-105. The silver vessels for the banquet found in "Philip's Tomb" are distinguished by their exceptional quality. This bucket, with its elegant handles, was certainly used as a wine container. Its "mouth" shaped like a lion's head, was most suitably adjusted to its use. The moulding of the lion head is perfect.

104

spine and various finishings of the surface gave each its own moulded shape; the gracefully executed shape of at least the two biggest testifies to artistic ability as also to the happy result of the craftsman's labour. It is thus easy to arrive at the justifiable conclusion that these weapons, like all the others, are not only examples of the most perfect weaponry which the warrior-king could command, but also true works of art. They thus contribute to our knowledge of the technological and the artistic level both of the men who created them and of those who used them.

The greaves

The sole bronze objects amongst the armour found in the chamber were three pairs of greaves. These, perhaps the most common piece of armour, were not made with any special care and were not distinguished by any particular stylistic or artistic merits. Had we not found a pair of gilded greaves in the antechamber (see below) the breath-taking overall picture of the royal panoply with its matchless shield, the splendid cuirass and helmet contrasting with the almost carelessly made greaves would have been difficult to explain. I doubt very much if, except on the battlefield, the dead king would ever have worn any of the three pairs of greaves; and in battle, mounted as he would have been, he might well have felt more at ease wearing high, stout leggings (such as those we may see worn by the mature rider in the wall painting of the hunt) rather than the greaves where the bronze sheathing would have chafed the rider's shins. For his official appearances in peacetime, the answer is given by the gilded greaves from the antechamber (and the similar ones from the "Prince's tomb", see below).

VESSELS

Vessels for a banquet

We noted earlier that these vessels were found heaped against the north wall of the tomb. We suggested that they may have been placed on a wooden table in front of the couch. Together, they made up a group of vessels used at banquets; nevertheless it is worth observing that almost all were made to hold liquids (wine, of course) and only one bronze and four small clay vessels can have served

106

107

108

106-111. Six silver vessels for the banquet found in "Philip's Tomb". Two kylixes (106-107); two skyphoi (109-110); and a crater (111). The elegance of the shapes and the exceptionally careful technique used in their construction marks them off from all the vessels of the same type known up to now. The strainer is especially graceful and particular care has been taken over its shape and style; the gilding which decorates the braids on the flange of the lip enhances the overall picture by adding colour. There is an inscription on the undersurface of the flange – MAXATA – the genitive of the Macedonian name Machatas. We know that Philip had a brother in law of that name.

148

any other purpose; the absence of vessels suitable for food (for example a fish dish like that found in the "Prince's tomb") is certainly strange. Twenty of these vessels are silver, six clay and two bronze. Many of the silver are pairs; thus we have two kantharoi, two pairs of stemless kylixes, two "amphora" and two oinochoe (to which we should add one of bronze identical in shape and size and another of clay). Of the rest, three are large – the situla (bucket), the "crater" and a deep "phiale" of individual shape and five smaller ones, a skyphos, a small jug, a strainer, a spoon and a ladle. There is no need to dwell on the use of most of them. The kalyxes, the kylixes, the kantharoi and the "skyphos" were drinking vessels. Their small size confirms our information from Athenaios (*Deipnosophists*, XI, 461a-d) derived from older texts that "the ancients" used small *"ekpomata"* and one would find large vessels amongst the barbarians and despots, a custom which was later adopted by the Greeks. Two of them contained wine, unadulterated or mixed with water; it would have been ladled out with the ladle or the small jug and decanted into the oinochoe to be poured into the *"ekpomata"* (that is the cups from which it was supped). The large "phiale", uniquely shaped, (I know of nothing similar) must also have been for drinking wine; more possibly, it was for the use of some hard drinker who got bored emptying the dainty little vessels designed for more restrained and dignified drinking. The strainer, placed either against the top of the "cups" or more probably of the oinochoe, filtered the residue of sediment which the wine might contain so that no disgust should be generated amongst the assembly.

There is a difficulty attached to the two long, narrow amphora. As far as I know, their shape is unique; the existence of a lid shows that the liquid they contained needed protection or, at least, was not to be exposed to air. Their presence amongst the other vessels for a banquet forces one to accept that these vessels also held alchohol. Their individual shape suggests to me that they were designed to hold some special drink, difficult to obtain and not in plentiful supply. I do not regard the suggestion that these transported a rare wine to the banquets as out of place. It might have been an aromatic wine drunk in small quantity or one that was mixed with another to achieve a smoother taste and bouquet.

109

110

111

112

113

Before any definitive or correct conclusions can be drawn about the way in which these vessels were made they will need careful study. At this point I can say reasonably certainly that the silver vessels were fashioned out of hammered silver sheets and that a wheel was employed for the moulding of the shape. Clear traces of a wheel can be seen on their surfaces. Some parts, such as the bases and the handles, were made separately and were later stuck to the body. That some kind of organic matter must have been used to stick the two together I regard as certain, for all the separately made parts were found detached from, and scattered around, the vessels, for this organic substance had decomposed and lost its adhesive property.

The vessels from "Philip's tomb" at Vergina make up one of the three large groups of silver vessels found recently in Macedonia. The first group is that from tomb B at Derveni (the same tomb as the large relief crater) and the third was that found subsequently in another unplundered tomb at Vergina (the "Prince's tomb"). All three groups date to the third quarter of the fourth century BC (350-325 BC) and thus furnish us with the richest collection of silver vessels of the fourth century known to date. Comparing the twenty vessels from "Philip's tomb" with the others in the Museum of Thessalonike and with all the known contemporary vessels from other groups, we are struck by the outstanding excellence of their quality. The shapes of the vessels, and even more their decoration, testify that they were works constructed with exceptional meticulousness inspired by skill of the highest order. If the hallmark of every true work of art is to be unique, then we may see this in a wholly objective fashion in all the paired vessels. Not only are their decorative elements not absolutely identical with each other, but even the dimensions of the same pair are slightly different. It is perhaps superfluous to refer to the gracefulness of the shape and the handles of the

112-114. This pair of kalyxes was amongst the most exquisite silver vessels from "Philip's Tomb". The tasteful decoration the outside of the body was complemented by delicate gilding. A medallion with a relief head of a Silen embellished the base inside one of them; the moulded rendering of the facial features emphasized by careful gilding produces a marvellous impression of Bacchic euphoria.

150

four kylixes or of the single ladle. The shape and decoration of the "strainer" when compared with the other examples, and especially with that of Derveni which is the best made, far outstrips them all in tasteful artistry. The delicately gilded braided swags on the flange together with the plant decoration on the surface of the handles reveals the sensitivity and care of an unusual craftsman; this is borne out by the exceptionally aesthetic shape of the whirling rosette formed by the very carefully placed open holes in the bowl. (I shall discuss the inscription which exists on the under surface of the flange later).

However, the craftsman's creativity and his very high standards become even clearer and more impressive in the relief heads which decorate the bases of the handles or the inside of some vessels. The bases of the handles and the interior of one of the two kalyxes are embellished with such heads. Finally, we should mention here the lion head spout of the situla.

At the base of the smaller amphora are two small heads of Pan. The god, charmingly youthful, tiny horns above his forehead, hair spread in short curls, laughing and happy, is more of an agreeable dionysiac figure than one akin to his panic-provoking ugly ancestor to whom he bears little resemblance. The iconography of fourth century art was already stocked with these humanized beings who, from their mis-shaped daemoniac form retained only as much as was necessary for their recognition – in this case, the horns.

The bases of the handles of the other amphora were decorated with the figure of Heracles. The mythical forebear of the Macedonian kings is depicted as young and handsome; his unwrinkled face is shown full-front within the rich lion skin which encircles it; the whole mane of the lion-head spreads out impressively round the youthful face while below the chin the skin of the fore-paws is tied in the "knot of Heracles". Only rarely has the lion's skin round the face of Heracles been so completely and so impressively depicted in Greek art; the lion's snout is at the vertical extension of the hero's nose; the eyes, the ears but especially the richly ordered mane of the noble beast surrounding the hero's face form the most suitable framework, a lion-crown, vigorous symbol of the attributes of the demi-god. The severe profile is under-scored by the definite vertical line of the nose and even more by

the wide open fearsome eyes which fix the viewer. The closest parallel I know is the depiction of the same hero on coins of Alexander, except that on these the side view cannot convey either the intensity or the fullness of this frontal view. The many small differences between the two heads are worth noting, because they are undeniable evidence that

115-116. One of the two silver oinochoe from "Philip's Tomb". In addition to the delicate decoration on the lip and the handle both oinochoe were embellished by heads of Silens; the sculptural finish of each face possesses a direct tangibility and exactness both in the rendering of the flesh and in the hirsute parts which characterize the figure.

116

117

118

154

117-120. Two silver "amphorae" from "Philip's Tomb". This vase with its well fitting lid is not a common shape and may have contained an aromatic wine of high quality. The relief heads which decorate the lower attachment of the handles are excellent examples of Greek toreutic art of the fourth century BC. The smaller amphora is decorated with heads of Pan; the youthful, enchanting god is shown as a rather agreeable dionysiac figure and bears little resemblance to his ugly forebear who provoked panic. The larger amphora bore heads of Heracles. The legendary ancestor of the Macedonian kings is depicted as a handsome youth, the "halo" of a lionskin spread impressively over his head and tied in the "knot of Heracles" under his chin.

they did not result from the mechanical use of the same mould.

Though in all these creations of miniature toreutic art the high standards and dexterity of the craftsman is clear, the figures of Silens which decorate the two oinochoe allow us to class them as rare examples of Greek modelling at a high point in its history. I do not think that I am far from the truth if I say that these two Silen heads must have been sketched by a great artist and executed either by him or under his supervision in his workshop. The sculptural detail of the faces renders both the flesh and even more specially the hirsute parts which characterize the figure with a unique precision and accuracy. The thick, flowing moustache droops to interlace with the smaller wavy curls of the beard which frames the greater part of the face. The engraving of this part with the ceaseless unbroken movement of the relief curve succeeds in creating the impression of a disordered and carelessly-trimmed beard on this non-human figure, and yet it is carefully integrated into the disciplined frame required by every work of art. The upper part of the hairless surface, fleshy over the cheeks, stretched over the balding pate, the nose a bridge between them, creates a single illuminated surface in strong contrast to the shadows of the lower part. Between the two goat's ears the eyes under the shaggy brows draw the viewer's attention to that which they are looking at with the unexpectedly deep gaze.

I know of no other Silen with such a total concentration on the inseparable mixture of beast and human. Socratic introspection and bestial sensuality, reflective man and scarcely suppressed lust after carnal indulgence are rarely to be read so clearly as in the eyes of these two Silen-philosophers.

It is obvious that the roots of these two figures lie deep in the classical tradition and that they have not been tainted by the violent currents of the world which would give birth to the new art – that which would be called Hellenistic. Their entire structure, though it betrays greater elasticity and shaping, something more flowing and simultaneously more fragile, nevertheless has not lost solidity or com-

121-122. The two pottery vessels from "Philip's Tomb", the black-painted oinochoe and the red-figure askos. Both come from an Attic workshop. When they were placed in the tomb they had not been used, for the under surface of their bases is completely unrubbed.

position, the referral of its parts to an indivisible whole and a cohesive core. I think therefore that it would be neither exaggerated nor far-fetched if one ventured to formulate the view that the true ancestors of the Silens of Vergina are some of the Centaurs to be found on the metopes of the Parthenon made by Pheidias; perhaps amongst those which caused one of the most perceptive archaeologists of our time, E. Buschor, to seek the true portrait of Pheidias in their faces and one of his peers, Christos Karouzos, to claim them as parallels to the creations of Michelangelo. Certainly these creations must lie artistically much closer to the portrait of Socrates than to the indifferent Roman copies which have come down to us.

Though the spirit of expression is other, the same quality and standard is attained in the Silen who decorates the inside of one of the two kalyxes; (the medallion of the second was not found, but it is very unlikely that it was not also decorated; it must have come unstuck before the vessel was placed in the tomb). The gold-red tint of the hair and the wreath which crowns it – the curving ends of the skin which covers the head – with the curious play of light over the silver parts, is the first time the expression on the face of a Silen is shown in gilding, studied and skilful. However, the fundamental formulation is concentrated in the moulded execution of the facial features, lips, nose, forehead and above all the eyes

in which the instinctive sensuality focusses and from which the bacchic euphoria of intoxication is reflected.

However, irrespective of their artistic importance, these silver vases (together with the twenty-nine found in tomb III (see next section) offer us more valuable evidence both for technique and, more generally, for Greek metal-working. A full exploration of the topic is precluded by the nature of this book, but it demands especially careful and exhaustive study of the material which so far has not been possible. It is, however, useful to present some information here, even if, of necessity, the final sifting and scrutiny of the conclusions has not yet come to an end. In particular, I wish to discuss the inscriptions which exist on a number of the silver vases.

On the under surface of the lip of the strainer is the inscription MAXATA △△△△ ⊦ The second part, △△△△⊦, signifies the number, 41. We know that the ancient Greeks weighed objects of precious metal (gold, silver) against the drachma as a

123. This vessel in the shape of a frying-pan, a patera, was found in "Philip's Tomb" alongside other vessels for the banquet. Other similar objects have been found in tombs in Macedonia, but we are not certain what purpose they served. They may have contained food, but it is perhaps more probable that they held hot water to rinse the hands.

123

124. With the silver vessels for the banquet in "Philip's Tomb" was this bronze oinochoe. Though the material is not precious this does not deprive the object of any of its artistic merit. Its shape, and even more the excellent decoration, are the equal of the finest silver vessels. The female head, probably of medusa, retains the severely classical structure.

124

unit of weight; we also know that such records of weight exist on other silver vases. We may therefore infer that the indication 41 denotes the weight of the strainer, which weighs 171.45 grammes, that is 4.18 gr. the drachma. The first word must be the genitive of the known Macedonian name Machatas; it could refer either to the name of the craftsman or to that of the owner. I think it is more probably that of the owner. We know of a historic personage at this time within the circle of the Macedonian court; the brother in law of Philip II by his (?) second wife, Phila. On the base of the situla there is the incised combination $A\!\!\!\wedge\!\!v$ and on one edge of the handle the letter A. I have not yet succeeded in finding any satisfactory interpretation for the cluster $A\!\!\!\wedge\!\!v$ (which is incised whereas all the other inscriptions are formed by dots); I think it is possible that the letter A may be a mark made by the craftsman to ensure the placing of the handle in its correct position, that is on the main face (where there is also the lion head spout). No interpretation has been found for the two letters on the outer surface of the bottom of the small crater, ΣI, or for the three letters EPB on the outer surface of the base of one of the kylixes.

The letters on the lip of the two kalyxes and on the external surface of the base of the two kylixes are of special interest. On the former we may read φ B – and φ $\Delta = -$ and on the latter $\Xi B = -$ and $\Xi\Gamma = -$. On the alphabetic system of numeration the first gives the numbers 92 and 94 and the second 62 and 63 (I refer only to the letters). In Greek inscriptions horizontal lines usually represent marks indicating fractions (an obol or fractions of an obol). Given that recording the weight of a vessel in drachmae is not an unusual occurrence (we also have the example of the strainer) and interpreting the horizontal incisions as some fraction, we might think that we had a true record of the weight in drachmae. If we examine these figures (omitting ambivalent horizontal lines) it emerges that the probable unit of weight for the kalyxes must have been the equivalent of approximately 2.08 grammes (to be absolutely exact 2.0819 gr. for the kalyxes) inscribed φ $\Delta = -$ (=94) and 2.0891 gr. for that inscribed φ B $= -$ (=92); the total weight of the first today is 195.7 gr. and of the second 192.2 gr. Unfortunately I do not know of such a unit of weight for the ancient drachma. This particular unit does not match with the weight of the two kylixes, the first of which weighs 266.2 gr. and is inscribed ΞΒ =- (= 62) which gives us 4.29 gr. and the second 269.8 gr. and the inscription ΞΓ =- (=63) giving a unit of 4.28 gr.; this at least falls within the limits of the weight of a silver drachma of the fourth century BC (which is around 4.30 gr.). It would be curious if different units of weight were used for measurement although on the other hand it cannot be coincidental that the unit of measurement for the same shape is almost identical (2.08, 2.09 gr. for the kalyxes, 4.28, 4.29 gr. for the kylixes). The use of alphabetic numeration creates a difficulty for this interpretation, since it is not the usual system for recording numbers in the fourth century BC (we do have the striking example of the strainer inscribed ΔΔΔΔ⊢ representing the number 41).

An alternative interpretation might be that the figures corresponded to some catalogue of the vessels; the coincidence that the numbers are continuous – 92, 94 and 62,63 – would strengthen this suggestion. But this view leaves the horizontal lines which follow the numbers unexplained, which must now indicate something else which escapes us. Thus, at least for the moment, a flaw remains in providing any acceptable interpretation of these letters.

Four of the clay vases are small, with a shiny black surface; their shape is that known to the archaeologist as "salt-cellars". Their use is uncertain; the most probable is that the ancients placed what they termed condiments – vinegar, silphium, cumin etc. – in the hollow bowl. The other two vases are an oinochoe, with a plain black surface and an askos with some red figure decoration. The pottery oinochoe completes the group of silver vessels. That it should be amongst the vessels for the banquet is not strange, although it is less easy to understand why this inexpensive and simple item should have been placed alongside the valuable vessels. Greater doubt is raised by the askos, the peculiarly-shaped but commonly found vase which we know was used to contain oil. We may account for its presence in the group if we recall that those attending a banquet first washed their feet and then anointed them with perfume. Hence a vase for aromatic oil finds its place amongst the other vessels required for a banquet. Finally it is worth noting that all the pottery vases seem to have been unused when they were placed in the tomb; the

bottom of the oinochoe and the askos for example are completely unrubbed.

A bronze oinochoe complements the pair of silver ones; its measurements are roughly the same and it was made with at least as much care. It too bears very delicate decoration on the lip and on the external surface of the handle, while on its lower attachment the severe beautiful head of Medusa rivals the heads of the Silens in sculptured perfection. It too still retains the chunky solid shape of the classical tradition not yet overturned by the exuberance of the new age.

We do not know to what use the bronze patera, the frying-pan shaped object, was put; it was found with the other vessels for the banquet. Similarly shaped objects, usually of bronze, have been found in other Macedonian tombs; in the "Prince's tomb" (tomb III) there was a similar one in silver. The long handle which terminates in a ram's head is

125. The iron tripod from "Philip's tomb" is a rarely found example of its kind. It was designed to be placed in the fire to support the bronze cauldron in which water for a bath was heated.

125

typical; this implies that its usage required it. We may suggest that it served either to hold food or to hold hot water for the washing of hands during the banquet, although neither explanation seems to me to be very convincing; certainly there is nothing to support either.

One general comment on all the vessels for the banquet is that, with the exception of the pottery items, they were not unused when they were placed in the tomb, but had been the property of the dead man and had been used by him in this world before they accompanied him to the next.

Vessels for the bath

As I noted in the description of the finds bronze vessels and the weapons of the deceased had been placed in the southwest corner of the chamber. I think that most of the bronze vessels and the iron tripod were there for the same purpose, the "care" of the body as the ancients would have expressed it. They are the vessels used for washing. The tripod held the cauldron when the water was heating, the situla (bucket) was for the transport of water, the jug to empty it from one container to fill another, the four "phiale" to shower the whole body and lastly the basin for rinsing off. To these should be added the sponge which we know the ancients employed in the same way as we do ourselves for washing the body.

The iron tripod was preserved in very good condition and is almost perfect (only the terminals of two of the three rods over the crown which supported the cauldron are missing). Its shape is very simple, as its use demanded, and there is no attempt at any particular embellishment; it is purely and simply an object to be put in the fire, on which the cauldron containing the water was balanced. Indeed the bronze cauldron was found above the tripod; it had slipped and lay on one side which was certainly not its original position when it was first deposited in the tomb; it is virtually certain that it was placed as though it were in actual use (see the photograph). This cauldron, 0.37 m. high and maximum diameter 0.41 m., was furnished with two circular ring handles opposite each other on the shoulder for its safe positioning above, and removal from, the fire. The handles were suspended within the ring formed by the neck and the

beaks of two ducks with open wings attached to the body of the cauldron with nails. Although this vessel was intended for practical use, a great deal of care was taken over both its shape and the tasteful decoration of the handles; on the other side the shape of the spout which had a diameter of 0.26 m. (that is 0.15 m. smaller than the belly) was the most suitable for its purpose, wide enough to pour the boiling water easily and as narrow as was feasible so that the exposed area of dangerous steam was restricted.

The bronze situla in which the water was transported was found on the floor, tipped over on one side. In front of its mouth was a fairly large sponge which was preserved in relatively good condition. We know from ancient sources, even as early as Homer, that the sponge was used for washing the body, but I personally know of no other example where an archaeological find bears out in such convincing fashion what we learn from the texts. The situla, like the cauldron, was well made and survives in very good condition although dents can be discerned both on the circumference of the base and below the lip. It is also noteworthy that the thickness of the lip was double that of the rest of the body; this was certainly contrived for reasons of safety since the carefully executed handle was suspended from the lip by means of the two ring handles. Next to the attachment of the handle on the side face of the lip is the letter Σ formed in small dots. The word ΣΙΚΩΝΟΣ was formed on the side face of the handle in the same way.

126. Bronze bucket from "Philip's Tomb", in which water could be transported. Its carefully constructed handle is remarkable; on the side is the incised inscription «ΣΙΚΩΝΟΣ»

127. Bronze basin. Its separate base, well-balanced handles, carefully designed curve of the neck and the thin lip make it one of the finest examples from Macedonia, where a nymber af basins, approximately contemporary with this one, have been found.

128. Bronze jug, squat, wide-bellied and narrow mouthed. Its elongated twisted handle made it possible to hold it firmly without danger of scalking from hot water and without fear that it would slip from wet hands.

129. Large bronze *phiale* used in bathing. Three smaller ones were found associated with it. Their shape and dimensions are reminiscent of the items later used in Turkish baths.

The most painstakingly executed and the most elegant of the vessels for the bath is undoubtedly the basin. With a separate base, the well balanced handles, the carefully designed curve of the neck and the thin lip it is the finest example of a basin we know of from Macedonia where a considerable number of examples roughly contemporary with that of Vergina have been found. The difference in quality which we noted between the silver vases of Vergina and those from other areas is immediately clear also in this example of a bronze product. The first and foremost contribution to the general artistic picture is the carefully calculated proportions of the measurements (height 0.211 m., diameter of the lip 0.412 m., diameter of the base 0.147 m.), but each delicate curve, one succeeding another to build up the outline, has its place.

The smaller vessels found near the larger ones are just as essential to the bath; the jug, the biggest phiale and the three smaller ones. The jug, small and squat, with a broad belly and narrow mouth has a tall twisted-rope handle so that there is a distance between the hand and the hot water and less risk that it slipped from wet hands. The difference from the shape of the graceful oinochoe shows what effect the function of the vessel exerted over its shape. I believe that the four phiale were used for bathing; indeed the shape and the dimensions (height $\pm$ 0.05 m. diameter $\pm$ 0.17 m.) of the three smaller ones recall the similar vessels which were used until recently in Greece and other countries of the East in the Turkish baths *(hamam)* which are probably the descendant of the Roman baths. The water from the bucket may have been emptied into the largest (height $\pm$ 0.15 m., diameter $\pm$ 0.32 m.) via the jug and then emptied into the smallest so that the body could be wetted all over.

Four unrelated bronze items

In the preceding section we mentioned three other bronze items amongst those found in the southwest

130-131. Bronze lampstand, one of the finest and most valuable objects found in "Philip's tomb". The opening in the upper part was covered by a circular lid; double circular handles made it easy to carry or to hang up. Below the attachment is a magnificent head of Pan (131). Inside, an iron support to hold a clay lamp was attached to the base.

132. Bronze torch; an iron extension is attached to the lower part, into which fitted the wooden shaft by which it was borne aloft by the torch-bearer who walked in front of the king in procession.

133-134. Bronze tripod; the inscription on its rim (134) shows that it was a prize won in the Heraia games held at Argos. The shape of the letters and of the lion's feet suggest that it should be dated around 430-420 BC.

corner of the chamber; a bronze object with perforations, a bronze tripod and a large bronze shield-shaped object. None can be classed within the preceding groupings (weapons, vessels for the banquet, vessels for the bath) except perhaps indirectly and even then not all. However, each in its different way if of interest; each is unique.

The first of these, the perforated object, is one of the most elegant and valuable found in the tomb. It is egg-shaped, a delicately curved outline narrowing towards the bottom where there is a separate circular base to which three legs with moulded lion feet are attached. The opening at the upper end is covered by a circular lid, while a moveable double handle on the shoulder allows it either to be carried or to be suspended. Below the attachment of the handle there is a relief head of Pan (one of the two heads is missing). For about two-thirds of its height from the base the entire body of the object is perforated with small holes (diameter 0.002 m.) arranged in straight parallel lines. On the shoulder the perforation has been executed in such a way as to leave solid surfaces which form spirals of tendrils from which sprout ivy leaves pointing alternately up and down. There is no perforation on the upper part of the body which is decorated with silver-plated triangles, their apex to the bottom. The height of the object is 0.305 m. and the maximum width 0.205 m.

A similar object was found in a fourth century BC tomb at Derveni near Thessalonike; it was much simpler and more homely. At the time it was difficult to find an explanation for its use. However, the excellent example from Vergina gave us an immediate answer to our difficulty. A slightly curved iron base was attached to its bottom by an iron pin (0.03 m. high); the former held the clay lamp (which we also found). This object is therefore what the ancients termed a λυχνοῦχος (= lamp-holder) which up to now has been interpreted incorrectly as a lampstand (λυχνοστάτης). Its shape and position next to the utensils for the bath allow us to suggest that it may have been useful there too, to protect the flame of the lamp from the water which was likely to splash onto it.

The shield-shaped object was found propped against the west wall of the chamber. As we mentioned elsewhere the remains of a chryselephantine shield were found in a heap on the ground behind it. This is a large object (diameter 0.91 m.) its external surface slightly convex flattening into a fairly wide flat rim at the circumference. Its shape is strongly reminiscent of a bronze shield, but it is absolutely certain that it is not a shield. Many factors could be adduced to exclude the possibility; one is sufficient, the absence of a handle. A second suggestion might be that it is a large basin for use with the other vessels we have seen for the bath; and to rule out this interpretation I think one observation suffices; the absence of handles. They would have been essential to assist its easy transport. The only possible interpretation which remains is that which I gave from the very first moment; it is a protective covering for the valuable and exceptionally delicate shield which had to be safeguarded against every chance and unexpected knock. Moreover, the position in which it was found testifies that this was its purpose in the funerary chamber; it is therefore logical to suppose that this was its function in this world too. Admittedly, I know of no comparable example, but then there is no example for comparison with the shield.

The bronze tripod is another find of particular importance. Its shape and use are not of course unknown. However, its presence amongst the other utensils for the bath is not entirely justified for, as we shall see immediately, this tripod serves no practical purpose. Its crown is 0.305 m. in diameter and is supported on three straight rods whose upper end forms the head of a duck and whose lower stands on the upper surface of lion's feet. The ends of other rods spring from the same surface to curve upwards, forming an arc and are also attached to the crown. It should be noted that one of the three straight rods is missing. Even the least initiated layman is immediately struck by the excellent rendering of the lion feet; the toes, the hair and especially the nails are stamped with a unique modelled finish and finesse. However, while appreciating their high artistic standard, the historian of ancient Greek art will also easily recognize their stylistic language as being much older than the middle of the fourth century BC and that the tripod is separated in time from all the other finds. This chronological comment is borne out by the inscription discovered on the crown when the oxidization was removed. The following phrase has been executed in dots;

ΠΑΡΗΕΡΑΣΑΡΓΕΙΑΣΕΜΙ ΤΟΝ ΑΓΕΘΛΟΝ
which means "I am from the games of the Argive

Hera". The letters are in the Argive style; the use of H (= h, aspirated) and of F (digamma), the writing of E instead of H and of O instead of Ω and finally the shape of every letter confirms that it was written before 410 BC. My original dating, to around the middle of the fifth century BC (450 BC) has been modified by a French colleague, Pierre Amandry, who suggests a date of around 430-420 BC by comparing it with a similar inscription on the lip of a cauldron found in Athens and which is now, along with other finds from the same tomb, in the British Museum. Almost the same inscription is to be read on three other bronze hydriae.

It is clear that all such bronze objects – hydria, cauldron, tripod – were prizes awarded to the victors in games held at Argos in honour of Hera and known as the Heraia (or as Ekatomboia). Thus the tripod which was found in the main chamber of the tomb at Vergina was won as a prize by some victor in these games at Argos somewhere between 450 and 425 BC. I think that the participation of a lowly Macedonian athlete in such an event is unlikely at this time. If, however, we reflect that the Macedonian royal family was proud of its Argive descent from the family of the Temenids to which Heracles himself belonged, and if we recall that later two Macedonian kings, Demetrios Poliorcetes and Philip V were *agonothetes* of these games, we may appreciate that the possibility that the victor who carried off the trophy was a Macedonian king is quite strong. Moreover, we know from Herodotus that Alexander I, who ruled Macedonia from 479 to 454 BC himself took part in the Olympic Games. Thus the presence of the tripod in the chamber of the royal tomb means that it was deposited there because it was a valuable family heirloom, a fitting tribute to a worthy scion of the house.

Close to the west wall of the chamber, a little to the north of the marble sarcophagus, one more unique bronze object was found. This is an open cylinder, 0.304 m. in length and 0.0705 m. in diameter; to one end an iron rod was attached. This formed a conical pipe (0.261 m. long), into which a wooden rod could be fitted. The cylindrical shaft

135. The large gold larnax which was found inside the marble sarcophagus in the main chamber of "Philip's Tomb". On its lid is the sixteen-pointed Macedonian star; each side is richly decorated.

has two bands at each end and one in the middle bearing relief decoration of spirals and small circles. When it was found traces of smoke were preserved inside the cylinder which means that some kind of burning had taken place. It is easy for anyone to suggest that this is a torch which by means of a long rod could be raised high above the "torchbearer". Beyond the iron pipe traces of disintegrated wood and fragments of very fine gold leaf were seen on the floor; I imagine that these came from the wooden rod belonging to the torch which would have been gilded. As we have no other example of a torch from a tomb it is not possible for us to know what purpose it served. However, a piece of information from Xenophon is relevant (*Constitution of the Lacedaemonians*, 13.2). He tells us that before the king of Sparta set out on campaign he made a sacrifice at the temple of Zeus and the "firebearer" who went at the head of the army to the frontiers of the kingdom lit his brand from the altar. There, there was a second sacrifice to Zeus and to Athena; after which the army crossed the border and again, the torch, which was always ahead and which was never extinguished, was lit from the altar. This means that for the Spartans the torchbearer with his torch was a sacred symbol of war who stood alongside the king in the front line. If we consider how many common elements the institution of kingship in Macedonia shared with that of Sparta, it is not difficult to interpret the presence of a torch in the tomb of a Macedonian king who was also a great commander.

THE SARCOPHAGUS
AND THE GOLD LARNAX

As we said, the point of reference for all the grave goods was the marble sarcophagus which stands at the centre of the western end of the chamber. The sarcophagus is a solid almost square block 0.70 × 0.615 × (ht.) 0.595 m. out of which was hewn a suitable empty space in which the funerary larnax could sit. The sarcophagus was closed by a lid of the same marble (which measured 0.80 × 0.655 × 0.15 m.) Neither the main body nor the lid was particularly carefully hewn and one might say that the work betokens hasty execution.

The wealth and quality of the grave goods found in the chamber led us to think that the contents of

the sarcophagus must also be valuable, especially artistically, the more so since the vase which serves as an ossuary is the most important object in a burial. My own mind ran on the impressive crater from Derveni and I had visions of something similar, even though the dimensions of the sarcophagus showed that it would be much smaller. Nevertheless, the opening of the sarcophagus took us by surprise; we could never have dreamt of the sight which met our eyes or of what our fingers touched, since up to then nothing similar had been found. The sarcophagus housed a solid gold larnax. Its dimensions (0.409 × 0.341 × 0.17 m. plus the height of the feet ± 0.035 m. giving a total height of 0.205 m.) and its weight (7.790 gr.) alone were sufficient to induce us to believe that it was one of the most valuable finds from the ancient Greek world. Additionally, this unique larnax was clinching evidence for the view that we had already formed, namely that the tomb was royal. The contents, discovered when we opened it, were the final confirmation of this opinion.

The larnax is the same shape as comparable wooden boxes which we know of mainly from painted vases. It is emphasized by the addition of vertical bands which represent the four basic uprights of a wooden skeleton, thus retaining the ancient shape while at the same time endowing the larnax with a structural stability. The countless details of construction cannot be described within the bounds of this book. It suffices to say that the body of the larnax consists of two sheets bent at a right angle thus forming the four vertical sides. At the bottom a narrow ledge formed by the sheets supported the square sheet which formed the base and allowed it to be fastened in position by gold "nails". A fourth sheet, bent over at right angles on three sides formed the lid. This opened and closed by means of a hollow cylindrical tube on the back edge of the cover and two similar ones on the upper part of the rear side of the body into which fitted two identical narrower rods, like pins which terminated

136. The large gold larnax, its lid open, showing the reverse side of the star which decorated it. On the rear side of the cover and on the upper edge of the back sheet of the box there is a hollow circular tube into which a gold pin fitted, forming a hinge by which the box opened and closed. At the bottom the two lion's feet on which the larnax stood can be seen.

168

in shield-like ends resembling bosses.

The decoration of the larnax is rich, carefully thought-out, and delicately designed and executed. On the lid a narrow relief band makes a square border; in the middle of the enclosed area is a relief star with sixteen rays, eight smaller rays lying between eight larger. At the centre of the star is a circle with a relief surround within which is a double rosette with gold petals and a small gold globule at the centre. The petals of the inner rosette are filled with glass paste, rather like enamel. On the front surface and the two sides of the body the broad band of the base is covered by a wide flowing relief plant composition consisting of two symmetrical parts left and right of a central kalyx acanthus. This plant decoration unfolds with admirable simplicity, its succulent stems curving in twists and spirals from which sprout acanthus, flowers and lilies.

An upper band bears more restrained ornamentation of vertical palmettes and lotus blossom whose stem ends are twined into a continuously curved line. The raised band formed between the two strips is occupied by "enamelled" rosettes. Rosettes also embellish the vertical surface of the corner strengthening bands. The decorative scheme is completed by the relief lion-like feet at the four corners of the larnax. Lastly two bosses on the front side and two corresponding ones on the front edges of the cover served both a decorative and a functional purpose since they were used to shut the box.

It is superfluous to stress that, out of all proportion to the value of its material this unique larnax stands second to none as an example of the goldsmith's craft at a level we could not have imagined before its discovery. This immediately raises the question; was this object made solely for funerary use? If it was, then was it fashioned after the death of the deceased, and intended only for this purpose? The answers to these questions are far from easy and certainly cannot be based on incontrovertible evidence. I believe that it could have been made within a very short space of time by an experienced craftsman who had the gold sheets and the moulds for the decoration to hand. However, I think it is very probable that this valuable casket, like similar ones, formed part of the royal treasure; in it, the royal family may perhaps have kept jewels or other valuable objects. The four bosses on the

front made it possible to close it in some way, so preventing it from being opened surreptitiously. The fact that it was not so shut when it was placed in the tomb, (not that there was any need for it to be closed) does not exclude such a thought. However, I realize that this view, as every other view, is entirely subjective.

We knew that inside the larnax we would find the bones of the deceased; but it was impossible to have imagined what we actually saw when we opened it – the carefully placed burnt bones, perfectly clean, and in the left corner the two pieces of a very heavy wreath of oak leaves and acorns pressed against the bones. In the upper layer were the bones of the skull, many of which had a dark blue, almost aubergine, hue. Spots of the same colour could be seen on the base of the larnax (later, when we lifted the bones out, we saw that the colour spread over quite a large area). There is no doubt that the bones had been collected up after cremation with the utmost care. They had then been washed – in wine, of course – wrapped in an all-purple cloth and placed in the larnax. The cloth had disintegrated leaving only dye stains on the bones it had touched and on the base. For the first time we saw with our own eyes what the Homeric epics narrate about the two most ceremonial burials in the Trojan War; those of Achilles and of Hector. The burial of Achilles is recounted in the last book of the *Odyssey* (24.40 ff.) After the body had been burnt

"in the morning we gathered thy white bones, Achilles and laid them in unmixed wine and unguents"

The burial of Hector concludes the last book of the entire *Iliad* (24.788 ff.). When the fire was extinguished, his brethren and comrades

"gathered the white bones and placed them in a golden urn, covering them over with soft purple robes. . ."

The correspondence between the Homeric description and the archaeological discovery is incredible. The archaic structure of the Macedonian kingdom perhaps explains the similarity between Homeric customs and the royal tombs of Vergina. But this literal re-enactment of the heroic and mythical burial suggests that we are not witnessing common custom, but a deliberate imitation of the Homeric description in every detail. From this it is an easy step to associate this with Alexander's love for the Homeric epics, which in turn directs our thoughts to the identity of the dead man whose bones are in the gold larnax.

One further detail, observed both by myself and by my anthropologist colleague, N. Xirotyris, is worth noting. Our experience of cremation in other burials is that the bones which were collected and placed in a funerary urn are only part of the skeleton, the number fluctuating, being sometimes more and sometimes less. In this case almost all the bones have been very carefully gathered together; very few are missing. This, together with everything else, reveals the exceptional care devoted to sifting the remains of the pyre.

The gold wreath found above the bones is as precious as the gold larnax. On examination clear traces of the effects of fire could be seen at certain points; this means that at the moment when the pyre was set alight for the cremation of the body the dead man was wearing the wreath which was removed, hastily, immediately the first flames shot up around his body. This view is corroborated by some few gold acorns which were found outside the tomb in the heap of sun-dried bricks above the vault which were, apparently, taken there from the site of the funeral pyre. A second observation completing this picture is that a number of leaves are missing from the delicate little branches of the wreath which must have fallen off when it was wrenched, roughly and in a rush, from the dead man's head.

After the excellent restoration carried out in the Museum of Thessalonike, the wreath as we see it today is the most impressive and the heaviest gold wreath to have survived from antiquity. Fifty-seven large leaves and thirty-two smaller shoots sprout from a hollow cylindrical rod which forms an elliptical ring, (maximum diameter 0.185 m., minimum 0.139 m.) whose two ends fasten together with thin gold strands. Smaller leaves sprout from the small boughs, from which acorns also peep up. A total of three hundred and thirteen leaves and sixty-eight acorns survive, but it is clear that before it was damaged there were many more. Thus its present weight, 714 gr., is less than the original. As with the larnax, the precious material is not the most important aspect of its worth. Perhaps of course the glitter of the gold distracts us from a scrupulous appraisal of the craftsman's excellent work. With consummate insight and sensitivity he rendered not only the external form of the leaves and the fruit

but their internal substance. He was interested in the reality of the things he was recreating more than in their "naturalness".

We have said that this wreath is the heaviest to have survived from antiquity. This is of course chance and a matter of luck; there could have been other, heavier wreaths which have either been lost over the centuries or are yet to be found. However, I believe that there exists one very substantial piece of evidence which permits us to maintain that in antiquity such a wreath was a rare and uncommon object. The catalogues of the Treasury of Delos which list the valuable offerings mention a series of gold wreaths, each with its weight. All are lighter than that of Vergina, even though many of these are the offerings of kings of the Hellenistic period to Apollo. Only one, dedicated by a Ptolemy which weighs 192 drachmae, that is about 810 gr., is heavier than the Vergina example. If, however, we allow for the leaves missing from the latter and secondly for the difference in date – the Delos wreath belongs to the period after Alexander's conquests when gold from the East and from Egypt was in the hands of the Diadochoi – we may come to appreciate its truly royal weight.

THE ROYAL DIADEM

We noted in the relevant section that next to the iron helmet a circular gilded silver object was found. It consists of a hollow cylinder which is bent into a circle; its two ends fit into a separate piece identical in section but slightly larger in diameter, whose curve continues that of the main part; thus it forms a normal closed diadem, or crown, whose diameter could be increased or decreased. The outer side of this smaller piece bears a relief knot of tresses whose four ends extend respectively two each to left and right. Incised lozenges decorate the outer surface of the cylinder. This circular object is

137. The gold wreath, found on top of the burnt bones of the dead king placed within the gold larnax. It is the heaviest gold wreath to have survived from antiquity. More important than the weight of the precious metal is the excellent workmanship and delicate feeling which went into the making of the oak leaves and acorns. A total of 313 leaves and 68 acorns has survived, but we are certain that many others have been lost.

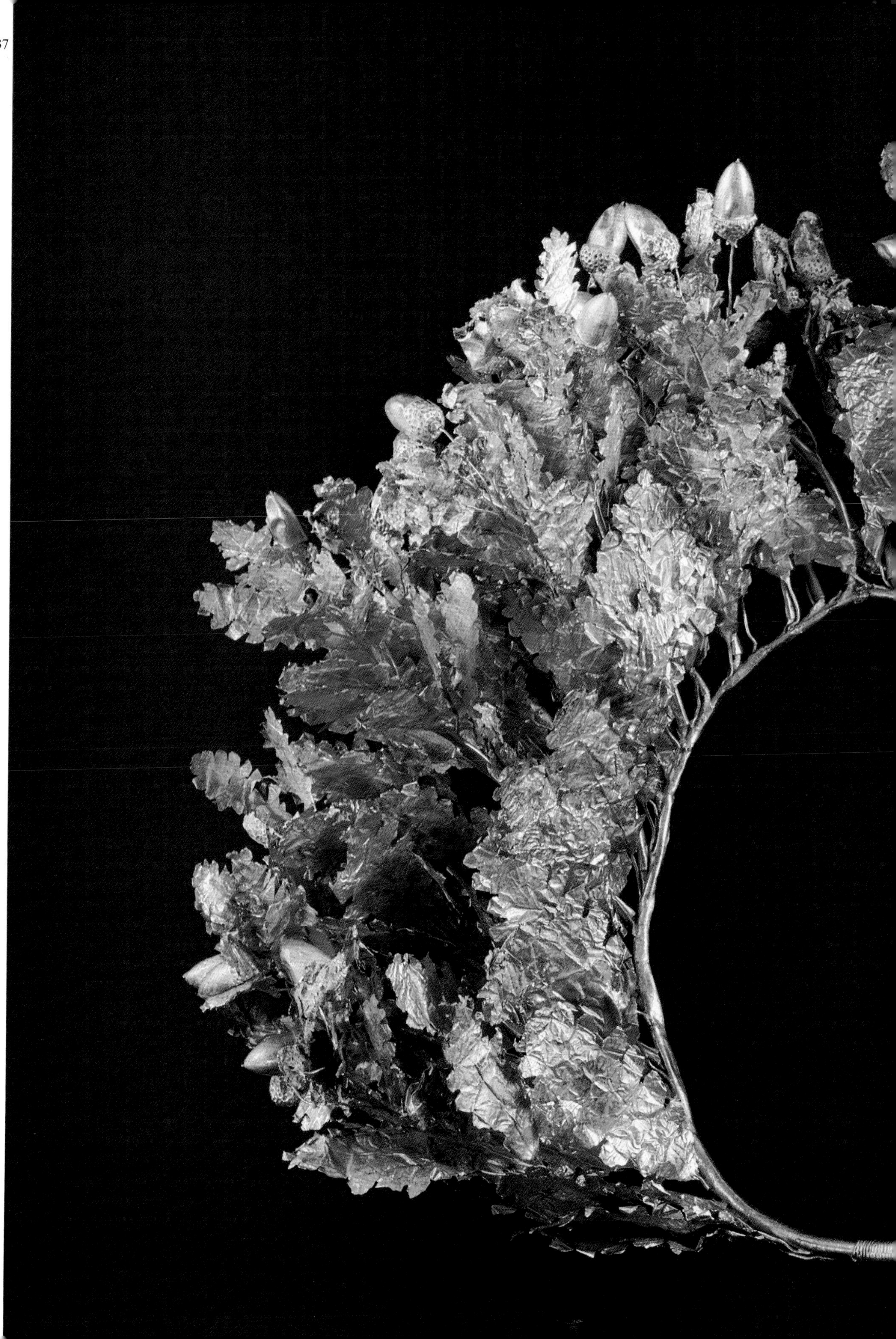

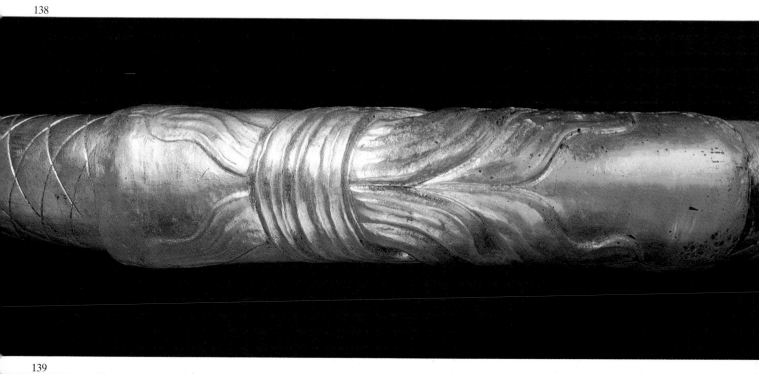

of solid silver and the whole surface has been gilded. However, the lozenges which fall in the central horizontal row – the ones that were especially visible that is – have been carefully scraped to remove the gilding thus showing the silver beneath. The internal diameter is 0.21 m. while the external is 0.24-0.27 m. Traces of some organic material, leather or cloth, are to be seen on the inner surface.

This is a unique find; nevertheless I think it is undoubtedly a chaplet. We know that similar chaplets or diadems were worn by priests as we may ascertain from a number of marble portraits. This same diadem is also seen in the portraits of many poets (Homer, Sophocles, Pindar and others). Finally an identical diadem is shown in the portraits of several Macedonian kings in the Hellenistic period, for example of Antigonos in a portrait from the Boscoreale, though its identification has been called in question; of Attalos III, where again there are certain doubts about its identification, in the Ny Carlsberg Collection in Copenhagen; of Antiochos III in the Louvre; and in two portraits of Alexander the Great, one at Rossy Priory, England and a second in the Museum of Fine Arts, Boston. In addition to these, where Hellenistic coins portray the king, his head is always crowned by such a diadem. Finally the two portraits of Philip we know of at the moment, one on a gold medallion from Tarsus now in the Bibliothèque Nationale, Paris, and the other preserved in a Roman copy in the Ny Carlsberg Collection are both crowned by a similar diadem.[23]

I therefore regard it as certain that this find from Vergina is also a diadem. The unlikely chance that the deceased was a poet must of course be ruled out. Two possibilities thus remain; that he was a priest or a king. But, since we know that the king of the Macedonians was the high priest of the people,

138-139. The "royal diadem". This unique object discovered in "Philip's tomb" has excited interest amongst both historians and archaeologists. It is a work of contrasted techniques. The diadem is made up of two parts; the larger section is decorated with incised lozenges; its two ends fit into a smaller section at the back, decorated in relief with the ends of a ribbon. The diameter was thus adjustable. It is very probable that this silver gilt object is the rendering in precious material of the royal Macedonian "diadem" which could be worn above the "diadematoforos kausia" = hat with a diadem).

these two possibilities are reduced to one and to one only. It is beyond doubt that the dead man was a warrior as his many shining weapons testify indisputably; so the diadem from the Vergina tomb, whether it is interpreted as the wreath of a priest or of a king, confirms, I believe, that the dead man was not only a member of the royal house but was himself the king. Even the mechanism which allows for the size to be adjusted can be adduced to support this interpretation; because the size could be increased, the crown could be worn directly on the head or above the *kausia*, the familiar Macedonian head covering which we know was described as the "καυσία διαδηματοφόρος" or, lastly, on top of a helmet, when the king wished to make an appearance in full armour and to be viewed as the symbol of royal authority.

Thus the finds in the main chamber gradually led us to the belief that the tomb was royal – to the view that the tomb belonged not simply to a member of the royal family, but to the king himself. Who could that king have been? I shall endeavour to answer this question, which has provoked so much interest not just amongst non-specialists but also amongst historians and archaeologists, in the last section.

THE ANTECHAMBER AND ITS CONTENTS

The antechamber of the tomb is unusually deep (3.66 m.) so that it creates a spacious second area, the largest of all the antechambers in the Macedonian tombs we yet know of; (its width is the same as that of the chamber, 4.46 m.). The surface of the walls present a sharp contrast with those of the chamber. The plastering is of exceptionally good quality; the lower part of the walls is painted white while the upper part is a deep Pompeian red; the vault is white. At the spring of the vault there is a cymation, immediately below it a band and, below an indentation of the surface, a second band decorated with rosettes. There are nails in both bands, from which material or various other objects were probably hung. They subsequently disintegrated and fell to the flooor.

At many points the plaster of the walls has blistered and fallen to the ground; other lumps were still hanging from the walls when we first entered. The same was true of the plasterwork of the floor,

140

141

140-142. Decorative gold sheets found in the antechamber of "Philip's Tomb". Here, as in the main chamber, there was an elegant piece of wooden furniture (a couch or a throne). Its legs were lavishly decorated with ivory, glass and gold. Nine rectangular sections, which we found also on the couch from the "Bella Tumulus" existed on its upper part. These too were embellished by gold sheets which were covered by transparent glass. The first, with the glass, was found together with corresponding one next to the upper spirals of the foot (see the drawing of the bed).

142

176

especially in the northern section where it had lifted considerably. I suggest that this happened because the tomb was covered by the mound immediately after its construction, so that the plaster had not had time to dry out before the air ceased to circulate freely.

Many surprises awaited us in the antechamber, each more pleasing than the one before. The first was that close to the southern (side) wall there was a marble sarcophagus (1.01 × 0.56 × 0.68 m. high). In front of it and next to it a thick layer of decomposed organic material covered the floor. In this material, still being treated by the conservators in the laboratory at Vergina, one may surmise the existence of another wooden couch, even though at the moment the evidence for its existence is less firm than it is for one in the chamber. I have reason to think that this material is derived from a greater selection of wooden objects, amongst which it is not impossible that there is a magnificent chair, a kind of throne, wooden boxes etc. These objects, once temporary fixatives had been applied, were, like the objects from the chamber, taken to a laboratory for conservation and treatment. It is necessary to add that the thickness of this layer of remains has proved to be rich in content, so that their rescue has demanded devotion and unusual care. It is only thanks to the skill and dedication of our conservators, especially of Mr G. Petkousis, that today we have the satisfaction not only of having hardly any loss, but even more, that we succeeded in spotting the successive layers of remains which in some cases are more than six or seven. A mass of decomposed material was found on top of the sarcophagus lid. Large numbers of small thin circular disks, with an eight-pointed star in relief, were found scattered amongst all this material and in most cases above it. The way in which they were strewn about and especially the fact that three were found on the lid of the sarcophagus compels us to accept that they fell from somewhere higher up and were unevenly distributed because they were so light. It is not easy to be sure of their original purpose; one probable suggestion is that they decorated some large piece of material which was – in some unknown way – above the sarcophagus, and when that disintegrated the disks fell and dispersed. It may be that in the course of treatment and subsequent study further light will be shed both on this problem and on the many others produced by

the present state of the material. Indeed, as we shall now see, the finds from the antechamber are almost all very problematical.

I think it is useful here to give a brief description of the state of the antechamber when we first entered it, as I did for the main chamber, to pinpoint the spot in which each object was found.

One group of finds, the most numerous, was found in the recess formed by the two marble door jambs and the door which leads from the antechamber to the chamber. The "gold" gorytos was found upright in the left corner of the recess,[24] or more exactly the gold cover of its outer side, since the gorytos itself must have been entirely of wood or leather; at the bottom, now detached from the main body, the leaf-shaped gold part belonging to the base could be seen. Immediately to the right of the gorytos, fallen onto the threshold, were the two gilded greaves. In front of the gorytos, on the threshold, was the iron head of a spear or a javelin while a second was found on the other side of the recess next to the right jamb. At least ten alabastra were disposed along the length of the door sill and immediately in front of it. Finally a clay amphora, almost intact, and a second, broken one, completed the group. When we moved the gold casing of the gorytos we saw a thick sheaf of arrowheads and abundant traces of wood; some of this must have been from arrows though the rest of it probably came from the case of the gorytos. Broad gold hoops were visible amongst these remains.

On the floor at the right (northern) side of the chamber could be seen traces of paint on what had presumably been wood which had almost completely disintegrated, amongst which lay a few gold filings. It is difficult for anyone to decide what they came from. At the edge of these remains, a small distance from the dividing wall, was a gilded pectoral rather well preserved. Beneath it and amongst the fallen plaster two gold gorgoneion were found, while a little way from them were a number of silver rings and rosettes. Finally, next to the dividing wall – on its northern half – was another iron spearhead.

On the floor, between the sarcophagus and the dividing wall – on its southern half – below the fallen plaster was a small gold wreath made from myrtle leaves and blossom; many of its leaves were found scattered quite a distance from the threshold. This means of course that the wreath had been hung somewhere high up and when it fell

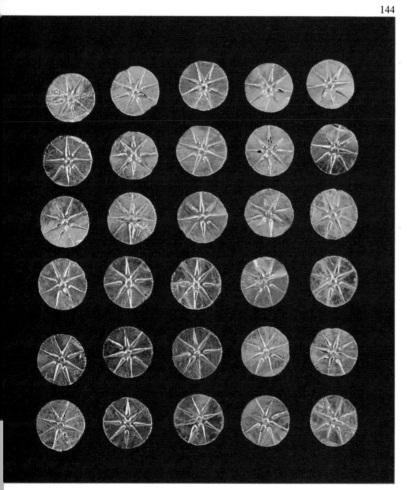

many of the flowers were dispersed.

Lastly on the lid of the sarcophagus was a gold brooch of "Illyrian type" as archaeologists call it.

This collection of finds is somewhat bizarre, and it is difficult for anyone to ascribe them to the burial of one particular person. There were weapons, perfume vases, a valuable pectoral, jewellery which was not of the usual sort (the two gorgoneions) a unique brooch and the gold wreath. We had still to see what the sarcophagus contained; its shape and size gave no certain clue to its use. When we opened it one more pleasant surprise awaited us; inside it a second gold larnax, smaller than the first, had been placed. The size of the sarcophagus bore no relation to the size of the larnax. We tried to lift it out and found that it was held fast in some way; with a little effort we succeeded in freeing it for it had been fixed only by a dab of stucco. When we had placed it on the floor and opened it we were confronted with a most unexpected sight; a gold and purple fabric, unique, covered the bones while squashed against one side was a delicate gold diadem.

We had therefore a second burial in the antechamber, something unique in a Macedonian tomb. The gold and purple cloth, the gold diadem which seemed to be for a woman, and the myrtle wreath testify that the bones were probably those of a woman (this was subsequently confirmed by the anthropological examination). However, in such a rich female burial there ought to have been correspondingly rich jewellery, bracelets, necklaces, rings and such like. But except for the wreath and the brooch nothing of this sort existed in the antechamber. On the contrary, there was a large number of weapons. The problem created by the presence of a female burial and weapons in the antechamber is certainly strange, and as far as I know there are no other archaeological parallels which can assist us to solve it. We can only search for the possible solutions from the finds themselves and the position in which they were found.

The first and simplest answer would be that all the objects which were found in the antechamber belonged to a woman's burial. This implies that the woman buried there could have had some kind of Amazonian leanings, or could have had some a liking for, or familiarity with, weapons. But this answer does not face the problem squarely nor acount for all the details. And even if we accept – as some scholars have maintained – that the dead woman was a warrior, it still remains to examine the kind of weapons found with her. We have arrows, javelins or spears, and greaves – it is a jumbled and ill-assorted collection. I should perhaps include the comment of a French archaeologist who, when I broached the matter, said that the greaves must have belonged to a man because their shape excludes any possibility that they were associated with a woman's leg.

A second answer might be that these weapons belonged to the dead man buried in the main chamber. It is certainly strange that they were not deposited in the chamber alongside the other armour. If, however, we recall everything we have said about the construction of the tomb in two phases and posit that the construction of the antechamber and the facade continued after the interment of the first dead person in the chamber, this could explain the delayed placing of certain further objects which had belonged to him in the antechamber, since by then the door of the chamber would have been closed. These considerations perhaps explain the position in which the weapons were found, placed in the recess of the jambs and leaning against the door of the chamber. It is a position which might be interpreted as declaring that they belonged not in the antechamber but in the main chamber.

But even this alternative cannot be considered entirely satisfactory. Even if it is accepted as the more probable, there remain still the doubts raised by the absence of woman's jewellery, for which in my opinion only one explanation is to be found; that the gold ornaments were burnt along with the body on the pyre. This would mean that she was wearing them when her body was placed on the pyre. This view is corroborated by a detail we

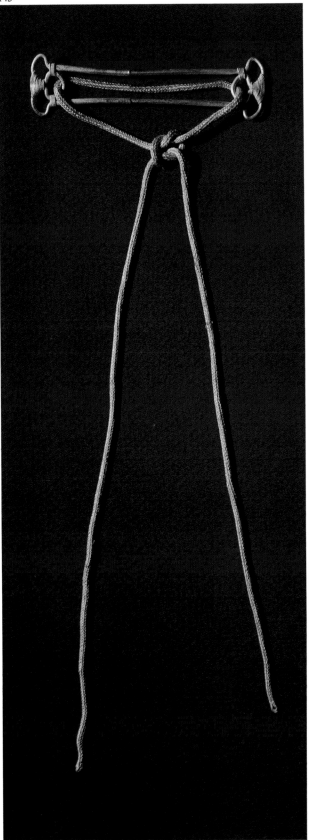

143-144. Small gold discs. Many small gold discs bearing the Macedonian star were found scattered over the disintegrated organic material of the antechamber. They were probably attached as decoration to a large piece of material which was hung high up.

145. A gold buckle of "Illyrian" type. This was found on the sarcophagus in the antechamber. Its gold chain has also survived which, tied in a knot, held the two sides of the clasp together and made it secure. It was the only piece of female jewellery other than the diadem to be found in the antechamber.

observed during the restoration of the gold diadem. At one end of the diadem there is a rod 0.063 m. long which terminates in a lion head; in its mouth is a small ring. At the other end of the diadem the twigs end abruptly, showing that they have been broken. It is clear that the ring which, together with the lion head, served to fasten the diadem on the head existed at this point. It therefore follows that at the moment the diadem was roughly snatched from the head of the wearer, the ring snapped off from the body of the diadem and lodged at the other side in the lion's head. This could have occurred as they set light to the pyre to burn the dead woman, just as we have seen that it must have happened in the case of the large wreath and the shield belonging to the dead man. One further observation supports these conclusions, namely that several blossoms and palmettes are missing, just as they are from the wreath.

The gorytos

The gorytos – or to be more exact its gold outer sheath – is one of the most striking finds from the antechamber. This sheet, silver on the inside and gilded on the outer surface, was moulded to the shape of the gorytos which is a kind of quiver in which both the arrows and the bow could be placed. The upper part was cut away in the middle to help the archer grasp the arrows. At its maximum, the sheet measures 0.465 m. in height and its greatest width is 0.255 m. while at its base it narrows to a breadth of only 0.19 m. This single sheet is divided into three main zones, the two widest of which bear pictorial relief decoration while the third is covered by a decorative relief braid. On its lower part, also in relief, is a heart-shaped lesbian cymation; a similar decorative motif separates the band with the relief figures from that with the braid. Other intermediate zones are decorated with the ovoid ionic cymation.

The only figure to follow the upright position in which the gorytos would have hung is the one on the upper right rectangular projection. Here there is a young warrior in relief; he wears a short tunic under a cuirass, a cloak and a helmet with a curious triple crest. A sword hangs from its strap, he holds a shield and spear and may possibly be wearing greaves. To the right a bare tree is visi-

ble, on the ground is an ox-head (boukranion). It is difficult to be sure whether the youth is to identified as man or god. I personally feel that a mere mortal has no place on the most conspicuous corner of the gorytos; but on the other hand I find it impossible to place such a deity in the Greek pantheon. I should also add that, unconnected with the problem of his identity, the stance and shape of this youthful figure can be related to the left hand warrior on the funerary relief of Lykeas and Chairedemos in the Piraeus Museum.

The remainder of the decoration unfolds on the bands which are aligned on the long axis of the sheet, ignoring the fact that the gorytos would have hung vertically. Thus to view them clearly it is necessary to place the gorytos horizontally on its longest side. In this position we observe immediately that the relief depictions which cover the two bands share a common theme which starts on the right hand edge of the shorter middle band and develops towards the left. The flow of movement turns in the opposite direction on the upper band, whose narrow, almost triangular termination is covered by inanimate objects (such as shields, a helmet, ox-heads (boukrania). The narrative begins, as we said, from the right hand edge of the middle band with a warrior who moves with a bold stride to the left; he wears a helmet and grasps a shield and spear; to his left is another beardless, kneeling warrior; there follows a warrior who, turned towards him, is about to strike him with his sword. These three figures form a group, and it appears that the first is running to the assistance of his kneeling comrade. The scene continues with a second group of three figures; between two men bearing shields with uncovered swords a third, unclothed figure has fallen face forwards against his shield, possibly dead. Next to this a female figure is depicted running terrified to the left, cradling the statue of a deity on a base in her right arm. Below the base and a little to the left is a low altar; a warrior stands on it, the toes of his right foot curled up. He balances himself with his right hand against the base of the statue while his left hand brings up his shield in an attempt to protect himself from the warrior approaching from the left drawing his sword from its scabbard ready to strike him. Behind the man on guard the upper part of a column can be seen. The last figure on this band is a frightened young woman fleeing from the enemy.

The upper band starts from the left; a young warrior crouches against an altar, his left leg bent, ready to spring to the right, brandishing his sword. Immediately right of the altar the first female figure races to safety to the right and a second, clutching her infant in her arms, runs in the same direction. Next come three warriors; the one immediately beside the woman turns sharply to the right, his sword in his extended right hand prepared to attack; to his left, a second warrior, turned to the left but with his head twisted to the right, attempts to defend himself, while the third moving quickly towards him has grabbed the rim of his shield. Further right, a female figure kneels on a base or an altar and, panic stricken, gazes at the clash of the three fighting men while beyond her another woman, also seated on the base, tears her hair distractedly; her left arm is curled around the statue of a deity; to the right there is a second statue of a goddesss. Beyond lie the objects we have already mentioned, the helmet, an ox-head, a shield, a cauldron(?) and a second *boukranion*, a felt hat and second shield.

Above this second band is one last border decorated with birds in flight, probably geese.

We noted that the theme of the representation is the same in both bands. The subject is clearly warfare; the presence of women with babes in arms means that it refers to the capture of a city; finally, the presence of altars and statues implies that the enemy has penetrated the shrines where the conquered, especially the women and children, had sought sanctuary. In seeking to throw light on the scene, one's first reaction is that it depicts the Fall of Troy, a much loved theme in Greek art. But it is not easy to link the representation on the gorytos with any of the iconographic models we know of in the Greek repertoire. Moreover, the most familiar and most important figures in the Fall of Troy are missing from the scene on the gorytos; Priam with Neoptolemy, Cassandra and Ajax, Aeneas and Anchises etc. We must therefore look for some other interpretation outside the Trojan cycle. However, I find some difficulty in defining the mythical event depicted with any certainty; a second possibility, that it may be linked with the fall of Thebes to the Epigonoi I fear finds no convincing support.

If the interpretation of the scene is fraught with difficulty, the presence of the gorytos in the royal tomb at Vergina (in addition to the fundamental problem of its positioning in the antechamber) is equally problematic. This gold sheath for a gorytos is a unique find on Greek soil, for archers, though they fought in battle, were few in number and were infrequently of native birth. This is true also of the Macedonian army, at least so far as the information we have about the army of Alexander tells us. On the other hand, the find has parallels in the Scythian world. In excavations of the tombs of Scythian rulers in south Russia a number of such gorytos sheaths have been found, of exactly the same shape, almost the same dimensions and similar decoration. Only the theme of the depiction is different. Amongst them is one of silver, the greater part of which has been destroyed and only seven fragments of which have survived. It was found at Karagodeuashkh in the Kuban; the largest part to have survived is the section of the tall rectangular protrusion of the gorytos on which is the upright figure of a warrior with a shield and a triple-crested helmet which we saw also on the gorytos from Vergina. The other fragments show only broken figures of warriors and parts of clothing. After the find at Vergina the Soviet archaeologist Mrs A. Mantsevitch was able to place them correctly; they formed part of the right edge of the two bands which depict the Fall. My original hypothesis, that we have not only the same subject but exactly the same presentation and that the two gorytoi must have been fashioned in the same mould is wholly confirmed by my Soviet colleague. It is illustrated by the new photographs she has published in the journal of the Hermitage Museum. If from one point of view these observations shed some light on the problem, from another they make it more complicated. What is the inter-relationship of these two valuable accessories of the armed man, other than their common origin? and more, where

146. → The gold gorytos discovered on the inner threshhold of the tomb. Arrows were found inside the gorytos, as they had been left. Similar gorytoi have been discovered in southern Russia in tombs of Scythian rulers. The relief scene starts on the lower band at the right and continues on the upper band from the left. It depicts the capture of a city. Defenders, women and children have fled to a sanctuary (altars and statues are visible).

181

did they originate?

However, before we answer these questions, or more correctly, in order to answer them at all, we must study the find from the Vergina tomb more carefully. There is no doubt that it is valuable and striking. The material, its perfect state of preservation and above all the lively and completely integrated scene in which the fighting warriors alternate with the frightened women fleeing to the shrines, the depiction of holy altars and sacred statues, immediately distract the viewer while provoking his admiration. But the more observant viewer, who does not stop at first impressions, can easily discern that the overall design and composition, which undoubtedly testify to a skilled and talented craftsman, are not matched for sensitivity and exactness in the execution of the work. If one compares the figures of the gorytos with any of the relief figures on the silver vases or the ivory decoration of the couch, the immense difference in quality is immediately apparent. It is impossible to introduce a detailed discussion of this subject into the brief presentation of the finds I am attempting here. The reader will perhaps allow me to express my opinion somewhat dogmatically. I believe that the gorytos was made by Greek craftsmen, like all the other objects, but that it was not intended that a Greek should use it. It, and the gilded pectoral, are the objects least elegant and most lacking in delicacy amongst all the finds from the royal tomb of Vergina. This means that it can easily be classed alongside the other gorytoi which belonged to Scythians. The workshops which made them might have been in a Greek city on the Black Sea, for example Pantikapaion, as many archaeologists have maintained, or in some region of northern Greece as Mrs Mantesevitch believes. In either case, those who made them knew that they would be sold to the wealthy Scythian rulers who, as many finds from their tombs show, had succumbed to the charm of Greek products.

The conclusion which follows from this chain of thought is that the Vergina gorytos is a work separate from those objects made for the use of the Macedonian kings; and that this gorytos, like the others which have been found in the Scythian tombs, was part of the panoply of some Scythian ruler. Its presence in the tomb at Vergina is not wholly inexplicable if we recall the frequent

148

149

147. The base of the gorytos; it was attached to the body of the gorytos by small gold nails.

148. Detail from the scene on the gorytos; two frightened women, one holding a baby in her arms, flee from the victors who chase them even inside the sanctuary.

149. Detail from the scene on the gorytos; one of the defenders of the city tries to avoid the blows of his rival. His weight is on his left leg bent against a low altar and he holds his shield, decorated with a large eagle, in his left hand. A column can be seen behind the altar and to the right, on a tall base, is the statue of a goddess.

clashes between Macedonians and Scyths, which allow us to regard it as the spoils of war. Even the reflection that it may have belonged to Ateas, the Scythian king conquered by Philip in 339 BC during his campaign against the Danube region of modern Dobrudja does not seem to me to be in the least far-fetched. Ateas, then about ninety years old, was killed in battle; 20,000 hostages and inumerable animals were the victors' loot (see J. R. Ellis, *Philip II and Macedonian Imperialism*, London 1976, pp. 185-186). What then is more likely than that amongst the other valuable booty Philip also acquired this magnificent gorytos, which was a most fitting "weapon" for a Scythian king, a people famed for their skill as archers? The date of its relief decoration, around the middle of the fourth century, is decisive support for such a theory which in its turn supplies the answer to all the doubts created by the unexpected presence of this foreign "weapon" in the tomb of a Macedonian king.

Inside the gorytos were the arrows and perhaps the bow. As we noted earlier, when we removed the gold sheath we found the arrowheads *in situ;* even small pieces of their wooden shafts had survived. The existence of broad gold bands leads me to suggest that the arrows had been separated into sheaves, each bundle being held together by a gold hoop. We have left the arrowheads the way we found them, and have not separated them out. This has made counting difficult, because it is not impossible that one or more have not been noticed in the pile; nevertheless we have tried to count them and make the total seventy-four. We also observed that they are not all the same size, but can be divided into three categories; the largest are 0.044 m., the smaller 0.038 and the smallest 0.0245 m. This difference in size of arrows all in the same quiver, must, I think, lead us to accept that they were not all employed against the same target. If this is indeed correct, then it implies that they were not for use in war but perhaps in the hunt where the size of the prey would require a different size of projectile.

When the arrowheads were found they were green, the familiar colour of oxidized bronze. After cleaning those which had become detached from the bundle we noticed that their surface had the same silvery colour that the surface of the spearhead has now that it has been cleaned. Chemical analysis showed that it was made up of a mixture of bronze, tin and lead, the two latter in an unusually high proportion so that the tip was very hard and not easily broken.

The greaves

Next to the gorytos was a pair of greaves. There would be no reason to concern ourselves particularly with these if they did not present two unusual features; a) they were gilded; b) they were of different size and different shape. As far as I know, they are the first example of gilded greaves from ancient Greece (another pair was found in the subsequent excavation of the "Prince's tomb"). This indeed can be accounted for if we accept that this is a royal tomb where we shall come across several unique and valuable objects. More attention should be paid to the difference between the two greaves. I noticed the inequality from the moment they were found, for it is as much as 3.5 cms. (the right 0.415 m., the left 0.38 m.; diameter of the right 0.097 m.; diameter of the left 0.09 m.). However, in no text of mine have I advocated the view that because of this the tomb could be that of Philip II, even if I have sometimes alluded to the lameness of the Macedonian king. A number of sources (Demosthenes, Justin, Plutarch) tell us that Philip was lame; we can even be precise about the date of the accident since both Justin and Plutarch connect it with the serious wound in the thigh caused by a spear in the attack on the Triballoi as he returned from his victorious campaign against the Scyths in 339 BC. The first thought that comes to mind is that the difference in size is due to a limp and thus it becomes the undeniable proof for the identification of the dead man as Philip. But even before I had consulted orthopaedic surgeons I had grave reservations about such an interpretation. The opinion of orthopaedic specialists only reinforced my doubts, though stopping short of the necessity for completely discarding such a correlation. The comment that in many other examples there is a difference between two of

150. The gold greaves which were found next to the gorytos against the marble door between the antechamber and the chamber. Both the difference in height (3.5 cms.) between the left and the right leg and their different shape – the left is narrower – are interesting.

186

a pair of greaves is not sufficient explanation, for in every case I know of the difference is only a few millimetres which is certainly due to sloppiness, whereas in this case the difference of 3.5 cms. rules out this explanation.

I can offer two possible interpretations, for the moment at least. a) That the difference is really to be ascribed to Philip's lameness. Being obliged to move and to bend each leg differently, one greave had to be shorter so that it did not impede the bending of the knee; the disparity therefore is not due to a difference in the size of the tibia, but was to ensure a certain ease of movement. For the same reason, one of the two greaves was narrower so that it fitted better. b) The co-existence of gilded greaves and the gold gorytos may signify a common use; that is, the owner of the greaves wore them when he was shooting with bow and arrow; in this activity he would be obliged to kneel which would create the need for a different fitting for the greave on the left leg from that of the greave on the right. A third explanation might be offered; the owner of the greaves had a natural limp and his legs were not the same size. But this merely creates additional problems and opens the door to uncontrolled surmise. It is therefore preferable to leave the problem open, at least for the moment, and to avoid searching for any historically based argument for this curious disparity.

The pectoral

Another unexpected find in the antechamber was a gilded pectoral. I say that it was unexpected a) because these pectorals formed a complement to the cuirass, protecting the neck and chest of the warrior where they were left uncovered by the cuirass, and b) because the pectoral of the deceased in the chamber was found, as we might have expected, next to the cuirass. There was no trace whatsoever of a cuirass on the spot on which the gilded pectoral was found, whether of leather or even of linen. This find is therefore isolated from the others and adds one more problem to those already generated by the objects in the antechamber.

The pectoral is made from leather, an iron sheet and its silver gilt sheath. The whole of the broad crescent-shaped surface and that of the main pectoral bears relief decoration, much of it consisting of rosettes. But on the main inner band, which is also the widest, four youthful horsemen are depicted, within circles; each wears a short tunic and sandals. On either edge, to left and right, there are two smaller circles and within these is the frontal depiction of a beardless youth, probably Heracles, if I am correct in interpreting the schematic head covering as a lion.

If the type and the shape of this pectoral is not unknown to us up to now (as we noted above a similar one was discovered in the chamber of the same tomb) it is unique for its decoration and in its valuable sheathing. We know of comparable examples from Thracian tombs which have been excavated in Bulgaria where, however, as far as I know, even the most sumptuous are only silver. This correlation with Thracian finds can be taken further. I think that we may reiterate what we said about the gorytos. This pectoral is impressive both for its precious material and for its rich decoration; if, however, we take a careful look at the decoration, we will observe that it does not possess the grace and delicacy which distinguish the other finds in the tomb. We are left again with the feeling that the craftsmen who fashioned it were aware that it was designated for someone who had to be impressed by its over-abundant decoration, but not by the high quality of the work. In other words, we are entitled to reach the conclusion that such an object was not made for the court of the Macedonian kings, but probably for some Thracian ruler. If this is the case there is no difficulty in explaining its presence in a royal Macedonian tomb when we consider how close were the contacts between the two peoples, whether in friendship or in emnity, and that even inter-marriage between their rulers was not uncommon.

151. Gilded "pectoral" from the antechamber. It is made of leather, an iron sheet and a gilded silver covering. The entire broad surface together with the horizontal band of the main pectoral are richly decorated in relief. Similar pectorals have been found in the wealthy tombs of Thracian rulers in Bulgaria.

Gorgoneions

As we noted at the beginning of the section two small gold gorgoneions, rosettes and silver rings

152-153. Two gold medusas found in the antechamber; their dimensions are the same and their overall shape is identical. There are, however, enough differences to show that they are not two exact copies originating from the same mould. Their high artistic quality becomes obvious when we compare them with other known medusas.

190

were found next to the pectoral. It is difficult to establish what all these decorative elements originally embellished; the most probable suggestion is that they must have come from some small wooden chest which has completely disintegrated. The Gorgoneions are the same size (height 0.036 m., width 0.035 m.) and on general lines are similar, but a number of small differences, mainly in the arrangement of the curls, show that they are not two faithful copies issuing from the same mould. A provisional comparison with every other gorgoneion known from the entire ancient world persuades us of their high quality and of the particular position they occupy in the pictorial development of this very important figure. As far as I know, it is one of the oldest gorgoneions of the type called "beautiful".

The myrtle wreath

One of the most elegant and valuable finds from the antechamber is the gold wreath made of myrtle leaves and flowers, which was found on the floor next to the sarcophagus covered by a large lump of plaster which had fallen from high up. Many leaves and blossoms from the wreath were found quite a distance away in front of the door sill to the main chamber. Both the spot in which it was found and the pieces scattered from it show that it must have been hung high up and that the pieces dispersed in its fall. As we have it now, after restoration, there are eighty leaves and one hundred and twelve flowers. The main wreath, from which the small twigs sprouted, consists of a narrow cylindrical rod, whose two ends have been flattened and which fastened by twisting together. The internal diameter of the main tube is 0.18 – 0.16 m. while the external is 0.26 – 0.23 m. The delicate rendering and calculated arrangement of the flowers and leaves together creates an admirable whole and I believe that it is no exaggeration to say that this wreath, as a work of art, is the equal of the impressive, heavy wreath from the main chamber, complementing regal majesty with noble grace.

The larnax and its contents

A second gold larnax was found in the marble sarcophagus of the antechamber. Its dimensions are a little smaller than those of the first (0.322 × 0.377 × 0.202 m.) and its decoration less, but the shape is basically the same, as is the ornamentation – a large twelve-pointed star on the lid, rosettes on the vertical corner strips and on the protruding band at the sides. The same small shield-like bosses decorate the two front edges of the lid with two corresponding ones on the vertical (front) side. The absence of plant motifs and of the lion feet lightens the decorative load so that it presents the structure and the simple lines of a wooden construction more clearly. Inside, traces of a disintegrated purple fabric can be observed.

As we have seen, the burnt bones of the dead woman were wrapped in a gold and purple cloth next to which the woman's gold diadem had been squeezed. Thus within this modest, simple larnax two unique and valuable finds were preserved.

We have said that the fabric was photographed immediately while still in the larnax, but this photograph cannot give a distinct picture of the state in which it was discovered. It presents the fabric in only two dimensions while in reality it lay in undulating folds over the uneven surface of the bones it covered. Right from the beginning we had to face the problem of its conservation; the larnax was tightly sealed up and transported to the Museum of Thessalonike with the utmost care. Our first act there was to sterilize its resting place to prevent the growth of fungus. Next we sought expert advice, from Greeks and from foreigners, on the methods which would best serve our needs. The problem was acute because parts of the purple had completely disintegrated and had turned into a watery substance like an ointment. Moreover, the parts made of gold thread could not either easily or safely be removed, for in reality they were much cracked and were no more than a mass of tears. I think I may now disclose the difficulty, which approached distress, of making any selection from the different and totally conflicting opinions advanced by experts. We all had a great responsibility; but, whether I wanted it or not, the weight of the decision would rest on me. I had to assess the pros and cons and to come to conclusions as soon as possible. Mulling over the calculable, predictable options open to me and logically marshalling all the instinctive reactions which the archaeologist develops from years of familiarity with the materials and with men on the job, I determined that my safest, and in practical terms, only possible answer was for the technicians of the Greek Archaeological Service to undertake the operation. I had known Mr Tasos Margaritov for years and there had been many occasions to admire not only his knowledge but even more his adroitness and ingenuity, the result of long experience and even more of a love for the objects in his care. I hope that he will one day have the opportunity to describe in full detail the arduous and absorbing processes which took him and his assistants two and a half years to restore this magnificent fabric. I am entitled to feel only satisfaction in my fortunate choice and the remarkable results.

Work on the restoration of the material resulted in the knowledge that the remains found in the larnax belonged to two separate pieces with the same trapezoidal shape, of almost the same size and with the same decoration. One of them seems to have been placed on the base of the larnax and the other covered the bones; probably both were folded at the ends so that the bones were covered from all sides. The purple of the bottom piece had suffered greater damage and traces of the purple could be seen on the base of the larnax.

It is difficult to interpret either the shape of these two pieces or their use. They are already being examined in detail, and this may perhaps allow us, if not to solve, then at least to offer solutions to these problems and to the many others posed by this unique find. One of the most interesting is the technique; how was this material made? It would have been difficult for it simply to have been woven, for it combined a gold and a purple surface. The gold, which forms the background setting off the purple decoration, was made from gold "thread"; the purple part had disintegrated before it was found and there was no way to distinguish the fibres since they had already coagulated into a mushy mass as we said above. It is very probable that the purple threads were of wool.

Its shape, as we said, was that of an upside down trapezium, with the shorter side at the base. The bottom measured 0.41 m., the top 0.615 and the height was 0.285 m. All four sides had a border of spiral meanders coiling from right to left; on the two slanting sides the purple in the spiral meanders formed triangular protrusions to the inside, not of equal size which was probably determined by the space left by the plant decoration on the inside. It

was this pattern which chiefly engaged the designer's attention.

The viewer is left with a general impression of a lifelike, almost naturalistic, rendering of plant life. Pliant stalks, succulent and well-drawn leaves, buds, blossoms and rosettes enfolding two swallows riot over the surface with a freedom and flexibility so true to life that he might think he was encountering the natural, untamed setting. But at the same time the more observant viewer will notice that all these plant motifs are sagaciously organized and subordinated to their decorative function which denotes order and discipline (= κόσμος). From a centrally placed kalyx in the middle of the lower edge, its base bordered to left and right by narrow leaves a stalk shoots off to either side. With a flowing movement and flexible curve it extends and develops over two-thirds of the surface, finally terminating in a long narrow flower which turns horizontally in towards the centre. From inside the kalyx at the centre two large curved leaves sprout to right and left, their veins pronounced, and in the middle another flower sends forth two others, turned upside down. Right and left of the tip of the central flower two swallows face each other; behind their tails are two more flowers linked to an almost invisible stalk with two large leaves. Finally, the upper corners are covered by two broad leaf-shaped embellishments.

Naturally very little fabric has survived from the ancient world, and much of that is in a fragmentary state. The best examples come from southern Russia and are now in the museums of the Soviet Union. As far as I can judge from the published accounts none compares with the completeness, the sumptuousness and the decorative richness of the two pieces from Vergina.

Inside the larnax was a woman's gold diadem, as we have seen, crushed and folded against one side next to the bones. Its skilful restoration by Mr Demetrios Mathios, the conservator at the Archaeological Museum of Thessalonike, permits

154. The gold wreath of myrtle leaves and flowers is amongst the most elegant and most valuable finds from the antechamber. Many leaves and flowers were found scattered over the floor; today there are some 80 leaves and 112 flowers. It is yet another wonderful creation fashioned by a Greek goldsmith.

155. The small gold larnax found in the marble sarcophagus in the antechamber; it is both smaller and plainer than the larnax found in the chamber.

156-157. The two pieces of gold and purple material found in the small gold larnax, after restoration; in them the burnt bones of the dead queen had been wrapped. The lower side measured 0.41 m., the upper 0.615 m., and the height was 0.285 m. Spiral meanders border each of the four sides; within this are pliant branches, leaves, blossoms, flowers and rosettes amongst which sit two swallows.

155

158

159

us to enjoy this superb creation of some ancient Greek goldsmith. There is no over-statement in saying that this diadem is the most beautiful piece of jewellery to have come down to us from the ancient world. It is not possible to study its style nor describe each detail in this preliminary presentation. Here a brief account must suffice which, together with a few comments, will aid the reader to a deeper understanding of the underlying technique and to a fuller appreciation of the photograph, though only a sight of the real thing can properly do it justice.

It is important to note that the diadem is made up of three separate parts joined together by hinges of small cylinders at the end of the three sections – four at the centre, two each to right and left and two at either end; a gold wire is threaded into the cylinders. This ensured the adjustability of the diadem, essential for its close fit against the curve of the head. In addition to the three sections, a special fluted rod ending in a lion head was fitted to the right end of the diadem; as we noted above, this was positioned at the back of the head and served to connect the two edges; the small ring from the opposite edge fitted into the lion's mouth (as we have it today).

Careful observation shows that its full length has not survived undamaged; some flowers and blossoms are certainly missing from several points. Damage is clearest at the right edge, from which the two inner spirals are missing. This, in conjunction with the position of the ring in the lion's mouth and the destruction of the other end, is to be interpreted as the result of the violent seizure of the diadem from the head of the dead woman who was wearing it when her body was placed on the pyre and it was necessary to rescue it hurriedly from the flames licking round the corpse.

At first glance the viewer is struck by the wealth of vegetation which runs riot in untrammelled vitality. Stalks twine and tangle endlessly, bearing leaves, flowers, rosettes and palmettes, many of them on twigs of twisted wire ready to sway at the slightest tremor; bees suck pollen from many flowers while a miniature bird nests in the central palmette. The finish of the detail stamps each as a faithful reproduction of the shapes of the natural world. However, both the immediate impression and the rendering of detail are subordinated to an overall plan, delimited by the shared elements in the general pattern as also by the naturalistic details which are employed to show off the shapely restraint of each element. Even just a little attention will reward the viewer with an appreciation of the underlying form of the composition; a central section whose core is the delicately wrought knot of Heracles filled in with a proliferation of ceaselessly twisting spirals, flowers and palmettes, its top surmounted by three crowning palmettes and finished at the bottom by four hanging chains which end in small balls. Right and left of the knot at the centre of the wreath the horizontal line of a thick bough passing through the composition forms three lyre-shaped motifs, essential to the pattern and enriched by spirals and rosettes; thinner stalks sprout from the central bough, spreading out in flowing waves above and below it; to these are attached the spiral-like twigs which end in flowers and palmettes. The trumpet-shaped flowers on the upper part, like some of the large and several of the smaller ones on the inside of the pattern, have preserved traces of glass paste of a deep blue hue, rather like enamel. It has disappeared from many others.

We should add that the technician who carried out the restoration confined himself to working on the damaged pieces. Only after definitive study shall we perhaps be able to arrive at a more exact placing of the many plant elements which depend from very thin wire stalks and were thus easily displaced.

158-159. The gold diadem worn by a woman found inside the gold larnax in the antechamber. The proliferation of plant elements in the composition is striking; coiling twigs, leaves, flowers, rosettes and palmettes. Bees hover round many flowers while on a central palmette perches a minute bird. Without exaggeration it is the most beautiful jewel from antiquity found to date.

THE "PRINCE'S TOMB"

THE BUILDING

The "Prince's tomb" lies a short distance northwest of "Philip's tomb". I have given it a conventional name based on the only reliable fact, that the deceased was a young man no older than sixteen. It too is Macedonian; that is, it consists of a vaulted building and a facade. As we noted in the revelant section it too was found unrobbed and was thus the second intact Macedonian tomb.

The structure consists of two rooms, the main chamber which is 4.03 m. wide and 3.00 m. deep and the antechamber of the same width and 1.75 m. in depth. The external measurements are 6.35 × 5.08 m. It has none of the anomalies presented by "Philip's tomb", neither is the outer surface of the vault plastered. Its facade also is much more simple, having only two pillars at the edges and the marble jambs which support the marble lintel of the door; it lacks columns to right and left. On the upper part a doric epistyle rests on the two end pillars, above which are the triglyphs and metopes. The paint on both the pillar capitals and on the triglyphs has survived in very good condition (deep blue on the triglyphs, and the *guttae*, red on the *tainiai*). Two decorative relief shields are fashioned in stucco on the upper parts of the walls between the jambs and the pillars; their convex surfaces bear painted decoration poorly preserved; a garland of leaves can be seen on the outer rim of one, and we suspect the existence of a Medusa at the centre. A small doric cornice protrudes above the triglyphs; above that, as on "Philip's tomb" there is a frieze 5.06 m. long and 0.63 m. high crowned by a second cornice. On it, at regular intervals, (almost above each triglyph), are roof tiles.

There are plentiful traces of colour on the frieze as well as remains of organic substances, probably leather and wood; the latter is clearer. I suggest that the only possible interpretation of all these elements is that there must have been a painted frieze there which, however, had been executed on a moveable panel (of wood or leather) which naturally has decomposed. The only difficulty with this theory is that I have not succeeded in finding traces of the nails which would have held the board in place; it is not impossible, however, that it could have been attached with some kind of glue, since the entire facade was to be covered with earth.

The outer door of the tomb consisted of two marble leaves with the typical characteristics in imitation of a wooden door with its bosses; the circular bronze knocker also exists here. The second, inner door between the chamber and the antechamber was similar, except that one of the two marble leaves had fallen into the chamber and broken into three parts.

THE INSIDE OF THE TOMB AND THE GRAVE GOODS

The walls of the main chamber were well plastered in white; at the spring of the vault (2.40 m. above the floor) is a narrow tainia-frieze (0.23 m. high) deep blue in colour with nails at intervals. The vault is plastered in the same way as the walls.

Very close to the rear (western) wall (0.17 m.),

160. The facade of the "Prince's tomb". Its architectural details are the same as those of "Philip's Tomb", though simpler. There are only two end pillars; the intermediate doric half-columns are absent. On the walls, left and right of the door, are two decorative shields. The frieze was probably decorated with a portable painted panel of wood which rotted and disintegrated.

162

163

161. General view of the main chamber of the "Prince's tomb" immediately it had been opened. The marble door, which had fallen and broken into three pieces, the "table" with the silver hydria for the ashes and the gold wreath on its shoulder can be seen. In the corner, top left, are silver vases; in the bottom right corner is a pair of gilded greaves.

162. The northeast corner of the chamber where most of the silver vases were piled; the two buckets (the upper one upside down), the oinochoe (left), the patera whose handle has become detached (right), the kalyxes and the perfume flask are visible.

163. Roughly in the middle of the main chamber, next to the fallen door, was a rectangular piece of leather, decomposed wood and fallen silver vases; above right is the unique silver fish dish.

201

centred between the side walls, stands a built "table", 1.10 m. long, 0.67 m. wide and 0.54 m. high. In the middle is a circular hollow in which the silver hydria containing the bones had stood; a heavy gold wreath of oak leaves and acorns had been placed on its shoulder. The fallen marble door leaf covered a large area of the space between the door

164. The northwest corner of the main chamber of the "Prince's tomb". Next to and below the fallen door is the iron silver-gilded lampstand and two large bronze silvered vessels.

165. The "table" close to the west wall of the main chamber; a silver hydria containing the burnt bones of the dead youth was placed in a hollow in the middle of the "table". A gold wreath of oak leaves and acorns can be seen around the shoulder of the hydria.

164

and the "table" and it is quite probable that its fall caused certain objects to shift, in particular the light silver vases.

On the floor in front of the "table" remains of decomposed organic substances, mainly wood, were preserved. From them, we may deduce the existence of a low wooden couch. On the floor further to the east, that is towards the door, and immediately in front of the couch could be seen a very thin sheet of leather, totally decomposed and preserved in an aqueous condition. Above it were a few silver vases. Most of the silver vases were found scattered in the northeast corner of the chamber while in the northwest corner were two large bronze-plated cauldron-shaped vessels. Next to these an iron lampstand stood upright; the lamp itself had fallen to the ground (it is important that whereas the body of the lamp was found close to the lampstand, its nozzle had been flung against the door sill of the chamber). The gilded bronze greaves, a gilded bronze wreath and two gold sheets with light relief decoration which probably belonged to a cuirass were found in the southwest part of the chamber.

As we noted above, the burnt bones of the deceased had been placed in a silver hydria, specially made for this funerary use, since it was constructed in two parts, one from the base to the shoulder, the second from the shoulder upwards; the parts were joined together by a kind of hinge. A purple cloth now completely rotted to a paste-like consistency had been laid over the bones.

So far it has only been possible to remove the metal items (except for the two large bronze vessels) and the piece of leather (together with a layer of the floor). The door has not yet been shifted, and for technical reasons almost all the organic substances have been left untouched as they were found. We broke off only two groups of the ivory reliefs which decorated the couch.

The walls and the vaulted ceiling of the antechamber had the same good white plastering as the chamber; here too, at a height of 2.05-2.10 m above the floor is a frieze (0.237-0.245 m. high), its upper part bearing a painted ionic cymation. The frieze of the antechamber is decorated with scenes of a chariot race, or more exactly, with a series of two-horse chariots, one coursing behind the other for the whole length of the wall. In all, twenty-one chariots are shown, five on each of the side walls, three on the three sections left and right of the doors and two on the southeast section.

Thus, up to a point, the absence of a wall paint-

167

168

ing on the facade is compensated for by this very well preserved decorative wall painting. Naturally the dimensions of the frieze and its obviously decorative character did not lend themselves to a wall painting of the same high standard as the works in the other two tombs (the rape of Persephone and the Hunt). Nevertheless, within the confined space the painter had at his disposal, and despite the obvious absence of ambition, he succeeeded in demonstrating notable artistic talent and knowledge. First of all he shunned the formal and uninspired repetition of the same motif, which one might have expected in a case like this. On the contrary, each chariot has its own character and is depicted from a different angle, so that the rendering of the charioteer and even more, of the horses, offered the viewer an exceptionally wide range of figures in perspective. This testifies not only to facility in design, but also to considerable knowledge and experience, attributes which are confirmed by the truly felicitous, I would even say inspired, rendering of the horses' bodies through a range of moments in their plunging, impetuous movements. The ability of the painter to mould the mass of the bodies in outline by dexterous and sparing introduction of highlighting is also obvious. Lastly, the simple but correct rendering of the uneven surface of the ground on which the horses' shadows are painted with a few brush strokes displays the chariots with their white horses racing across the deep blue background of the frieze with the fullness of sculpture.

On the floor of the northern half of the antechamber, on the right as one enters from the outer door, there was a mass of decomposing material preserved as a paste-like consistency. It gave an impression of having been a leather uniform which had fallen down the parts of which had crumpled against each other. At a number of points, decoration of gold rosettes and shoots could be seen while another piece was shaped like the inside of a small circular shield. Technicians are not unanimous as to the material, and the preliminary chemical analyses do not provide clear guidance. Because their safe removal was not easy, we deemed it convenient to leave them *in situ* for the time being, meanwhile maintaining the very high level of damp in the tomb so that they might suffer no further damage. Amongst these materials there is another object which looks like a staff. I am now in position to add that thanks to the dexterity of the conserva-

tor Mr. G. Petkousis these materials have been transferred to the workshop at Vergina and treatment has begun.

On the northern side of the antechamber there are also remains of organic material, much less in quantity and even further dissolved. This too has been left *in situ*. Amongst it were found gilded bronze and iron strigils and, next to these, almost upright, was the lower part of a spear; its iron butt and the gold casing which covered the wooden shaft had survived. The iron head, with traces of gilded decoration, was found on the floor where it had fallen.

Of the organic material in the main chamber we removed only the piece of leather and a few ivory reliefs from the decoration of the couch, as I noted above. It is not easy to produce any clear or definite picture of the extent or arrangement of the decorative themes from the reliefs. However, the quality of these ivories is undoubtedly exceptionally high; we may even deduce that the themes were connected with the Dionysiac cult. In addition to the purely decorative elements, such as spirals and cymatia, there are five figures amongst the sections we have so far removed to the laboratory. Two of these are identical and must be the corresponding motifs at either end of the couch; this is a bearded figure wearing a sleeved himation; the hands, extended to right and left, probably held branches; a belt encircles the waist below which the figure forms a reversed acanthus. Until now we have known this strange figure only from relief Roman copies; it owns to eastern descent or inspiration. Archaeologists differ about its identification; some identify it with Sabazios, some with "Sardanapa-

166-168. ← In the antechamber of the "Prince's tomb" there was a narrow frieze painted with scenes from a chariot race. Two-horse chariots move at speed; the white horses and the red chariots are depicted against a deep blue background. The two detailed pictures (167,168) show clearly that each chariot displays individual characteristics and has been painted from a different angle; the simple but correct rendering of the ground is remarkable.

169. Ivory relief from the couch in the "Prince's tomb"; on the left a goat-footed Pan plays his pipes, his music guiding the couple behind him – a bearded man and a young woman. In his right hand the man holds a thyrsos (? a torch). It is undoubtedly the most marvellous relief of Greek miniature sculpture.

170

lus" and others still with a Dionysiac figure. Most indeed believe that it is a figure created in the late Hellenistic period; only H. Moebius, one of the most perceptive archaeologists of the preceding generation, maintained that this strange figure must be a creation of the mid-fourth century BC. Fifty years later this find at Vergina proves his opinion correct; it can be dated to the second half of the fourth century.

Alongside this very singular find were discovered three other figures, which form a thematic unity. To the left a young goat-footed Pan plays on a single pipe, his music leading on the couple, a mature bearded man and a young woman, who follow him. The man's right hand, holding the thyrsos (or a torch?) is extended in front of him, and his left balances him against his female companion; he has clearly been imbibing; his steps have the swaying uncertainty of the "bacchanal". The woman follows, her step also light. One might easily consider that the pair depict Dionysos and Ariadne, if one did not also know that in fourth century BC art Dionysos was shown as a beardless youth. And though it is not this divine couple, it is certainly a couple who belonged to the Dionysiac circle. The quality of the work is more important than the identification of the figures. It is undeniably a unique masterpiece of Greek miniature sculpture, designed and executed by a very experienced, and inspired, artist. The modelling of the mass, the nobility of the flesh, the grace of the drapery and movement and the unrivalled finishing touches to the details of all three figures create a captivating sequence of sculptured forms.

The metal objects

The grave goods in this tomb were very remarkable, though few in number and restricted in variety. The largest and most important group consisted of the silver vases; in addition to these there were two bronze vessels, the lampstand, two spear heads, the greaves, a pectoral and a large bronze wreath. In the antechamber were the strigils and two spears. The absence of clay vases is significant; there was nothing other than the lamp and a few sherds from some small vessel. Only a single alabastron completed the objects considered essential for the eternal residence of the young prince.

Most of the silver vases were found on the floor in the northeast corner of the chamber; more accur-

171

208

ately, they were found on the remains of wood. A second, smaller group was found above "leather" a short distance in front of the "table" with the funerary hydria. Everything had shifted from its original position; amongst the reasons for this was the collapse of the marble door leaf, though this might not have been the sole cause. It should be noted that many of the vases were of the type made up of three pieces (body, base, handles) stuck together and were found with their parts broken off and scattered.

We observed that the silver vases from "Philip's tomb" fell into the category of vessels used at banquets, and this is true of those from the "Prince's tomb". Many of the latter also formed pairs; the two kantharoi, two kalyxes, two kylixes, two "salt-cellars", two situlae, two dishes and seventeen bowls. Next to these were a fish dish, a strainer, a ladle, an oinochoe and a small jug, an askos, a perfume flask and a patera. It is evident that all these items were used either for food (dishes, "salt-cellars", bowls) or for wine. The situlae were used to pour the wine into the crater, the ladle to take it from there to the kantharoi, kalyxes and kylixes for consumption. The oinochoe of course was used to fill the drinking-cups and the strainer to purify the wine. The askos and the perfume flask were probably used to scent the hands after rinsing. What we said about the patera in "Philip's tomb" is true also of the one found here.

Taken as a group the silver vases are of very high quality, and are a group valuable both for their number and for their shape. Nevertheless, if we compare them with those from "Philip's tomb" they pale before the quality and superior artistry of the latter. This difference becomes even more marked in the decorative relief heads on the kalyxes and in other decorative elements on the surfaces of the vases, for example the palmettes on the situla. We must, however, make an exception fall to the floor, and on impact one of the nozzles

170-171. A silver perfume flask and a silver askos which contained perfumed oil to scent the hands after they had been rinsed at the end of a banquet.

172. A silver oinochoe used to fill the wine "glasses" during a banquet. The precious metal used to make these vessels (170-178) reveals the high standard of life enjoyed by the Macedonians and confirms literary references describing the sumptuous banquets held at the Macedonian court and by the Macedonian nobility.

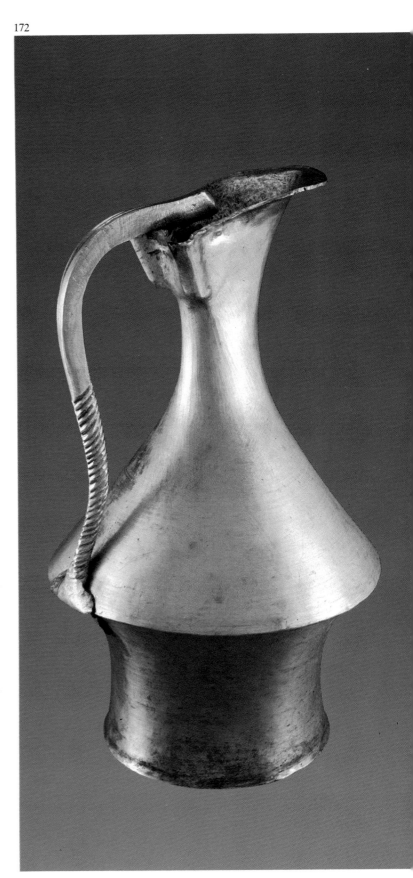

173

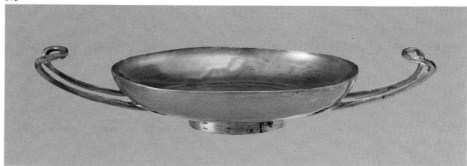

174

175

173-178. Silver vases for use at banquets from the "Prince's tomb". The stemless kylix (173) and the kantharos (174) served as "glasses"; water was mixed with wine in the crater (175), the small buckets (176, 177) were used to carry wine and the strainer (178) to cleanse it of impurities. There were a large number of silver vessels in the "Prince's tomb" in a rich variety of different shapes.

178

179

180

of the patera, both because it is an unusual shape in silver and, even more, because of its outstanding quality. Its peculiar long handle is embellished with a row of rings which project from the cylindrical surface and it terminates in the usual ram's head. The sculptural rendering of this head makes it a masterpiece and without exaggeration it is to be described as one of the highest-ranking creations of Greek metalwork. The linking of a realistic reproduction of the animal's features to their skilful schematization, the sculptural finish and finally the colour differentiation by the consummate exploitation of gold and silver in the rendering chiefly in the hairs of the ram all testify to the unrivalled talent of the craftsman as well as to his experience and sensitivity of feeling.

The fish dish, a shape well known in Attic pottery of the fourth century, is a unique example in silver, despite the fact that it is better suited to being worked in metal than to being thrown in clay on a wheel.

The silver ossuary-hydria, 0.45 m. tall, does not belong to the group of vessels for the banquet. As we have said, this hydria was specially constructed for use as a container of bones, since it was cut in half immediately below the shoulder so that the burnt bones might easily be placed inside. The two sections were held together by square hinges placed on the touching edges. The lower part of the hydria which was found within the hollow of the "table" had suffered considerable corrosion from having been in contact with the damp surface of the stone, and it had disintegrated into many small pieces which have been reunited. At the starting point of the neck is a rough inscription ΜΝΑΙΕ (= Μναῖ, five) and below it; ΔΡΑΞΗ (= drachmae 68) which represents the weight of the hydria (modern equivalent 2.300 gr.).

A gold wreath of oak leaves and acorns was found placed round the shoulder of the hydria. It is not as heavy as that found in "Philip's tomb" but, second to that, it is one of the most beautiful and most impressive gold wreaths to have survived from antiquity.

The silver-plated iron lampstand 1.315 m. high, stood upright almost at the centre of the western side of the chamber. It is one of the few known examples of the type. On its upper side there is a disc, 0.11 m. in diameter, on which the lamp would have been placed. The lamp itself had two nozzles and was large and of high quality. The vibrations from the collapse of the marble door caused it to

179-180. Relief heads of tiny Pans which decorated the inside of the bases of kalyxes.

181-182. The "frying-pan" shaped object, a patera, from the "prince's tomb" is the only example of its kind in silver; particular care has been taken over the large cylindrical handle which ends in a ram's head. The sculptural moulding of this head, especially the rendering of the hair and the horns, and the exceptionally well-applied gilding, has achieved a magnificent result.

183. → The silver ossuary-hydria with the gold wreath on the shoulder, after restoration. This hydria was specially constructed for use in a tomb and this is why it was cut at the height of the handles and given hinges to hold the upper and lower sections together after they had been closed. There is an inscription on the neck which gives us its weight; 568 drachma (= 2.440 grammes approx.).

184. → The gold wreath of oak leaves and acorns found on the shoulders of the ossuary hydria.

181
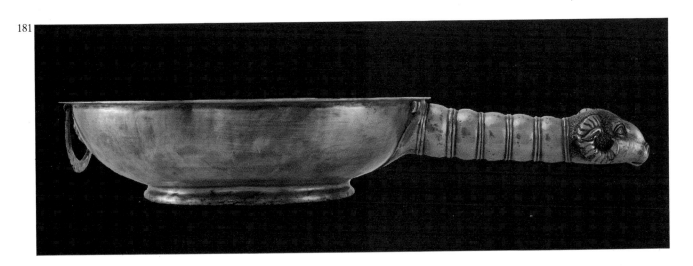

182

broke and was thrown as far as the door between the main chamber and the antechamber.

In the northwest corner of the chamber there were two large bronze vessels. One of these, cauldron-shaped, was pinned below the end fragment of the broken door and is still intact in this position. The second is the circular, almost flat dish 0.67 m. in diameter and 0.14 m. deep. Both had been silver-plated; the plating of the dish had covered the whole surface, inside and out. It was executed in very thin square sheets of silver, which is why the silvering had peeled off from large areas.

The weapons of the dead man must have been deposited towards the southwest corner of the chamber. The two thin square gold sheets found near the western (rear) wall came from the cuirass, probably made of linen. The gilded bronze greaves with the meticulous decoration at the ankles and the pectoral made from iron plates, bronze and leather which preserved gilt decoration at a number of points, were found near the south wall.

Finally, not far from these a large broken wreath of myrtle leaves and berries was found. It must have hung on the wall and shattered when it fell. Its almost circular (slightly elliptical) rod is of ivory; in it are small holes which held the wire stalks of the leaves and berries; the leaves were of gilded bronze, while the berries were of gilded terracotta. A thin leather strip passed inside the rod. Lastly, close to the corner of the "table" two iron spear-heads were found.

The discovery of an iron hammer on the floor of the main chamber was totally unexpected. Almost certainly we should not regard it as part of the grave goods for the deceased. Some workman must have forgotten it, probably before the burial ceremony. It is certainly a most welcome find since, though it is not a unique example, these objects are rarely discovered.

Taken as a whole, the finds form a display of uncommon wealth; the unique nature of some (the gold spear, the gilded greaves and strigils, the gold "epaulettes" of the cuirass) and the exceptionally high quality of the ivory reliefs substantiates the view that the dead man in this tomb was a member of the royal family.

185. The gilded bronze greaves which were found in the main chamber of the "Prince's tomb". The breadth of the greave at the calf shows that the young man who wore them have been of sturdy build. Their meticulous decoration at the ankles is noteworthy.

CONCLUSIONS

After this all too brief presentation of the buildings and the finds contained therein, it is necessary to attempt an answer to the questions they pose. Of course, the final answer can only be given when the study of all the finds is complete and only within a strictly academic framework; in other words, it must incorporate the conclusions of the detailed and systematic archaeological publication, which will require a long time. However, even in this preliminary and generalized presentation I can, indeed I must, set out in simple terms the problems which arise and the solutions I regard as probable. It is essential to repeat something which I have said and written many times already, that I am fully conscious of the difficulties and I recognize that though it falls to me to have the first word, I am certainly not the person who will have the last.

In the six years which have elapsed since the discovery of the first tombs and the writing of this book a number of articles written by historians and archaeologists referring to the finds from Vergina, as well as my own brief reports, have been published. Almost all my colleagues have been concerned with the identity of the dead man in "Philip's tomb". Their observations have been based on information which I in the meantime had set before them. It cannot be otherwise. Sometimes they have not paid enough attention to this information, sometimes they misinterpret it; on most occasions the arguments employed have been selective and certain factors have been isolated in order that more general conclusions may be reached. Not infrequently they mentioned views published in newspapers or magazines with a wide circulation; there have even been articles which attributed to me opinions I have never expressed. It is in keeping with such writing that the word "rumour" has been used to describe sources of information. Perhaps the basic responsibility for all this lies at my door, because I regarded it as an obligation to make news of these finds public immediately; thus I deviated from the accepted archaeological practice of making a single solemn announcement, proceeding to a fuller exposition of the results only after the end of the excavation and the completion of the systematic study of the finds. But I have no regrets, and I believe that I had not only the right, but still more, the obligation to let the whole world know about the discoveries as fast as I could, even if this exposed me to certain criticisms from more orthodox archaeological quarters. My respected colleague, Georges Daux, the first who spoke and wrote of the finds at Vergina only a few days after the first announcement, observed that this speed created dangers for me of which, as he himself observed, I was well aware. I should like to add that I adopted this position because of the concern implanted in me by my teacher Constantine Rhomaios that archaeological research should not be restricted only to a handful of specialists, but that it is an obligation that findings should be communicated as quickly as possible to a wider public. For this reason he published his first announcement both of the excavation of the palace and of the tomb at Vergina in journals with a wide, and I would even say popular, circulation.

Now, in the present attempt to provide a more extended presentation of the finds – though still not the final and strictly academic report – I have no desire to reply systematically to everything that has been written up to now. It is obvious that I cannot ignore it; nevertheless I shall try to summarize my thoughts in the same way as I would have done had nothing been published and, perhaps of more importance, with every intention of avoiding polemic involvement. Many of the objections advanced and questions raised in print arise from my own halting thought processes, still not resolved in every case; these very doubts compelled me to proceed to formulate answers as convincing as I could make them, at least to myself.

As my thoughts have developed, the reader may perhaps discern an underlying dialectical relationship; it would be a mistake – and erroneous – for him to imagine that my thinking has progressed in a vicious circle, and that it suffers from the fault that Aristotelian logic knows as a *petitio principii*. That is, if I maintain that premise A leads to conclusion B and then that conclusion B in its turn reinforces the authority of premise A, it does not in the least mean that my thinking has progressed in a specious manner; on the contrary, I believe that only by such a dialectical approach, as I have called it, can academic thinking move to its ultimate conclusions which will underpin or overturn all the premises under discussion.[25]

This dialectical method also encompasses the cumulative value of arguments and factors adduced in proof, even though by itself none is convincing or incontrovertible proof and can easily be upset. However, subversive logic must also possess a corresponding cohesion and cumulative value. In these few words I am trying to put on their guard some of those who have attempted to confront my positions, restricting their arguments to one or two points selected from the whole array I have presented and maintained up to now.

First of all let us summarize some useful facts.

1) Up to the time when these tombs were discovered (October 1977) fifty-one other Macedonian tombs were known, larger or smaller.

2) Except for one, all fifty-one had been robbed; the only unrobbed one was found near Karytsa, Pieria but its contents were exceptionally poor and insignificant.

3) The fifty-one tombs were either found by chance or were known to inhabitants of the area of old.

4) In the Vergina region three Macedonian tombs had been excavated up to 1977; during further excavation we discovered another six; thus at Vergina we have a total, to date, of nine Macedonian tombs.

5) Almost all the Macedonian tombs were found in isolation; only at Lakkoma in Chalcidice were two small destroyed Macedonian tombs found one next to the other. The two exceptions we have are the tombs of the Great Tumulus at Vergina and the three tombs of the "Bella Tumulus" also in the Vergina region and excavated in 1981.

These facts mean that a) we have plenty of monuments for comparison, and b) that we have scarcely any comparative material for the contents of the tomb because in very few cases are the remains of the grave goods anything but fragmentary. The second conclusion is susceptible of further subdivision because in a number of instances stone objects such as couches, sarcophagi, "tables", "thrones" and similar items have survived in robbed tombs.

One further general observation has, I think, its place here. All the known Macedonian tombs, or at least all those with a carefully constructed architectural facade present a particular architectural form. No two tombs have an identical facade. This is important because with a construction so simple architecturally, where the dimensions do not differ significantly, one would expect a greater degree of similarity and standardization. However the tombs of the Great Tumulus present anomalies other than the simple architectonic variation of the frieze. I shall attempt to list them:

1) The rectangular tomb with the painting of the rape of Persephone, though it is not unique, is a rarely found example of its type of such a size. Its wall paintings, covering all the empty surfaces of the walls, of course are unique. I shall speak later of the quality of the work which we have already noted in the relevant section.

2) The frieze which crowns the facade of both vaulted tombs is unique. If indeed my observation is correct, that in the smaller tomb the frieze was decorated by a moveable wooden panel, we also have an additional peculiarity. Finally, the existence of the frieze depicting the chariot races in the antechamber of the same tomb, apart from the frieze on the facade, is an unusual element which is worth noting.

3) Particularly important – and problematical – are the anomalies of "Philip's tomb".

a) the brick wall which rises slightly above and next to the vertical wall of the facade. It has no intrinsic link with the tomb, and was probably used to retain the earth which would cover the vault in the first phase of construction.

b) the plastering of the upper part of the vault, which at certain points at least, is more than ten centimetres thick. Where one part of the plastering of the back projects sufficiently from the stones of the vault and overlies the earth which covered the rear (western) wall, it indicates that the plastering was executed after the vault of the chamber had been covered up to a certain point with earth. This is confirmed by the layering of the plastering.

c) the vault is interrupted exactly above the wall between the chamber and the antechamber; the vault of the antechamber is a few centimetres lower than that of the chamber. It is clear that these two parts were built at different times and not as a unified whole.

d) the constructional differences noted between the chamber and the antechamber confirms and strengthens the preceding observation. The positioning of the stones in the side walls suggests that in the first phase of the work the side walls were erected for their whole length to the facade, but not to their full height; construction reached the row below the spring of the vault. Work continued in the main chamber and when the vault of this part was completed (and probably the plastering as well), work continued in the antechamber.

e) the most unexpected and problematical anomaly of the tomb is the plastering. The main chamber has only the first two coats and even these are not always evenly applied or of the same colour; the final, thin coat is nowhere to be seen and certainly nowhere has the plasterwork been painted. It is obvious that the work was carried out very hurriedly and was confined to a token covering of the uneven surface of the limestone. In contrast, the plastering of the antechamber was completed and it has the usual thin, final coat and smooth surface known from other buildings in the area. Indeed, it has been painted and decorated with rosettes. This very striking difference is consistent with what we noticed about the construction of the building in the previous comments (c,d).

f) Although this is not the only exception, it is worth noting that the back surface of the marble doors boasts no more than a coarse finish which contrasts with the sumptuousness and wealth of the tomb.

g) Above "Philip's tomb" – in one case almost directly above the tomb – the remains of pyres with the remains of many burnt potsherds and animal bones were found. At least three of these pyres were connected with the tomb and the only interpretation that I can offer is that they are connected with offerings made to the dead man. A similar pyre was noted above the smaller vaulted tomb (the

"Prince's tomb"). A far as I know, nothing comparable has been noticed in any other Macedonian tomb, even though the earth which covered the vault had not been disturbed by robbers.

h) The heap of sun-dried bricks which was found above the vault of the chamber is unique. The detailed investigation of the pyre shows that it was not a funerary altar, as I originally suggested. Now that this interpretation has been excluded, the facts which have emerged lead in another direction, which turns out to be the only possible explanation. These facts are the following: (a) many of the bricks bear clear traces of burning; (b) two burnt swords, a spearhead, the bronze bridle and the iron parts of harnesses were found between the bricks and the earth; (c) scattered about at one point in the pile were hundreds of small fragments of burnt ivory which probably formed the decoration of wooden objects; (d) in the pile six gold acorns and a small piece of a gold oak leaf were found. These pieces certainly belong to the large gold wreath found in the larnax in the chamber above the bones of the deceased.

All this convinces me that the sun-dried bricks in this heap come from the site of the pyre on which the deceased was cremated. They were probably part of a square structure on which the inflammable material was placed. Similar structures have been found above a tomb in Thessalonike (the Maternity Hospital) and at Leukadia (the tomb of Lyson and Kallikles). After the interment, they were moved, together with the objects that had been burnt on the pyre, and heaped above the tomb (we shall discuss the presence of the gold acorns below).

As we noted above, the fact that all the Macedonian tombs which had been discovered up to 1977 – and the three new ones discovered in 1981-82 – had been robbed deprives us of the possibility of comparing the contents of the two unrobbed tombs with others. It also excludes the marshalling of many conclusions which could have been of decisive help in reaching a better-based and more certain interpretation of the contents. There is, however, one very important piece of comparative evidence. I mean the existence of two marble sarcophagi in which the gold ossuary larnax was found. Up to now stone vessels which probably contained an ossuary vase have been found in three cases. In all three the container was of stone, not marble. But the most important fact is something else again; that neither in these three instances nor in any others was any evidence found testifying to burial in the antechamber, while the existence of more burials in the main chamber is very common. In only one example, in a tomb at Amphipolis, is there a stone construction in the antechamber which was probably used for burial (this exception should perhaps be attributed to the lack of space in the main chamber, but this does not apply to the Vergina tomb).

At this point it is useful to recall that in the heap of bricks which was found above the vault of the tomb and which came, as we have noted, from the pyre on which the corpse was cremated, was a number of burnt objects (swords, a spearhead, horse trappings, bronze, ivory). All these testify that in addition to the objects which were deposited in the tomb and had indeed been offered to the dead man, still others were placed on the pyre, amongst them a number of valuable items as the innumerable fragments of burnt ivory show.

THE DATING OF THE TOMBS

The date of any archaeological find is the key to its understanding and interpretation. The establishment of the date is especially useful in the case of the tombs at Vergina. It is therefore necessary to give the reader rather more information than the nature of this publication warrants. However, he must permit me to re-iterate that only in the scholarly publication of the finds shall I be in a position to state my final, detailed and proven position in regard to this problem.

The inquiry into the chronological limits within which we must operate began even before the discovery of any archaeological feature. As I noted above, sacrificial pyres containing burnt bones and potsherds were found in the overburden of the Great Tumulus. The pyre was located above the northern end of the mud brick wall which rose above the facade behind the cornice of the tomb. When we collected up the sherds we[26] ascertained that they must date to immediately after the middle of the fourth century BC (350 BC) and certainly to the third quarter of the century (350-325 BC). This conclusion was not influenced by any external factor, since we were as yet unaware of any other feature. When we had removed the sherds and the bones red, burnt earth remained below them. I myself cleared this earth with the greatest possible

care thus discovering for myself that a few centimetres below the burnt soil was the upper, narrow surface of the strange wall of whose function I was also ignorant. This means that the pyre and the sherds had sealed the strange wall and they could be dated with absolute certainty. I should add that I had not expected such an early building; this date, and the strange wall whose purpose I found impossible to comprehend, created many problems and teased our archaeological imagination.

Following the discovery of the three tombs – and later of a fourth one, destroyed – which had offered us abundant dating evidence, we may say that these initial guidelines for dating formed the firm basis which was reinforced by the rest of our observations.

It is well known that classical archaeologists have succeeded in dating the works of Greek antiquity within very safe, narrow margins which do not exceed a period of twenty-five years; indeed, in most cases and in particular for the sixth, fifth and fourth centuries an exact date, to within ten years, can usually be ascribed. The large number, and even more, the wide selection of the finds from Vergina provides a broader, firmer base for their chronology. The pottery vases are an initial, firm, starting point; but next to these rank both the silver and the bronze vessels whose shapes provide very useful evidence. Indeed, many of the metal vessels are decorated with relief heads which, by another route, give the archaeologist a date. The clues to be picked up from the ivory which embellished the furniture are also significant; the portrait heads and reliefs of mythological subjects, which form an important subdivision of the finds, amplify the picture of sculptural creativity. Finally, the gold gorytos with its rich relief decoration, ranks in this latter category. The weapons provide less information for dating, but it is not entirely absent even from them. Lastly, there is the architectural style of the facade and the wall paintings which, from another point of view, shed light on the dating of the finds.

I believe that the three tombs belong to a time span which does not exceed that of one generation. Nevertheless, it is possible to discern a small time difference between them. I shall discuss this problem below; what we may say immediately is that all these tombs fall within the fourth century BC. That is beyond doubt. I also think it is indisputable that we should exclude a date before the middle of the century (350 BC). Lastly, I believe that we may rule out the closing years of the century. This leaves us manoeuvring within a period of time which starts around 350 BC and finishes around 315-310 BC.

I deem it useful to start by trying to establish more exact chronological limits for "Philip's tomb" and to continue by discussing its chronological links with the two other tombs.

A few pottery objects were found in "Philip's tomb" amongst them a lamp. The type of lamp, as we know it from two series, from Corinth and from the Agora in Athens, falls comfortably into the third quarter of the fourth century BC (350-325 BC). The red-figure askos and the black glazed oinochoe which were in the tomb also fall within the same limits. It is worth noting that neither of these two pottery objects seem to have been used before they were placed in the tomb, since the lower surface was completely unrubbed.

The four pottery "salt-cellars" in the tomb also seem to have been unused. The recent dating of a related group of pots from the Agora in Athens to later than 325 BC demands their careful study; however, because a sufficient number of examples in the group were dated to the third quarter of the century, I believe that I have the right to place the Vergina examples within the same time limits to which I assign the other clay vessels. Finally, there is a "Cypriot" amphora (and sherds of a least one other) which, as far as I can judge, dates to around 350 BC or immediately thereafter. Thus the pottery finds from the tomb, like the finds in the pyres above it, suggest a preliminary time limit which covers the third quarter of the fourth century.

Two indications of date are offered by the silver vases; a) their shape and b) the decorative relief heads which embellished their handles. We should, however, say immediately that the quality of all the silver (and of the bronze) vessels in "Philip's tomb" is exceptionally high and immediately causes them to be distinguished from other similar vessels such as those for example found in the tombs at Derveni (near Thessalonike). This factor has a significance which goes beyond the artistic implications; it must be regarded as a useful contribution to the search for a date, because these objects cannot possibly be a mechanical repetition of known shapes. It is more probable that they were the models for others. This means that they are earlier than their derivatives.

However, independent of this comment, I believe that as a group these vases can be compared with the finds from Derveni. On first glance, and at

a first appraisal, we may say that they belong to approximately the same period which, at least for tomb B at Derveni is defined to a certain extent by the gold tri-obol of Philip which was found in the heavily sculptured crater. But a more careful examination would convince us that almost all the vases of the Vergina tomb have a much more severe and solid form. In none of them are the curves of the body and the handles transformed into satisfying and invitingly mobile surfaces or lines. The two small amphorae, for example, and even more the kantharoi and the two jugs, retain all the severity of the classical tradition, unaffected by the currents of the "hellenism" to come. If indeed the comparison with the vases of Derveni leads us immediately to a date which is still within the third quarter of the century, more careful observation and comparison of the shapes allows us, if indeed it does not force us, to accept the beginning of this period as the more probable date for their creation, (i.e. the decade 350-340 BC).

I believe that the relief heads of the handles lead us to the same conclusion. A comparison of the two Silens which decorate the two jugs with the portraits of the fourth century BC such as those of Plato, Aristotle and especially of Socrates, with the shapes of grave stelai of this period and lastly with the bronze head of the boxer of Olympia which is attributed to Silanion convinces us that a date of around immediately after 350 BC is the only possible one. If, however, as I believe, not without reason, these figures are indeed the creations of great masters and not of humble craftsmen, this date is further strengthened.

Absolutely identical evidence is revealed by the two bronze jugs both in their shape and in the head of a "Medusa" on one of them. This head, with its strict moulding, firm and immobile flesh on the cheeks, the shaping and arrangement of the curls would be very difficult to place later than the decade 350-340, though it could easily have expressed the language of sculpture prevalent even a little before this.

Rich material for discussion taken from modelling is provided by the small reliefs which decorated the wooden furniture. The attested dating and artistic inter-relationship of the many figures which have been preserved would need a longer analysis than can be presented within the limits of this book. I shall confine myself therefore to the comment that both the group of the mythological figures (a seated Muse playing a lyre, Dionysos and a Silen, a hermaic stele etc.) and the "portait" group can be ranged in the sculptural shapes of about the middle of the fourth century; it is, I think, impossible on the basis of the dated shapes we know to date them after 330 BC. Both the heads of Philip, of Alexander and of the others in the same group are with difficulty viewed as creations later in date than the sculptures of Tegea while the mythological carvings are undoubtedly earlier than the base of Mantinea. In brief therefore we may say that these reliefs also fall within the same time limits which have been established by an examination of the preceding evidence – that is to the period 350-325 BC.

Although destruction has deprived us of the opportunity to pass more exact comment, the stance and the general shape of the two figures which decorate the centre of the gold and ivory shield can be brought to bear to reinforce all the estimates we have referred to up to now.

The two gold gorgoneions and the decoration of the large gold larnax are amongst the remaining objects which make a contribution to the problem of date. Perhaps even more useful than everything else is the gilded gorytos with its two relief bands and its upright figure. The similar Scythian gorytoi which have been found in Russia have been dated to about the middle of the fourth century BC. This date is confirmed by the Vergina gorytos. A provisional comparison with the frieze of the Mausoleum suffices to convince us that we are in roughly the same period, while the figure of the upright "warrior", like some of the women on the two bands, echoes still older creations.

The sole deviation from the dates which emerge from the objects found in the tomb is the bronze tripod which belongs to the fifth century BC; it has no connection with the date of the tomb.

Thus the evidence at our disposal for dating the finds seems to be adequate and permits us to uphold the third quarter of the fourth century BC as the years in which they were created. However, this dating which in other cases would be deemed sufficient to date the tomb as well must in the instance of the Vergina tomb be backed up if this can be done, by the funerary monument itself, so that the conclusions which will be drawn about the identity of its occupant can be as well based as possible.

For the dating of the tomb we have the architectural evidence of the building and the wall painting.

The architectural members of the facade which can provide us with some indications of date are the column capitals and even more the triglyphs. However, I regard their certain dating to within the limits of a quarter century as impossible, even though I judge their shape which is preserved with quite sufficient clarity in the curvature to be enough to place them within the limits we have accepted for the rest of the finds.

An attendant objection may arise from another architectural feature – from the vault. The use of the vault in Greek lands is apparently a real stumbling block for some archaeologists, preventing them accepting a date for the tomb in the third quarter of the fourth century BC. It has been maintained that the Greeks were introduced to the shape of the arch and the vault during the campaigns of Alexander the Great in the East and that it was only adopted by the Greeks after that time. This matter cannot be debated in these pages. A brief answer to this objection has already been published in an archaeological journal. I shall therefore confine myself here to a brief recapitulation of the main arguments which give me the right to regard this objection as indecisive for a later date for the tomb (that is, after the campaigns of Alexander).

1) *The Laws* of Plato (who died in 348 BC) contain a description of a tomb with a vault which corresponds to the shape of a Macedonian tomb with remarkable accuracy.

2) Ancient sources tell us that Democritos was regarded as the inventor of the arch – he was a philosopher who lived in the fifth century BC.

3) The vault was not so widespread or characteristic an architectural shape in houses in the East.

4) The campaigns of Alexander were not the Greeks' first acquaintance with the East. Contacts with Persia were close and thousands of Greeks had had the opportunity to get to know the eastern world centuries before the time of Alexander.

5) Even if all the above were not known to us, I regard it as absurd to think that Greek architects could not have contrived the solution of the arch – which is technically very simple – when we know that centuries earlier tholos tombs had been constructed and men had arrived at solutions to far more difficult problems.

The discovery in 1976 of a large two-chamber tomb close to Katerini which had a flat roof and dated to the years of Amyntas III (381-369) will, I think, help us to understand how the Macedonians were led, quite logically, to the construction of large vaulted tombs when they perceived that the flat roof could not withstand the weight of earth piled on top of it. Once again we may understand that the search for foreign prototypes and theoretical solutions is not the answer to problems posed by buildings. I believe that specific needs led men to the solution they required.

Certainly the problem of the vault, even if its final solution has not been reached, is not a decisive hindrance to dating the Vergina tomb to before the campaigns of Alexander.

There remains the wall painting. The brief analysis I have already given I believe brings out the fact that this masterpiece has not overstepped the bounds of traditional classical taste. Despite the hints of dawning change and daring innovation it subjugated its form to the principles of this tradition. The opportunity for comparison afforded by the mosaic of the battle of Alexander permits us to observe the time difference which separates them. If, however, as nearly all historians of Greek painting agree, the original of the mosaic dates to around 315 BC (certainly it dates to the decade 320-310) then a date in the decade 340-330 BC for the wall painting seems the most likely. Such a date is accepted indeed by one of the men best versed in Greek painting, Karl Schefold.[27] But, as we have seen, and as we shall add later, the wall painting offers useful evidence not only for the dating of the tomb but for the probable identification of the dead man.

From this brief survey we may, I think, reach the conclusion that both the portable finds and the tomb itself can be dated with re-assuring certainty to the third quarter of the fourth century BC.

As we noted, the "tomb of Persephone" had been pillaged; only a few sherds were found in the earth which had covered part of the tomb. Some of these belong to a fish dish which can be dated to around the middle of the fourth century BC.

The wall paintings remain as a pointer to the most likely date for the tomb. The figures on the south wall, although not very well preserved, could be placed chronologically in the middle of the century. A similar date is reached from consideration of the seated figure of Demeter. More evidence is offered by the composition on the north wall, the rape of Persephone. The severe and mature modelling of the horses confirms that it cannot be much

later than the horses of the quadriga with the rider on the well known marble fragment from Herculaneum and from other similar themes on Italian vases from about the middle of the century. I think it is beyond question that the figures of Pluto, Persephone, Hermes and Kyane are to be convincingly placed, without contorting the evidence, within the artistic conventions of the middle of the century, as illustrated both by vase painting and by contemporary works of sculpture.

It is therefore inescapable that the "tomb of Persephone" dates to about the middle of the fourth century BC or immediately afterwards.

The third tomb must be the latest. This follows from its position in the original mound and from the archaeological evidence which showed that the tumulus had been disturbed at this point after its construction so that this tomb could be built. But the finds, which in general are to be placed around 325 BC, testify to a brief difference in time from the finds in "Philip's tomb". The clay lamp is a telling illustration for the dating, being of a newer type than the corresponding objects in "Philip's tomb". The silver vases, the ivory reliefs and the wall paintings also suggest that we should accept a slightly later date.

THE CHARACTER OF THE TOMBS

As we noted at the beginning of this section no other Macedonian tomb has been found unrobbed. We are thus deprived of the opportunity for comparison with the contents of other large Macedonian tombs and it is therefore possible to conjecture that these too may have contained the same rich, if not richer, objects. Were this so, the claim that the tomb of the Great Tumulus is royal – which I did not hesitate to advance in my very first announcement – would be arbitrary indeed. I therefore think it incumbent on me to expound, however briefly, the reasons which led me to such a description, even though no archaeologist or historian has challenged it, as far as I know.

Though the pillaging of the other tombs has taken away many of our other fundamental points of comparison, it cannot deprive us of the evidence to be derived from the monuments themselves. Perhaps by chance, this evidence is decisive for our argument.

I shall not invoke the size of "Philip's tomb"

which, as we have seen, is the largest of all those known up to now; nor its antiquity which constitutes an effective indication of its character. However, both here and in the "tomb of Persephone" wall paintings are preserved while in the "Prince's tomb", where the outer frieze has been destroyed, a painted frieze survives in the antechamber. Other examples of painted decoration in Macedonian tombs existed in four tombs at Leukadia, one at Dion and one of the three tombs recently discovered, again in the Vergina area. We should add also the tomb excavated by K. A. Rhomaios at Vergina. None of the other tombs offers anything other than the architectural form of the facade, executed with a greater or lesser degree of care. We have therefore one specific piece of evidence whereby I believe we may compare the other robbed tombs with the tombs of the Great Tumulus at Vergina.

The painted decoration of the robbed tombs, whether it is confined to decorative elements (the tomb of Lyson and Kallikles at Leukadia, Rhomaios' tomb at Vergina) or to a small scale scene (Kinch's Tomb at Leukadia) or is a combination of both (the tomb of Leukadia, Rhomiopoulou's excavation) is in no way comparable to the wall paintings of the great tomb at Vergina. Only the large tomb at Leukadia (Petsas' excavation) and the tomb of the "Bella Tumulus" at Vergina provide painted material sufficient for comparison with the tombs described as "royal". On the facade of the Leukadia tomb there are four figures, distributed between the four inter-columniated spaces. Thus, although the theme is a unity – the dead man, Hermes the conductor of souls, and the two judges of Hades – each figure has an independent existence: there is no link between them. In other words, there is not an artistic composition.

In the tomb of the "Bella Tumulus" at Vergina, three figures are painted on a single wall above the height of the door; in the centre the dead warrior, on the left a female figure extending her hand with a golden wreath and on the right the seated figure of a young warrior. Here too the figures are independent of each other and, although they probably make up a thematic unity, they are not linked into an integrated painted composition.

In both these cases the artist has confronted only one problem; the drawing and painting of one figure. And there is something even more important; the rendering of a figure in a definite position. The

dromenon is presented by intimation rather than by being painted. This means that the painter has limited his aims and there is no risk that his talent is outstripped by his subject.

This aspect therefore of the artistic composition gives us no point of comparison with the works of the royal tombs where the compositional force of their creator is peerless.

But if we were to confine ourselves to a comparison of the figures and of their drawing, we would again be in difficulties in the search for some common ground, since almost no figure in the paintings of the royal tombs is static. Even the seated figures in the "tomb of Persephone" betray some movement – whether it be of the hand, of the body or of the head, there is some intimation of inner life. Over and above this difference, the drawing and the colouring of the two groups separates them in no uncertain fashion; on the one hand we have a correct but almost lifeless drawing, completed by a banal range of colours, and on the other there is the dynamism of the design which soars to the extreme limits of its expressive strength complemented by the most inspired and inspiring chromatic composition.

Briefly, one group is perhaps the work of competent craftsmen lacking the creative touch, while the others are the works of large scale painting by inspired artists of the greatest ability.

This immense difference in the quality of the painting is enough to convince us that the tombs of the Great Tumulus are to be differentiated immediately from the other Macedonian tombs which we know of up to now.

A second point of comparison is provided by the foundations of the building which we have labelled the "heroon". No other instance of a similar structure adjacent to tombs is known. If the interpretation as a "heroon" is correct – and I at least can find no other explanation – this means that the adjacent tombs did not belong to common mortals, nor even to the well-to-do or nobly born like all the other Macedonian tombs. We shall see later that the existence of the "heroon" does indeed signify far more.

A third point which permits comparison and the mustering of conclusions is the existence of the huge mound, unique in its dimensions throughout Macedonia. There is no such unusual construction over any of the other Macedonian tombs. The original mound had a considerable diameter and height but was not of unusual dimensions. The importance of the mound we excavated lies in the fact that it was added to the original one many years after the construction of the tomb and the interment of the corpse. The significance of the mound extends beyond this, however.

With only these pointers to permit comparison with other known tombs I considered the conjecture that the tombs were royal was convincing. I think that the contents of the tomb confirms this belief. It may perhaps be questioned whether the wealth of the tombs is unique since we have no opportunity for comparison. But the quality of each object is unmatched and marks it out from every similar example we know of. It would be easy for me to remind the reader that the two wreaths of oak leaves are the heaviest gold wreaths to have survived and, as we noted, must have been unique in their time. The woman's diadem and the fabric are finds wholly out of the ordinary, and, in addition to all these, there are the two gold larnaces which contained the bones. If in any of the other tombs there had been something similar, it must have been protected by similar marble sarcophagi which have not been preserved in the tombs. Setting this aside, the exceptionally heavy gold larnax with the typical starburst would not have been used lightly for the burial of a mere mortal. Not only was gold a precious metal of great value, but it was a symbol of royalty. So too is the purple fabric in which the bones were wrapped. The sacrifice of horses and the burning of many valuable objects on the pyre all come together, adding their weight to the testimony of every preceding indication.

I shall conclude my presentation of the facts which indicate that the tomb is royal with two more which I believe are the least easily gainsaid. In the main chamber of the tomb a unique gold and ivory shield was found in a state of disintegration; together with this was part of another shield. Lastly, from the remains of the pyre were some small iron fragments of a third shield which was burnt along with the dead man. All three shields bore heraldic relief depictions of lions at the centre of the inner side and above the sheet which fits the handle. On the burnt piece, between the lion's feet, there is the Macedonian star. I think these lions can only be interpreted as the symbol of royal authority. Even by itself the unique gold and ivory shield would suffice to assure us that the occupant of the tomb was of royal lineage. But to cap this, a small,

rectangular gold sheet on the inside of this shield was decorated with the club of Heracles in relief. This I believe constituted the emblem or device of the royal family which regarded Heracles as its forebear as the inscription found in the palace of Vergina testifies – *ΗΡΑΚΛΗΙ ΠΑΤΡΩΙΩΙ.*

Finally, we have the unique circular diadem which, whatever interpretation we seek to lay upon it, we must accept as having belonged to the king. Even if, as has been suggested, it is taken as a priestly symbol, we know that the king of the Macedonians was also the high priest (although he would have been a strange figure of a priest or high priest with all the weapons he possessed!)

It is evident that if the great tomb is royal, as it appears to be, the two other tombs covered by the original mound and built side by side must also belong to members of the royal family.

THE IDENTITY OF THE DEAD

In my original announcement I summarized my first judgement on the identity of the dead man in the words "basing my judgement on firm archaeological evidence, I believe I have the right to claim this tomb as that of Philip II."

Today, its excavation is complete, and although the study of the finds has not yet been completed it is necessary for me to set forth my views on this problem in greater detail, the more so since, in spite of my original statement that the most important aspect was not the identity of the deceased but the finds themselves, the interest of many scholars has concentrated on the former.

We may regard it as certain that the tomb is royal, and, to be more precise still, that the dead man was a king. It is also certain that it dates to after 350 BC and equally certainly to before 310 BC. In my opinion the latter date is very late, and we might legitimately say that the latest chronological limit is 325-320 BC. However, to exclude any *a priori* objection and for the sake of logic and method I accept the possibility of dating the tomb between these two extreme limits; 350-310 BC. Three Macedonian kings died within this time span; Philip II; Alexander III (the Great) and Philip III Arrhidaios, son of Philip II and the half brother of Alexander. He was proclaimed king after the death of Alexander, but he suffered from a severe mental disability which prevented him from exercising military duties. Alexander was buried in Alexandria and so the dead man in the tomb at Vergina can be only Philip II or Philip III Arrhidaios.

Philip II was murdered at Aigai in 336 BC and was interred there. Philip III was assassinated in the autumn of 317 BC by Olympias. When, the following spring (316 BC) Cassander executed Olympias and in fact took over the kingdom, he had a royal tomb built for Philip Arrhidaios, his wife Eurydice and her mother Kynna. This means that Arrhidaios' "royal" tomb was in reality a re-burial in a new tomb, because his first interment had been carried out by Olympias, naturally without any ceremony.

As we have seen, there was a double burial in the Vergina tomb; the bones of a man were found in the main chamber and those of a woman in the antechamber. This immediately led to the speculation that the deceased could be Philip Arrhidaios and Eurydice. This, I think, was the reason which led several scholars to dispute my suggestion and support this alternative which seems to provide the most satisfactory answer. I ruled this view out immediately; and of course I had my reasons for doing so. I deem it useful now to set them out in full, though even by confining myself to the most effective I would completely vindicate my opinion.

1) The first – and I think conclusive on its own – emerges from indisputable archaeological evidence which permits us to define the chronological relationship between the interment and the cremation of the dead man with certainty. That is, we know that the burial of the burned bones in the great tomb took place immediately after the cremation of the dead man, in accordance with usual practice. This is demonstrated by the fact that many objects which came from the pyre on which the deceased was burnt were found above the vault. As we have seen, the heap of bricks must have belonged to the construction of the pyre. After the cremation of the dead man, and after the bones had been gathered up and laid in the tomb, all the remains from the pyre were also collected up and placed above the chamber. Amongst these remains were two iron swords, a spearhead, the iron horse trappings and innumerable pieces of burnt ivory. But the most important and revealing items are the gold acorns and the gold fragments of oak leaves which come from the large gold wreath found in the gold larnax. These were found together with the other burnt objects in the pile of sun-dried bricks and earth above the vault. Indeed, the bare twigs of the wreath testify to the number of leaves and acorns missing from it. On some leaves of the wreath traces of fire can still be seen, and they are visible also on the chryselephantine shield on both its outer side and on the gold sheets of the inside. All these facts permit us to deduce with assurance that the gold wreath and the shield, in addition to the plethora of other objects which were offerings to the deceased, were placed on the pyre. When the flames began to rise higher, the gold wreath and the unique gold shield were removed – of course in some haste. It was then that a number of gold acorns and leaves snapped off, and many were destroyed in the heat; some, however, fell towards the edge and survived; together with the other remains from the pyre they were placed above the tomb.

There can be no objection to these comments. But, are they sufficient, on their own, to persuade us that the dead man in the tomb at Vergina cannot possibly have been Philip Arrhidaios who was interred in a royal tomb a number of months after his death and first burial? In his endeavour to answer this argument of mine, one of my colleagues who maintained that the deceased was Philip Arrhidaios, wrote that we were equally ignorant of details about both his first and his second burial – as to whether there was a burial or a cremation. Thus we might speculate that the first burial took place without cremation and that before the re-burial there was a cremation. This suggestion lies beyond the grasp of the ordinary brain with which I at least am endowed, and I deem further discussion unnecessary.

2) The existence of a "heroon" has no justification if we accept that the dead man in the tomb is Philip Arrhidaios. To repeat the description of him by one of the leading historians of Macedonia, Peter Green, the worship of this man "the most insignificant and unheroic" king of Macedonia is incomprehensible.

3) The Great Tumulus was raised later than the first quarter of the third century BC. The date of its erection is supplied by the countless fragments of broken grave stelai which were found in the overburden of the vast mound. The existence of these fragments, which testify to a destruction of the cemetery out of the ordinary, is to be deduced from a piece of information from Plutarch about the

occupation of Aigai by Pyrrhos, the quartering of a small mercenary guard of Galatians in the town and the pillaging of the royal (and of course other) tombs by them. This took place in 274/3 BC, a date which exactly corresponds with the chronological limits of the latest stelai as they can be dated from the style of the lettering in the inscriptions. This huge tumulus for the great tomb was therefore constructed after 274 BC, on the orders of the Macedonian king Antigonos Gonatas. It is completely unreasonable to accept that Antigonos should have expended so much effort and taken so much care to erect the most impressive funeral mound we know over the tomb of the insignificant Philip Arrhidaios.

4) We noted earlier that this tomb presented certain unexpected anomalies in construction: a) it is beyond doubt that it was not built in a single operation but in two successive phases; the vault of the chamber was completed first and was followed by the building of the walls and the vault of the antechamber; b) the plastering of the main chamber was never properly finished; it was carried out in a hurry and probably the interment took place in the main chamber, the connecting door was closed and work continued in the antechamber where all the plastering is perfect, carefully painted and with some decoration (rosettes). The circumstances of Philip Arrhidaios' death do not warrant this unusual, and I would say irrational, plan of construction.

5) This curious constructional anomaly must be related to the second burial in the antechamber which in itself is uncommon in Macedonian tombs; it becomes unintelligible if we accept that Philip Arrhidaios and his wife Eurydice were buried in this tomb. It must be regarded as obvious, I would go so far as to say even obligatory, that the remains of both should be in the same chamber. Indeed one would expect to find the bones of Kynna, mother of Eurydice in the same place, since her re-burial by Cassander occurred at the same time.

These five reasons constitute objective facts which do not, I think, admit discussion, and which exclude the ascription of this tomb to Philip Arrhidaios.

In addition to these we might adduce several others which, though of themselves they do not carry the same weight of conviction, combine to corroborate the conclusions to which the first have inexorably led us.

1) The anthropological examination of the bones concluded that the deceased were a man aged between forty and fifty and a dead woman aged between twenty-three and twenty-seven. We know that when Philip Arrhidaios died he cannot have been older than forty, nor Eurydice older than twenty. This means that Eurydice must be ruled out, and it would be an inadmissible violation of logic to accept that the lower limit, of forty, allows us to identify the dead man as Philip Arrhidaios, who had only just attained that age.

2) The wealth and the quality of the armour found in the tomb is totally incompatible with the non-martial Philip Arrhidaios. The magnificent iron cuirass and the gold and ivory shield alone should be enough to convince us that the deceased must have been a much more important king than he was.

3) If the date of the wall painting can be called in question, its subject creates insurmountable obstacles to whoever upholds the identification of the dead man with Philip Arrhidaios. It is difficult for anyone to deny that the theme is connected with the dead man; and since there is no mythological content, it means that the picture reproduces some scene from the life of the deceased, if not with the exactitude of a chronicler, certainly with the intention of depicting the interests of and the way of life characteristic of the deceased. Nothing that we know of Philip Arrhidaios confirms a picture of him as a man who enjoyed hunting, still less the chase of wild beasts shown in the wall painting.

All these facts oblige me, justifiably I think, to exclude the supposition that the dead in the tomb of the Great Tumulus can be Philip Arrhidaios and his wife Eurydice.

Since therefore it is agreed that the tomb is that of a king, and that this king cannot be Philip Arrhidaios, there is no alternative to the conclusion that it is the tomb of Philip II. Logically, the chain of thought we have followed should suffice to support this conclusion. However, it will not come amiss to proceed beyond these negative arguments, and to see whether the observations which led to the exclusion of Philip Arrhidaios constitute positive evidence for the ascription of the tomb to his father, Philip II. In this enquiry I shall not repeat the order I followed in the first stage, because I judge that the coherence of the observations demands that they should be differently marshalled. I hope that it will be immediately apparent that the timing of the burial, the construction of the tomb part by part, the separate burials in the chamber and the antechamber and the establishment of a "heroon" formed a closely inter-related series of actions, reflecting all that we know about the death and burial of Philip II without straining the evidence at all.

It is completely customary for burial to follow immediately after cremation; this, of course, adds no positive evidence for the identification of the deceased. However, it is important that, as we have noted, the construction of the tomb was carried out in two phases, and it imposes the need to search for some probable interpretation since it is a unique instance amongst the fifty-five Macedonian tombs which have been found so far (1982).

This break in construction and the half finished plastering in the chamber – also unique – implies that the first part of the work was carried out with unaccustomed speed; this is confirmed by the plaster itself and by the putlog holes for the scaffolding in the walls of the main chamber which were never filled in. This hurry is to be interpreted by the circumstances of Philip's death and by the consequences it brought in its train. The murder of the king in the theatre at Aigai threw everything into confusion. Alexander was immediately proclaimed king, but he knew that he had to deal with enemies both at home and abroad. The sequence of events convinces us that he had to struggle to consolidate his position. It is obvious that he had reason to expedite his return to the capital, Pella. But he had first to complete the funeral ceremonies and the burial of his father as fast as he could. He made provision therefore for the construction of an imposing tomb but reckoned that he need not wait for its completion. When the burial chamber had been erected and hastily plastered he carried out the interment, closed the marble door and was free to leave for the capital. I believe that only the circumstances surrounding the murder of Philip, the proclamation of Alexander as king at Aigai, far from Pella and his excusable haste to be in the capital as soon as might be can illuminate the otherwise inexplicable peculiarities of construction in the tomb at Vergina.

If it is impossible to account for the "heroon" with the ascription of the tomb to Philip Arrhidaios this does not however exclude its attribution to Philip II, but on the contrary, it decisively strengthens it since we have explicit testimony in ancient sources for the "cult" of Philip and his father

Amyntas in Macedonia. The Pseudo-Callisthenes for example contains the information that Alexander erected a "temple" above the tomb of his father. Knowing how untrustworthy this source (the *Romance of Alexander*) is considered to be – and indeed is – I leave it to historians to assess the value of this testimony, noting simply the strange coincidence of unprompted testimony and an unexpected archaeological find. However, other reliable sources record that before Philip entered the theatre on the day of his assassination he was preceded by men carrying the statues of the twelve gods and, with them a thirteenth: – his own. The speculation that this statue was placed in the "heroon" after Philip's burial is attractive.

I regarded the construction of a vast tumulus for the tomb of the "insignificant" Philip Arrhidaios as strange – especially many years after his death. Such an exceptional construction can not, on the other hand, be regarded as unjustifiable for a king of such consequence as Philip II. But this very restrained judgement could be taken to be subjective had objective support for it, deriving from certain information in ancient sources, not been forthcoming.

Diodorus Siculus, who is one of the most important sources for the history of Macedonia because he apparently gleaned his information from older, authoritative historians, tells us that before his death Alexander gave written orders to Crateros for the execution of certain commissions; these orders are known as Alexander's *Hypomnemata*. One of the works envisaged by Alexander was the construction over the tomb of his father Philip of something similar to the largest pyramid in Egypt.

"A tomb for his father Philip was to be constructed to match the greatest of the pyramids of Egypt"

However, after his death his successors decided not to execute his plans because they were extensive and numerous and required intolerable expenditure.

I believe that Alexander's design for the construction of a "pyramid" over the tomb of his father was to some extent realized with the erection of the vast mound of Vergina by Antigonos Gonatas many years later. And I believe too that the explanation for Antigonos' decision is also to be found. The plundering of the royal tombs by the

Galatians of Pyrrhos in 274/3 BC from which "Philip's tomb" escaped by sheer chance while the "tomb of Persephone" was robbed and the "heroon" probably destroyed may have been the excuse for the execution of the work. For us to understand how Antigonos reached this decision we should remember certain facts. Diodorus drew his information from older sources. We know that in particular the eighteenth book (that which contains the information on the *Hypomnemata* of Alexander) is taken from the work of Hieronymos of Cardia who lived in the time of Alexander and his successors and who wrote a history of the years after the death of Alexander. We know also that Hieronymos was a close friend of Antigonos and lived at his court for many years. Finally, it is known that Antigonos was highly educated and interested in philosophy and literature. I therefore consider it quite likely that Hieronymos had discussed the *Hypomnemata* with Antigonos and indeed it is not impossible that he had read a text of them aloud. Thus, when Antigonos returned after the desecration of the royal tombs of Aigai by the Galatians, he regarded it as his duty to look after them and to protect those which had escaped profanation. Hence, influenced by his discussions with Hieronymos and his direct knowledge of the unfulfilled wishes of Alexander it is eminently probable that he decided to execute his great predecessor's behest.

We come now to the wall painting. If the subject, a hunting scene, is incompatible with a tomb erected for Philip Arrhidaios it is readily acceptable in the tomb of Philip II. When I analyzed the wall painting I formed the view that the young horseman at the centre of the composition could depict Alexander, and the horseman striking the lion with his spear Philip, while the other youths were the ΠΑΙΔΕΣ – the king's retinue which according to ancient sources, participated in the hunt. If indeed this view is accepted, on its own it constitutes proof of the identity of the dead man. But, even if the pictorial identification of the two figures is not accepted, it is still, I think, certain that the scene is that of a royal hunt in a sacred grove. And we may I think consider it as indisputable that Philip Arrhidaios did not join in such activities. Who then can the two main figures represent – the two figures whose faces we see? And what is the relationship of the adolescent horseman at the centre to the mature mounted man who attacks the lion? Because I

personally cannot find any answer to these questions other than supposing that the painter had Philip and Alexander in mind, this route too brings me to the same conclusions as before.

Finally I would add the evidence of the ivory decoration of the couch in the chamber. Although I am not at this moment in a position to restore its appearance completely, nor am I yet certain of the inter-relationship between the different figures which portray particular faces, nor, finally, to recognize all the faces, I think I may say with so much probability as to be virtual certainty that two of these faces are Alexander and Philip. The head of the first bears such a strong resemblance to the well known portrait on the Tarsus medallion that it allows us to identify both heads and in consequence accept that it is Philip. Over and above this external corroboration, the Vergina head offers its own evidence towards identification. A slight scar can be seen on the right eyebrow while the eye – much wider open than the left – seems expressionless, and lacking the power of sight. Philip is known to have been left blind in his right eye after an arrow wound received during the siege of Methone in 355 BC.

The portrait of Alexander is, I think, so characteristic that no argument is required to establish its identity. However, because some rather imprecise doubts have been expressed, I feel bound to dwell a little on those features of the face which endorse its unquestionable identity. First of all we have the long neck turned to the left, the very slight tilt of the head in the opposite direction and eyes raised in a gaze tender, yet also virile which we know of from Plutarch's description. If we compare this sideways view of the head with the most faithful portrait we have of Alexander, in the Naples mosaic, we may observe a striking resemblance, especially in the nose and forehead. The absence of hair perhaps distorts the appearance and hampers recognition; if we were to restore the hair we could immediately check the identification against the truest portraits which have survived. The same holds for the head of Philip. So, the faces of Philip and Alexander were carved on the wooden couch found in the tomb at Vergina. This couch was certainly not made specially for the tomb, but must have come from a palace, either that at Aigai or that at Pella. It is, I think extremely logical that such a couch should find a place in the tomb of Philip II and not in that of Philip Arrhidaios.

If the armour, especially the cuirass and the chryselephantine shield, seems to be completely mis-matched with the non-belligerent Philip Arrhidaios, it is yet a further feature which fits perfectly with the bellicose Philip II. Amongst the armour we find the gilded sheath of the gorytos which probably came either from the booty of Philip's war against the Scythians in the campaign of 339 BC or which was given to him as a gift from the Scythians in some other context. It is as natural for Philip II to have possessed such an object as it is unnatural for it to have belonged to Philip Arrhidaios.

We have already discussed the gilded greaves of differing height and differing shape. Although they cannot be considered a decisive factor for the identification of the dead man as Philip II, I think it is a pointer which we must take seriously. We know that this warrior-king was twice wounded in the leg, so that his lameness is explicable even if we postulate that the wounds had not affected the bones. Moreover, Demosthenes' phrase *"σκέλος πεπηρωμένον"*, "Philip limping in his leg", on conjunction with the immediately preceding remark, *"τὴν κλεῖν κατεαγότα"*, "his collar bone broken" although it may be no more than rhetorical flourish is perhaps not coincidental.

Lastly the inscription *MAXATA* on the strainer which probably refers to Philip II's brother in law, offers one more clue to the identity of the dead man.

All these reasons lead me to conclude that we have the right to attribute the Vergina tomb to Philip II whereas we are compelled to disallow the possibility that it is that of Philip Arrhidaios.[28]

I still regard my original suggestion that the dead woman in the antechamber may be Cleopatra, the last wife of Philip II, as probable, without however dismissing N. Hammond's suggestion that one of Philip's "barbarian" wives (for example Meda) was buried with him, according to their custom of following their spouse to the grave (suttee) or being sacrificed above it.

I have so far avoided any attempt to identify the occupant of tomb III of the Great Tumulus. We may undoubtedly regard this too as a royal tomb; its occupant was a very young man. The definitive anthropological study established that he was between thirteen and sixteen years of age. Some historians, such as N. Hammond and P. Green have advanced the view that the body is that of

Alexander IV, son of Alexander the Great and Roxane who held the title of king from 323 to 311/10 BC when he was executed along with his mother by Cassander. I can offer no other more probable interpretation, although I have some reservations about this one.

I regard it as certain that members of the royal family were buried in the robbed tomb with the wall painting. But other than this I do not think that I have any evidence to further the identification of the dead and I shall leave it to the historians to decide, without involving myself at the moment in the speculations which have already been voiced.

THE ASSASSINATION AND BURIAL OF PHILIP

The sequence of thought I have followed leads me, without, I think, violation of the evidence, from the general chronological framework 350-310 BC for the objects which cannot be challenged, to the almost inevitable conclusion that Alexander buried his father in the great tomb after his murder at Aigai. Continuing to follow the *spirale méthodologique* we shall revert to the problem of the dating of the objects and formulate the very useful conclusion that all the objects in this tomb date to before 336 BC. This gives a firm chronological terminus for a complete series of works of the fourth century BC for which our knowledge has so far been relatively uncertain or has at least obliged us to move within very wide and very elastic limits. The same line of approach gives us the exact date of the tomb and, more important still, of the wall painting. From another point of view the certainty that the "Prince's tomb" cannot be later than 310 BC nor earlier than 336 BC allows us to proceed to a comparative study of the finds (silver vases, ivory reliefs, wall paintings etc.) and to note the consequent morphological (and other) differences. Such a study of course has no place in a book of this sort, but will be undertaken in the detailed and definitive publication of the finds.

The archaeological evidence we possess so far permits us to attempt a reconstruction of the historical events linked with the assassination and burial of Philip II. It is now certain that Aigai was situated in the region of Vergina. It was here, then, that in

336 BC both the royal family of Macedonia and all the representatives of the Greek cities had assembled for the wedding of Cleopatra, daughter of Philip, to Alexander, king of Epirus. The royal family was housed in the palace which, if it was not the building which the excavators have uncovered, was probably on the same site. After the elaborate banquet came the day of the games. Even before dawn the crowds had gathered in the theatre; the procession set off at sunrise; at its head were the bearers of the magnificent twelve gods "very elaborately worked and wonderfully decorated with the brilliance of wealth", and with them a thirteenth statue of Philip himself, which showed that the king regarded himself as equal in rank to the Olympian deities. The *hubris* aroused was great. When everyone had taken their places the royal retinue made its appearance. The distance from the palace to the eastern passageway of the palace was less than one hundred and fifty metres. The king walked down it on foot, because as the sources tell us, the oracle had warned him "to beware of chariots"; we know now that the theatre was so close and that there must have been a magnificently paved road, that there was no need for a chariot. With him were the two Alexanders, son and son in law; all three were robed in white. Philip let them draw ahead of him, cut loose from his bodyguards and walked alone from the eastern passageway towards the orchestra. He got no further; Pausanias' dagger buried itself in his body and left him dead. The assassin ran towards the western passage and reached his fellow conspirators awaiting him with horses. The walls of the city were close by – less than one hundred metres away. If he had put them behind him he would have crossed the deep ravine west of the city and once into the foothills of the Pierian range he would have headed for his own territory of western Macedonia where he would have found shelter. Some of the king's bodyguards threw themselves on the king, others chased Pausanias and slew him before he could mount his horse.

It seems that after the first, momentary disturbance the usual procedure of accession followed immediately; "the King is dead, long live the King" is the modern phrase we might well apply, even anachronistically, to this case. According to established Macedonian custom Antipater presented Alexander to the Macedonians assembled at Aigai so that they might acclaim him. After this, two urgent duties awaited the new king; to punish the murderers and to bury his father. But a still more pressing need was for him to seize power and to face his rivals both at home and abroad. He was thus obliged to reach his capital at Pella as soon as possible.

But he had first to attend to the burial ceremonies for the dead man. The construction of the tomb began at once. At the same time preparations for the cremation of his father were put in hand; a fairly impressive brick construction was prepared for the pyre; when everything was ready, the dead king was placed on top of it. They had also to fetch his weapons; the heavy gold wreath was placed on his head and the magnificent gold and ivory shield was set at his side. All around were piled weapons and objects of all sorts. Of these we know at least of two iron swords, a shield, a spear and many wooden boxes with ivory decoration. It is virtually certain that horses were sacrificed on the pyre and indeed chariots too may have been burned with him. When the flames began to rise the gold wreath and the chryselephantine shield were hastily removed so that these were preserved without anything more than the minimal effects of fire.

The construction of the tomb could not be completed within this short space of time. The chamber was finished, roofed by a vault, while the walls of the antechamber had reached to one course below the spring of the vault. The inside of the chamber was hastily plastered, with only the first two coats.

When the body had been burnt, all the bones were collected with great care and washed in wine; the purple cloth was spread over the bottom of the gold larnax, which will have been a royal jewel chest, and the bones were carefully laid out in order – first the feet, then the trunk and at the top the skull which they covered with the purple cloth. Above this they placed the wreath, bent to fit the casket. They closed the larnax and took it to the funerary chamber to place it in the marble sarcophagus which too had been constructed as fast as possible. Lastly, in front of this they positioned the wooden couch and around it the weapons and the other articles. Then, closing the heavy marble doors of the chamber, they allowed the wedge which would lock it forever to fall.

The king had been buried. The rest of the building work (the antechamber, the facade etc.) could be continued at a slower tempo. However, it was thought prudent to heap earth over the vault on the outside since the tomb would remained uncovered for a longish spell before it could be completed. They later cleared the pyre of the ash and the burnt remains and, transferring the entire brick structure, they heaped it over the vault of the tomb. They took with the bricks as many objects as had survived the flames; the iron swords, the horse trappings, the spearhead, fragments of ivory, the iron remains of the shield and a number of gold acorns from the gold wreath. These, it seems, had fallen beyond the heat of the flames and were thus preserved.

The chamber was covered by earth to approximately the top of the vault, at least in its rear part. Work on the antechamber continued at a normal pace. The plastering was completed, the walls were painted and the architectural detail of the facade was finished off. It was probably then that the burial in the antechamber took place and the outer door closed. There remained, however, the execution of the wall painting which might have required some time. Thus when the outside of the vault of the chamber had been plastered, they then began again to heap earth over the tomb. To help prevent the soil from sliding over the facade the curious breastwork of bricks which rises a little above the cornice and extends right and left of the facade was erected. The two lateral revetting brick walls right and left of the entrance must have been built simultaneously with the facade.

When the wall painting on the facade had been finished the construction of a wall of limestone blocks to protect the outer door and the infilling of the descending *dromos* was started. It is quite likely that these works progressed in parallel, so that as the fill of the *dromos* reached the height of each course of stones the next could be more easily set in position. It seems that when the second and third row of stones was being erected the northern revetment brick wall was, through some carelessness, damaged by a large block and it collapsed. There was no point in rebuilding it since in any case the *dromos* would be filled up with earth. The work therefore continued and the tomb was covered. It was eventually buried under a mound some three to four metres high.

After an interval of time, which cannot be estimated with any degree of certainty, a small "heroon", probably resembling a temple, was erected a short distance southeast of the tomb. There the dead would have been worshipped. It is not impossible that it housed the statue of Philip which had accompanied the statues of the twelve gods to the theatre. This structure must have been destroyed before the erection of the Great Tumulus, at the time when the "tomb of Persephone" was pillaged by the Galatians. This is apparent from the fact that its foundations, together with those of the adjacent tombs, were covered by the Great Tumulus.

SUMMARY

When Léon Heuzey, the French archaeologist who initiated the excavation of the palace of Vergina in 1861, concluded his publication of the finds by expressing the hope that the work might be continued, it was impossible to foresee how fruitful this exploration would be. Heuzey took care not to leave the area which extends between the villages of Palatitsia and Vergina without a name; he called it Balla – the name of an unknown and insignificant city which was preserved only in an ancient lexicon. The archaeological excavation which recommenced in 1937-38 under K. A. Rhomaios and which still continues today, has progressed without assistance from any written source which might guide the archaeologist's spade. Today, one hundred and twenty-two years later, the monuments have spoken for themselves. The "speaking stones" as a pioneering student of Macedonian archaeology, M. Dimitsas, so accurately christened them in the title of his valuable work Ἡ Μακεδονία ἐν λίθοις φθεγγομένοις καὶ μνημείοις σωζομένοις, have allowed us not just to reconstruct an ancient Macedonian city but the ancient capital itself of the kingdom of Macedonia, Aigai or Aigeae.

The capital too was no more than a name, a name which suffered a curious fate in history. Somewhere towards the end of the fifth century BC it ceased to be the capital of the Macedonian kingdom; king Archelaos built a new capital at Pella down on the plain close to the sea. Ancient writers only infrequently referred to Aigai thereafter, the most notable occasion being in connection with the murder of Philip in the theatre of the ancient capital in 336 BC; the second is to its occupation by Pyrrhos in 274/3, the stationing of a garrison of Galatian mercenaries and the plundering of the royal tombs. Then it was gradually forgotten as other cities, such as Veroia, emerged during the years of Roman rule and in the subsequent centuries of the Byzantine empire. The most curious aspect, however, is that at some period it was depopulated and its very site forgotten. When, centuries later, men were interested in the historic past and sought to locate its ancient centres, they believed, because of a chance confusion based on a Roman historical compiler, that Aigai was to be identified with Edessa in western Macedonia. This belief caused them to overlook several obvious facts; first of all that it is preposterous, and without precedent, for one city to be known by two names; secondly, that the written evidence of the ancient geographer Ptolemy gives us separate geographical bearings for the two towns. It took the clear head and academic audacity of N.G.L. Hammond to reassign to each Aigai its proper site. In a paper read to a conference in Thessalonike in 1968 he advocated, for the first time, the view that Aigai should be located at Vergina where a magnificent palace and a Macedonian tomb with an impressive marble throne had been discovered. He based his theory on a series of abstract deductions and historical information. The continuation of excavation confirmed the correctness of his identification. Today it is accepted by almost all historians and archaeologists. Thus the finds from the excavation are possessed of particular importance because they throw light on the history of the very cradle of the ancient Macedonian civilization.

At the present stage of the excavation we may summarize, with a fair degree of certainty, our information about the city of Aigai.

The first inhabitants of the neighbourhood seem to have arrived on the site towards the end of the Bronze Age, that is, in the middle of the eleventh century BC, at the latest at the start of the tenth century. This is shown by the oldest burials in the Cemetery of the Tumuli which go back to this period. We cannot be certain of the identity of these settlers; it is however clear that their cultural level attests the continuation of an older Macedonian tradition and the introduction of intrusive shapes which originated in more northern cultures. This settlement certainly seems to have enjoyed a very real prosperity, if we judge from the wealth of the women's jewellery and the robust armour belonging to the men.

The view that these were Phrygian tribes – Phryges or Bryges – receives corroboration from the written testimony of ancient sources, that at some time the Phryges lived in this area of Macedo-

nia. It is difficult to know when they migrated; if, however, we consider that in the middle of the eighth century BC the Phrygian state of Asia Minor already demonstrates impressive prosperity, we are compelled to accept that the migration of the Phrygians from Europe to Asia cannot have occurred later than the ninth century BC. I find it difficult to follow historians in their attempt to place the various tribes and to trace their movements in northern Greece on the basis of archaeological finds – insufficient in my view – and even more difficult when efforts are based on later, still more obscure evidence. What I consider certain is that the first Macedonians arrived in the Vergina area no later than the beginning of the seventh century BC, though this latest date does not preclude much earlier settlement.

In this area the Argead dynasty established the first capital of the Macedonian kingdom, Aigai or Aigeae. Although there are no archaeological finds from this city at this time, we may suppose that it was sited on the heights south of the palace. When the capital was transferred to Pella, Aigai ceased to be the administrative centre, though it seems to have retained the glory of being the former capital. The evidence available allows us to regard as certain that in the middle of the fourth century BC Aigai enjoyed a period of prosperity, which was probably due to Philip. In that century the magnificent palace was erected, the theatre constructed, temples built and furnished with cult and votive statues. The city spread over a large area, some of it below the palace. It is highly likely that the fortifications which surrounded almost the entire city were built at this time, while a notable water supply system was also installed. The funerary monuments and the tombs of both the fourth and the following centuries disclose both the wealth and the highly sophisticated standards of the inhabitants. As well as the royal tombs a series of Macedonian tombs confirms that wealthy nobles continued to live in the old capital. After the Roman conquest there seems to have been a decline, but the city continued to exist as we may deduce from the remains of houses and from tombs. It seems that a slight shift towards the plain, which may perhaps have started earlier, continued in this period, as is shown in the ruins of buildings and especially in the foundations of a recently discovered early Christian basilica. We know nothing about the site in the early centuries of the Byzantine empire. However, a doc-

234

umentary reference of the fourteenth century reveals the existence of the village of Palatitsia where in the sixteenth century the church of Saint Demetrios was built, whose very splendid wall paintings still survive.

The archaeological investigation of the area has so far provided copious material both for our knowledge of the culture of the Macedonians and for our understanding of their historical physiognomy. Its continuation, and the systematic study of the finds, can only assist us to draw a much clearer and more accurate picture of this domain of Hellenism which from the fourth century onwards played a leading role in its historical progress and succeeded in spreading the Greek language and Greek culture over virtually the whole world. And it would constitute a genuine historical paradox – the like of which is not known – if we accepted that the participants in this oecumenical hellenization were a "barbarous" people whose rulers compelled them to cast off their national character, change their name, convert to a foreign religion, forget their language and metamorphose into the apostles of a more advanced, but foreign, culture. Regardless of the scholastic trivialities of the erudite there is, I believe, a meaningful approach to history which is not easily caged within either the pronunciation of a letter or the recondite pedantry of grammarians.

FOOTNOTES

1. G. Theocharides, Μιά διαθήκη καί μιά δίκη ὂυζαντινή, *Μακεδονικά*, Supplement 2, 1962, pp. 15, 22. 86, 31. 22, 66, 69.

2. L. Heuzey, H. Daumet, *Mission Archéologique de Macédoine*, Paris, 1876, p. 117.

3. Now that both these archaeologists are dead, these names do not really create a problem. But the name "Rhomaios tomb" was in circulation long before his demise, just indeed as happens with other tombs, Macedonian or not, which are unofficially referred to by the name of their excavator. This custom takes those outside the archaeological fraternity by surprise when they hear the terms.

4. The style of the marble door obviously imitates wooden construction; the impressive bosses (the heads of nails) are typical. We should add that the gilding of the reconstruction has not been authenticated.

5. K. A. Rhomaios' account of the tomb showed that all its measurements from the shortest to the longest are subordinate to a carefully calculated system of geometrical proportions.

6. Πρακτικά τῆς ᾿Αρχαιολογικῆς ᾿Εταιρείας, 1952, p. 213.

7. See M. Andronicos, Ancient Greek Painting and Mosaics in Macedonia, *Balkan Studies*, 5, 1964, pp. 287-302, pl. X.

8. ᾿Αρχαιολογικά ᾿Ανάλεκτα ἐξ ᾿Αθηνῶν IX (1976), pp. 124-129.

9. K. A. Rhomaios, *Ο Μακεδονικός Τάφος της Βεργίνας*, p. 12.

10. M. Andronicos, Deux stèles funéraires de Vergina, *Bulletin de Corréspondance Hellenique*, 79, 1955, p. 87.

11. *Idem*, p. 101.

12. M. Andronicos, *The Prehistoric Necropolis and the Hellenistic Palace*, Lund, 1964, p. 5.

13. M. Andronicos, *Βεργίνα Ι. Τὸ νεκροταφεῖον τῶν τύμβων*, Athens, 1969, p. 286 (in Greek).

14. Fanoula Papazoglu, *Les cités macédoniennes*, (in Serbo-Croat), Skopje, 1957, pp. 110-111, French summary p. 343. To be absolutely accurate and fair, I should mention that the first person to challenge the identification of Aigai with Edessa was an early explorer of Macedonia, T.L.F. Tafel. In his book, *De Via Militari Romanorum Egnatia*, Tubingen 1842, he refers to several important passages from ancient authors who accepted this identification. It is worthy of note that his arguments passed unheeded for a hundred years and have not been noticed even by more modern scholars who reached the same conclusions.

15. N. G. L. Hammond, *A History of Macedonia*, i, Historical geography and prehistory, Oxford 1972, pp. 156-158.

16. ᾿Αρχαιολογικά ᾿Ανάλεκτα ἐξ ᾿Αθηνῶν, IX, 1976, pp. 127-129.

17. *Τό Βῆμα*, 3.10.1976.

18. ᾿Αρχαιολογικά ᾿Ανάλεκτα ἐξ ᾿Αθηνῶν, X, 1977, pp. 1-2.

19. The need to be more widely understood frequently obliges the archaeologist to make use of a conventional nomenclature. Faced with this problem in a book which is aimed at others besides the specialist, I decided to "christen" the three tombs of the Great Tumulus for the first time. The name is but a vehicle of communication and carries no significance. To emphasize this still further I have put the title in inverted commas.

20. I wish to record here that the title "The royal tomb of Philip II" which headed a preliminary description of mine in the periodical *Archaeology* (31, 1978, pp. 33 ff.) originated with the editorial staff of the periodical. Up to now I have always used the appellation "the royal tombs of Vergina". Nevertheless its characterization as the tomb of Philip II was employed, without comment, by Professor K. Schefold in a recent article "Die Antwort der Griechische Kunst auf die Siege Alexanders des Grossen", *Bayerische Akademie der Wissenschaften, Sitzungsberichte Phil. Hist. Kl*, 1979, part 4, Munich 1979). This I think leaves me free to employ it also, always within inverted commas.

21. N. G. L. Hammond maintains that this custom belongs at least to the time of Archelaos (413-399 BC). *A History of Macedonia*, ii, Oxford, 1979 p. 168 n.l.

22. In connection with the original supposition, it was attractive to think that we had a distant reminiscence of the Pheidian shield.
23. A third portrait, on the base of a clay vase, also wears a similar diadem, as does the figure on an unpublished example in a private collection in Rome.
24. It is of silver with gold on the outer surface.
25. I wrote this text before reading the recent book by R. Ginouvès, *L' Archéologie Gréco-Romaine*, Paris, 1982, where he supports exactly this progression of archaeological thought, describing, it as the "spirale méthodologique".
26. The plural here refers to myself and to my two assistants, Dr. S. Drougou and Mrs C. Paliadeli. Miss Drougou's speciality is the study of pottery, in particular that of the fourth century BC.
27. The objection to this date contained in the argument that the lion hunt was an eastern element which once again presupposes the campaigns of Alexander. I do not believe to be insuperable if we recall that Xenophon in his treatise *On Hunting* (11, 1) explicitly mentions that lions, leopards, wolves, panthers, bears ..... were to be found in Macedonia .... (not in his time of course) and describes in detail the manner in which they were hunted.
28. This text was written before the team of English scholars Dr A. J. Prag (archaeologist), Dr J. Musgrave (anatomist) and R. A. Neave (artist collaborating with the Medical School) of the universities of Manchester and Bristol presented their reconstruction of the head of the dead man based on the bones of the skull to the 12th International Congress of Classical Studies. The discovery of the wound in the bone of the right socket from an arrow and the structural similarity of the face with that of the carved ivory head which I have identified as that of Philip II led them to conclude that the dead man was unquestionably Philip II. I might add that when the Hungarian anthropologist J. Nemeskéri first saw a photograph of the ivory head after having seen the skull he said "when I saw the bones of the skull that is how I envisaged the face of the deceased."

BIBLIOGRAPHY

Adams, John Paul, The Larnakes from Tomb II at Vergina, *Archaeological News*, XII, 12 (1983), p. 1-7

Adams, W. Lindsey, The Royal Macedonian tomb at Vergina, An historical interpretation, *Ancient World*, 3, 1980, p. 67-72

Ανδρόνικος, Μ., Ανασκαφή νεκροταφείου Βεργίνας, *Πρακτικά Ἀρχαιολογικῆς Ἑταιρείας*, 1952, 1953, 1957-1961

Ανδρόνικος, Μ., Μακαρόνας, Χ., Μουτσόπουλος, Ν. Μπακαλάκης, Γ., *Τό Ἀνάκτορο τῆς Βεργίνας*, Athens, 1961

Ανδρόνικος, Μ., Deux stèles funéraires grecques de Vergina, *Bulletin de Correspondance Hellénique*, 79 (1955), p. 87-101

–, An early iron age cemetery at Vergina, near Beroea, *Balkan Studies*, 2 (1961), p. 85-98

–, Vergina, *The Prehistoric Necropolis and the Hellenistic Palace*, Lund, 1964

–, Ancient Greek Paintings and Mosaics in Macedonia, *Balkan Studies*, 1964, p. 287-302

–, An early iron age cemetery at Vergina, near Beroea, *Atti del VI. Congresso Internazionale delle Scienze Preistoriche e Protostoriche (Roma 29 Agosto - 3 Settembre 1962)* Rome, 1966, vol. III, p. 3-6

–, Βεργίνα I. *Τό νεκροταφεῖον τῶν τύμβων*, Athens 1969

–, Sarissa, *Bulletin de Correspondance Hellénique*, 94 (1970), p. 91-107

–, Ἀνασκαφή στή Μεγάλη Τούμπα τῆς Βεργίνας, *Ἀρχαιολογικά Ἀνάλεκτα ἐξ Ἀθηνῶν* (IX), 1976 (1977), p. 123-30

–, Βεργίνα καί Αἰγαί, «*Τό Βῆμα*», 3.10.1976

–, Οἱ βασιλικοί τάφοι τῆς Βεργίνας, «*Τό Βῆμα*», 25.12.1977 (see. Μ. Ανδρόνικος, *Ἱστορία καί Ποίηση*, Athens, 1982, p. 53-64)

–, Βεργίνα. Οι βασιλικοί τάφοι της Μεγάλης Τούμπας, *Ἀρχαιολογικά Ἀνάλεκτα ἐξ Ἀθηνῶν* (X) 1977 (1978), p. 1-72 (in Greek, English, French, German, separately.)

–, The finds from the Royal Tombs at Vergina, *Proceedings of the British Academy*, 1978, London LXV, 1979, p. 355-67, (also off-printed)

–, The tombs at the Great Tumulus, at Vergina, Acta of the XI Intern. Congress of Classical Archaeology, (London 3-9 September 1978), p. 39-56

–, The royal tombs at Aigai (Vergina), in *Philip of Ma-*

cedon, Athens 1980, p. 188-230 (in Greek, English, French and German)

–, Οἱ βασιλικοί τάφοι τῆς Βεργίνας καί τό πρόβλημα τοῦ νεκροῦ, *'Αρχαιολογικά 'Ανάλεκτα ἐξ 'Αθηνῶν*, (XIII), 1980 (1981), p. 156-78

–, *Βεργίνα. 'Αρχαιολογία καί Ιστορία*, (forthcoming in the presentation volume for G. E. Mylonas)

Borga, Eugene N., The Macedonian Royal Tombs at Vergina: some cautionary notes, *Archaeological News*, 10, 11 (1981), p. 73-87

–, Those Vergina Tombs again, *Archaeological News*, 11, 1-2 (1982), p. 8-10

Calder, W. M. II., "Golden diadems" again, *American Journal of Archaeology* 87 (1983), p. 102-103

Calder, W. M. III., Diadem and Barrel-Vault: a note, *American Journal of Archaeology*, 85 (1981), p. 334-5

Daux, G., Aegeai, site des tombes royales de la Macédoine antique. *Comptes rendus de l' Academie des Inscriptions et Belles-Lettres*, 1977, p. 620-30

Fox, Robin Lane, *The Search for Alexander*, Boston 1980, (chap. 4: The Royal Tomb)

Fredricksmeyer, E. A., Again the so-called Tomb of Philip II, *American Journal of Archaeology*, 85 (1981), p. 330-34

–, Once more the Diadem and Barrel-Vault at Vergina, *American Journal of Archaeology*, 87 (1983), p. 99-102

Giallombardi, Anna Maria Peristiani – Bruno Tripodi, Le tombe regali di Vergina: quale Filippo? *Annali della R. Scuola Normale Superiora di Pisa, Sezione di lettere*, ser. III, 10, 3 (1980), p. 889-1001

–, La tomba e il tesoro di Filippo II di Macedonia: una nuovo proposta di attribuzione, *Magna Grecia*, 16 (1981), No. 3-4, p. 14-17

Green, Peter, The Royal Tombs at Vergina, in *Philip II, Alexander the Great and the Macedonian Heritage*, Washington 1982, p. 129-51

Hammond, N.G.L., Philip's tomb in Historical Context, *Greek, Roman and Byzantine Studies*, 19 (1978), p. 331-50

–, The evidence for the identity of the royal tombs at Vergina, in *Philip II, Alexander the Great and the Macedonian Heritage*, Washington, 1982, p. 111-27

Heuzey, Léon, *Le Mont Olympe et l' Acarnanie*, Paris, 1860

Heuzey, Léon, – Henri Daumet, *Mission Archéologique de Macédoine*, Paris, 1876

Hurtle, Robert Wyman, The Search for Alexander's Portrait, in *Philip II, Alexander the Great and the Macedonian Heritage*, Washington, 1982, p. 153-76

Huxley, George., Baanes the Notary on "Old Edessa" *Greek, Roman and Byzantine Studies*, 24 (1983), p. 253-257

Lehmann, Phyllis W., The so-called Tomb of Philip II: a different Interpretation, *American Journal of Archaeology*, 84 (1980) p. 527-31

–, The so-called Tomb of Philip II: An addendum, *American Journal of Archaeology*, 86 (1982), p. 437-442

–, Once again the Royal Tomb at Vergina, *'Αρχαιολογικά 'Ανάλεκτα ἐξ 'Αθηνῶν*, XIV, 1981 (1982), p. 134-44

Martin, Roland., *La Grecia e il Mondo Greco*, Torino, 1984 vol. II, chap. V, *Lo Sviluppo Artistico in Macedonia*, p. 111-133

Moreno, P., La pittura in Macedonia, VI, p. 703-721 in *Storia e Civiltá dei Greci, La crisi della polis. Arte, Religione, Musica*, Milan 1979

Oikonomides, Al. N., A New Inscription from Vergina and Eurydice the mother of Philip II, *The Ancient World*, VII (1983), p. 62-69

Παντερμαλής, Δημ., Ὁ νέος Μακεδονικός τάφος τῆς Βεργίνας, *Μακεδονικά*, 12 (1972), p. 147-182

Pantermalis, Dem., Beobachtungen zur Fassadenarchitektur und Aussichtsveranda in hellenistischen Makedonien, in *Hellenismus in Mittelitalien*, (Kolloquium in Göttingen von 5 bis 9 Juni 1974) Göttingen 1976, I, p. 387-395

Πέτσας, Φ., 'Ανασκαφή 'Αρχαίου νεκροταφείου Βεργίνας (1960-61), *'Αρχαιολογικόν Δελτίον*, 17 (1961-62), Α' p. 218-88 και 18 (1963), Β' 2, p. 217-232

Ritter, M., Zum sogenannten Diadem des Philipsgrabes, *Archäologischer Anzeiger*, 1984, p. 105-111

Ρωμαῖος, Κ. Α., Ὁ Μακεδονικός τάφος τῆς Βεργίνας, Αθήνα, 1951

–, Τό ἀνάκτορον τῆς Παλατίτσας, *'Αρχαιολογική 'Εφημερίς*, 1953-1954 (εἰς μνήμην Γ. Οικονόμου) I, p. 141-150

Schefold, K., Die Stilgeschichte der Monumentalmalerei in der Zeit Alexanders des Grossen *Acta of the XII International Congress of Classical Archaeology*, Athens, 4-10 September 1983

The following photograps were taken by Spyros Tsavdaroglou: 9, 20, 28-45, 56, 64-67, 72-74, 77-85, 87, 94-102, 104-139, 143-153, 155, 158, 161-180, 185

The following photographs were taken by Makis Skiadaressis: 6, 7, 8, 10, 13, 14, 15, 16, 22-26, 46-59, 57-63, 68, 69, 86, 88-93, 103, 140-142, 154, 156-157, 160, 166-169, 181-182, 183, 184

The drawing of the painting (59) is made by G. Miltsakakis. – Map by Tonia Kotsoni

INDEX

cylinder, bronze, 166
cymation, 206; ionic, 180, 202; lesbian, 142, 180

D

Danube, region of, 186
Darius, 117
Daumet, H., 20, 31
Daux, G., 218
Delacoulonche, M., 17, 20
Delos, 39; treasury of, 171
Demeter, 88, 224
Demetrios Poliorcetes, 166
Democritos, 223
Demosthenes, 24, 186, 231
Derveni; sculptured crater from, 150, 168, 222; tomb B, 150, 165, 222· vessels from, 150, 153, 222
diadem, see jewellery
Dimitsas, M., 233
Diodorus Siculus, 229, 230
Dion, Macedonian tomb of, 225
Dionysiac, circle, 208; figure (relief), 208
Dionysos, 208; relief of, 128, 136, 223; shrine of, 49; worship of, 49; see also thymele
Dobrudja, 186
door, 42, 73, 75, 179, 198; of marble, 31, 32, 35, 68, 69, 71, 81, 82, 106, 177, 210, 219, 232; knocker of, bronze, 198; marble leaves of, 198, 209
doorsill, 39, 65, 202
drain, 42, 47
dromos, 35, 233
Drykalos, 84

E

Edessa, 56, 59, 234
Egypt, 171; pyramid, 229; tombs of, 55
emblem, royal, 137, 140; see also Macedonian dynasty, emblem of
enamel, 170
entablature, 68, 106; ionic, 31, 32
"epaulettes", see cuirass
Ephesus, 124
Epigonoi, 181
Epirus, 58; see also Alexander, king of, and Pyrrhus, king of
epistyle, 68, 106; doric, 198
Etruria, tomb of, 55
Eukleia (ΕΥΚΛΕΙΑ), goddess, 24, 50; temple of, 46, 49 f.f., see also Athens
Europe, 234; central, 30
Euxeinos, 84
Eyrydice (ΕΥΡΥΔΙΚΑ), 24, 50, 51
Eyridice, the wife of king Amyntas III,
51
Eyridice, the wife of Philip Arrhidaios, 227, 228

F

facade, of the palace, 39; of tombs, 22, 24, 31, 32, 35, 37, 65, 67, 69, 82, 83, 97, 179, 198, 206, 219, 221, 223, 225, 232, 233
fish dish, see vase
fish-plate, see pottery
flake, of bone, 29; of sardis, 29
fresco, 114, see also wall-painting
frieze, 32, 81, 116, 128, 129, 198; doric, 106; painted, 35, 66, 67, 225, with scenes of chariot race, 82, 202 f.f., 219; stripe-frieze, 35; tainia-frieze, 198
funerary relief, of Lykeas and Chairedemos, 180

G

Galatian mercenaries, 84, 228
Galatians, 230, 233
gate, 38; see also Palaioporta
Gauls, 62
Geometric period, 26
glass paste, 170
gorgoneion, gold, 177, 178, 189 f., 223
gorytos, 177, 180 f.f., 186, 189, 221, 223; gold sheath of, 181, 231; Scythian, 78, 223
grave goods, 119 f.f., 168, 198, 208, 219; see also jewellery, pottery, vase and weapons.
Great Tumulus, 20, 21, 30, 38, 82, 83, 84, 86, 221, 224, 225, 227, 228, 231, 233; excavation of, 21, 22, 55 f.f., 131, 219; see also tombs, royal greaves, and weapons
Greece, 50, 51, 79, 162; ancient, 17, 29, 58, 186; northern, 58, 234; southern, 24, 30
Greek; ancient art, 117, 153, 165, 181; ancient world, 79; architects, 223; culture, 235; language, 235; metal work, 110, 157; miniature, 208; painting, 67, 87, 117, 224; see also wall painting; pantheon, 50, 180
Greeks, 149, 191, 223; ancient, 119
Green, P., 227, 231
guttae, 106, 198

H

Hades, 225
Haliakmon, river, 17, 20, 38
hall, circular, see palace
hammer, iron, 217
Hammond, N.G.L., 59, 62, 231, 234
harness, 69; iron parts of, 220
head, limestone, 37
headgear, Macedonian, 88
Hector, burial of, 170
Hellenistic; art, 156; coins, 175; painting, 36; period, 22, 24, 30, 39, 140, 171, 175; world, 132
helmet, see weapons
Hera, Argive, 165; Ekatomboia, 165; Heraia, 165
Heracleides, 56, 84
Heracles, 38, 42, 153, 166, 189, 226; club of (as the royal emblem), 137, 140, 226; knot of, 153, 197; shield of, 140
Herculaneum, 88, 224
Hermes, 88, 224, 225
Hermitage Museum, 181
Herodotus, 166
"heroon", 65, 66, 83, 98, 225, 227, 229, 230, 233
Hesiod, 140
Heuzey, L., 17, 20, 21, 31, 38, 39, 42, 55, 58, 59, 233; tomb of, 22, 32, 35, 106
Hieronymos, of Cardia, 230
Homer, 140, 161; portrait of, 175
Homeric, customs, 170; epics, 170
hoop, gold, 186
horse trappings, iron, 69, 98, 221, 227, 233
house, ancient, 39; court of, 46; foundations of, 46; remains of, 35, 39
hydria, marble, 83; funerary, 209; ossuary (silver), 82, 202, 210; see also vase

I

Indo-European (people), 29
inscription, 50, 83, 228; on the strainer, 231, see also MAXATA; see also stele, grave
Iron Age, 25
Irra, 51, see also Sirra
ivory, 69, 136, 137, 140, 145, 221; burnt, 98, 220, 227; decoration, in wooden boxes, 232; fragments, 121, 233; hands, 74; heads (portrait), 74, 115, 131; legs, 74; reliefs, 124, 129, 202, 206, 224, 231; see also couch, decoration of; rob of wreath, 217; sheath of, 123

J

jamb, marble, 31, 32, 35, 36, 68, 78, 177, 178, 198

235; *see also* Macedonian tomb at
palmet, 67, 106, 123, 145, 180, 209; re-
lief, 137; vertical, 170
Pan, 208, relief head of, 153, 165
Pantikapaion, 184
Papazoglou, Fanoula, 59
Paris, *see* Bibliothèque Nationale *and*
Louvre
Parthenon, *see* Athens
patera, *see* vase
Patroclos, funeral of, 69, 98
Pausanias, 50
Pausanias, the assassin of Philip II, 232
pectoral, *see* jewellery
pediment, 31, 32, 35, 37, 106
Pella, 39, 229, 230, 232, 233, 234;
couch from, 123
perfume flask, *see* vase
Persephone, 89, 224; *see also* Macedo-
nian tombs *and* wall painting, the
rape of Persephone by Pluto
Persia, 223
Persian wars, 51
Petsas, Ph., 225
Peukolaos, 57, 84
Pheidias, 157; portrait of, 157
phiale, *see* vase
Phila, the second wife of Philip II, 158
Philip II, 24, 49, 51, 73, 74, 82, 84, 116,
118, 186, 189, 226, 227, 231, 232, 234;
"cult" of, 229; murder of, 224, 233;
portrait of, 115, 130, 131, 132, 223,
230, marble bust of, 130; *see also* Tar-
sus gold medallion; statue of, 232,
233; tri-obol of, 222
Philip III Arrhidaios, 140, 226, 227,
228, 229, 231
Philip V, 166
Philistos, 84
Philotas, 84
Philoxenos, from Eretria, 118
Phryges, 234
Phrygian tribes, 234
Phrygians, Paradise of, 38
Pieria, *see* Macedonian tombs, Karyt-
sa's
Pieria, Mt., 17, 38
Pierian plain, 17
Pierion, 84
pillar, 68, 106, 198
Pindar, portrait of, 175
Piraeus, Museum of, 180
Plato, 223, portrait of, 222
Pliny, 91
Plutarch, 59, 62, 130, 144, 186, 227,
230
Pluto, 88, 89, 224; *see also* wall paint-
ing, the rape of Persephone by Pluto
Pompeian red, 66, 75, 87, 175
Pompeii, 21; *see also* Naples, mosaic
from Pompeii
Pontos, 17

portico, *see* palace
pot, *see* pottery
pottery, 30, 46, 64, 72, 119; alabastro,
78, 177, 208; amphona, 177, cypriot,
78, 222, from Thasos, 31, *see also*
vase; askos, 122, 123, 159, 222; Attic
pottery, 210; fish plate, 64, 224; jug,
26, *see also* vase; lamp, 202, 208, 210,
222, 224; lekythos, white Attic, 87;
oinochoe, 123, 149, 159, 222, *see also*
vase; pot, 26, 30, geometric, 30,
sherds of, 87; protogeometric, 30;
"saltcellars", 64, 122, 123, 159, 209;
sauceboats, *see* "saltcellars"; sherds
of, 33, 35, 55, 66, 208; tall skyphidia,
64; *see also* vase *and* vessel
Priene, 39
prodomos, see pronaos
pronaos see temple
"propylaia", *see* palace
propylon, *see* palace
Priam, 181
Proxenos, 84
Pseudo-Callisthenes, 65, 229
Ptolemy, 171
Ptolemy, geographer, 59, 234
Pydna, *see* Macedonian tomb
Pyrrhos, 228, 230, 233

R

relief, heads, 209, 222; *see also* ivory;
inscribed, 58; human figures in, 98
Rhomaios, C., 21, 31, 32, 33, 35, 38,
39, 55, 58, 233; *see also* Macedonian
tomb of
Rhomiopoulou, Katerina, *see* Leuka-
dia, Macedonian tombs of: Rho-
miopoulou's excavations.
ring, *see* jewellery
Roman baths, 162
Roman copies, 157
rosette, "enamelled", 170
Roumlouki, 17
Roxane, 231
Russia, 72, 181, 192, 223, *see also*
Soviet Union

S

Sabazios, 206
sacrificial pyres, 221
Saint Demetrios, church of, 235
"saltcellars", *see* pottery
sarcophagus, 37, 219; from Sidon, 116;
marble, 71, 73, 75, 78, 119, 120, 121,
122, 166, 168, 175, 177, 178, 191, 220,
232
"Sardanapalus", 206
sauceboats, *see* pottery

scabbard, wooden, 27
Schefold, K., 117, 118, 224
Scythian, rulers, 181, 184; panoply of,
184; tombs, 184; world, 181
Scythians, 184, 186, 231
secco, 114; *see also* wall painting
sekos, see temple
sheet, of gold, 123, 124, 128, 170, 202,
217, 226, 227; of iron, 189; of silver,
141, 145, 150, 217
shell, marble, 86
shield, *see* weapons
shrine, 184, *see also* Dionysos, shrine
of
Siganidou, Mary, 73
Silanion, 222
Silen, relief head of, 136, 156, 157,
159, 222, 223
sima, 65, 66, 81
Singer – Polignac Institution, 21
"Sirens", relief, 124
Sirra (ΣΙΡΡΑ), 24, 50
skene, see theatre
skyphidia, tall, *see* pottery
skyphos, *see* vase
Socrates, portrait of, 157, 222
Sophocles, portrait of, 175
Soviet Union, museums of, 192, *see*
also Hermitage Museum
Sparta, 168
Spartans, 168
spear, *see* weapons
spearhead, *see* weapons
sphinx, relief, 145
stairway, *see* palace
statue, 181, base of, 49; chryselephantine, 128; sacred, 184; votive, 46; *see*
also Philip II, statue of
stele, grave, 30, 55, 56, 57, 62, 64, 82,
83 f.f., 222, 227, 228, painted, 57, 58,
89, relief, 30, 83; hermaic, relief, 128,
133, 223
storerooms, *see* palace
strigils, 208, 217, of bronze, 82, 208, of
iron, 82, 206
sword, *see* weapons

Σ

σύριγγες, see jewellery
σφηκωτῆρες, see jewellery

T

table, built, 120, 202, 209, 210, 217,
219; sacred, 49; wooden, 146
tainia, 68, 81, 106, 198
Tarsus, gold medallion from, 74, 130,
175, 230
Tegea, sculptures from, 229